WILLA CATHER

A CRITICAL BIOGRAPHY

WILLA CATHER

By E. K. BROWN

WILLA CATHER

A CRITICAL BIOGRAPHY

Completed by LEON EDEL

Primus ego in patriam mecum . . .
deducam Musas.
                    VIRGIL

NEW YORK   ALFRED A. KNOPF
1 9 5 3

280677

Rov

L. C. catalog card number: 52–12204

THIS IS A BORZOI BOOK,
PUBLISHED BY ALFRED A. KNOPF, INC.

FIRST EDITION

6/65

Introduction

AND EDITOR'S FOREWORD

INTRODUCTION BY E. K. BROWN

IN the autumn of 1946 the *Yale Review* published an article of mine entitled "Homage to Willa Cather," in which I surveyed her fiction and tried to define its peculiar qualities and effects. Miss Cather liked the article and during the winter and early spring we exchanged a number of letters. Plans were laid for meetings in the summer of 1947 when I was to teach at New York University. It had always been Miss Cather's way to decide instantly and irrevocably whether she would give her confidence; to me she wrote warmly and vigorously, with no apparent shadow of restraint, concerning her books, the principles of her art, and the general values from which her achievement grew. Late in March she began to dictate a letter about the pleasure it gave her to have been visited by Yehudi Menuhin and his sister Hephzibah and their children—she was carried back to the time when the parents had come there to talk, play, and read Shakespeare with her more than a decade before. She hurried out of New York before she could finish the letter. It stopped in the middle of a sentence. Miss Cather died on April 24.

Her literary executrix, Edith Lewis, who had shared her life for forty years, remembered Miss Cather's pleasure in my article and was aware of the epistolary friendship that had begun and had grown to maturity so quickly. She asked me to write a study of her friend, a biography of the artist, and of the person, always keeping before me the principle that the person was to be studied not for herself but for the light her life and character might cast upon her art. In one of the stories in Willa Cather's first book, an admirer of the paintings of Sir Hugh Treffinger, visiting the studio soon after his death, grows curious about the life that lay behind the art and resolves to write a biography. "I mean," he says, "to touch only on such facts in his personal life as have to do directly with his work." It was a book of this kind that Edith Lewis had in mind. I had long believed that no American novelist since the death of Henry James was Willa Cather's equal in vision or in design and I was joyfully ready to attempt it.

In an essay of which she thought well, T. K. Whipple described the literary development of Willa Cather as the victory of mind over Nebraska. Like many another capsule of criticism this has value only when its elements are clearly defined. It will not be sufficient to define *mind* and *Nebraska; victory* also will require a gloss.

In 1883 Willa Cather's parents took their four children to join more adventurous members of the family who ten years earlier had started a Virginia colony on the unbroken prairie. Willa Cather, who was not quite ten, was excited by two violent contrasts: between the tumultuous polyglot mass of pioneer life on farms within an easy ride of the colony, and the homogeneous, somewhat humdrum life of the farming community in the Virginia she had left; and between the wind-tormented flatness of south-central Nebraska and the rich hill-and-dale landscape of her corner of Virginia. Her friend Dorothy Canfield, who met Willa Cather before she was twenty, has said that an imaginative and emotional response to the great shift from

Virginia to Nebraska is at the core of Willa Cather's fiction. Her own accounts of her response show that it gave her an awareness of her differentness from others, her individuality. Within a year or two of their coming to Nebraska the Cathers moved to town, to Red Cloud, a straggling village that was no more than a market center and a section point on the Burlington line from Kansas City and St. Joseph to Denver. Unlike the settlers on the prairie, most of the villagers were of old American stock and instinctively repeated in the appearance of the buildings and the way of life what they had known in small towns in Illinois, Ohio, and Kentucky, but in cheaper and rougher fashion. From her first visits to Red Cloud, Willa Cather had felt an unlikeness between the tight, rather mean aspect and pace of the village, and the vigorous, precarious, and in some ways exalting life of the farmers. When she began to live in the village, she threw herself impetuously against the way of the majority and sought out the exceptions, the dreamers, the nonconformists, the questioners. Visits to relatives who remained in the Virginia colony kept her sense of the land and its people vivid. In 1890 she began a five-year course at the state university in Lincoln, and this was to be the third and last tier in her experience of Nebraska. In Lincoln the dreary churchiness and bustling women's clubs could not repress the bold imagination of an occasional professor, or the theaters that gave Willa Cather so much pleasure, whether she was making friends with actresses backstage, seeing plays, or writing reviews of them for the *State Journal*. If Lincoln was very much a part of Nebraska, it also held a hint of the Eastern cities for which Willa Cather had begun to long.

In an obvious way Nebraska meant to her, when she was a girl and when she was a mature artist, the prairie and its foreign-born farmers, the crude village with its hard molds and its rebels, the college town where two worlds collided without requiring one to choose between them. In her early stories, a few of them recently accessible in James Shively's collection of Willa Cather's juvenilia, she rendered what was hard and bleak and cruel in the state's way of life—the collapse, for instance, of minds and bodies in the struggle with the land, the pressure of convention in the village, the imperviousness to art which was early and late for Willa Cather the chief expression of mind. Her first literary response to Nebraska was an almost unmitigated hate and fear: it was opposition to forces that seemed to her monstrously strong and a threat to her differentness, to the core of what she felt herself to be.

To look at Nebraska otherwise, to contemplate it with some objectivity and appreciation, Willa Cather needed to go away for a long time and to achieve success. She had gone east in 1896, and when twelve years later she was named managing editor of *McClure's Magazine*, she had finally the security of an established position and a firm foothold in the world of art. In "The Bohemian Girl," a long story published in the magazine in 1912, a new attitude toward Nebraska appears, and its main origin is plain. The young hero of the narrative, Nils Ericsson, returns to his home on a Nebraska farm after some years in a Norwegian port where he has had extraordinary success. He cannot persuade Clara Vavrika, who has married a stolid brother of his, to join him in admiring the vitality, force, and endurance of the pioneer grandmothers. She knows their thoughts of her, and feels in them a threat to her differentness. But she will find it an easy matter to recognize their values, Nils tells Clara, after she has gone away with him to Bergen—freedom and distance change the aspect of all things. So they did with Willa Cather.

Still, her new perspective toward Nebraska might never have been achieved, and would certainly have been retarded, if she had not come under the influence of an author whose name and work she had known when she was a child—the face appeared in a special pack of cards for the game of "Authors"—and whom she met in 1908. This was Sarah Orne Jewett. In 1908 Willa Cather was at the height of her enthusiasm for Henry James; some of the short stories she had been writing during the five preceding years were obtrusively Jamesian both in substance and in form, and in "Eleanor's House" she did what is really a pastiche of Jamesian implication. There is no record that Miss Jewett gave any warning against the cult of Henry James, whom she had known for some years; but her example and her precepts told powerfully against his influence. She showed to Willa Cather the possibilities of a simple rural subject, treated by an artist in profound sympathy with the places and the persons she dealt with, but also who, by a broad knowledge of the world, and of books, and by a habit of detached contemplation, could see her material from a distance. Miss Jewett was a supreme example of the artist who is both involved in her material and disengaged from it. Little by little Willa Cather's addiction to Jamesian substance and form wore off—there is a good deal of it surviving in *Alexander's Bridge*, written in 1911—and in her later years she would say that much as James had meant to her at one time, she knew that she would never reread his more complicated fictions. But there never came a time when she could not and did not reread the stories of Sarah Orne Jewett. The first sure evidence of the effect Miss Jewett had upon her was in the sketch called "The Enchanted Bluff," which appeared in *Harper's* in 1909, the year of Miss Jewett's death. It is severe in its treatment of Nebraska life, much more severe than "The Bohemian Girl"; and when one knows the works that were to follow, all of them seem implicit in this short piece about a few boys gathered by the river and what they made of their lives.

In the stories and novels that came after "The Enchanted Bluff" and "The Bohemian Girl," Willa Cather went far beyond those early works in the quality of her contemplation and appreciation of Nebraska. The dichotomy she had felt between the pioneer and the artist—one crucial form of the conflict between mind and Nebraska—began to disappear. The pioneer, it was true, did not often set any value on art, the old grandmothers would not have understood that art had much importance, would have agreed with the Northern Farmer that to stub Thurnaby waste was a prouder achievement than any bit of brain-work. Nevertheless the pioneer and the artist were generically one, they were both intent on creating. Underneath all the distinctions that separated them, and more telling than any, was the impulse they shared to turn from all the tracks of routine and convention to make a track of their own. A farmer like Alexandra Bergson in *O Pioneers!*, a farm-wife like Ántonia Shimerda in *My Ántonia* were creators just as surely as the artist in "A Sculptor's Funeral," at whom the villagers sneered while his body lay in his coffin. In later novels the conception of a pioneer broadened to take in those who planned the West and gambled fortunes on its future, building its railroads and filling its towns.

When Willa Cather lived in Red Cloud, the village had a number of extraordinary personalities who did not bend to the narrow standards of the majority. There was a dry-goods merchant whose *Iliad* in a Greek text lay on the counter before him and meant more than any number of customers, and a former Governor of Nebraska whose way of life had more to do with Denver and Omaha and Lincoln than with the little incidents of local progress. Everyone in the village who had an exceptional nature responded to that exceptional element in Willa Cather's, exactly as happened with Thea Kronborg when she was growing up in Moonstone in *The Song of the Lark*. Few of the dreamers or rebels read many books, but they had an obscure fellow-feeling for an artist's nature. In a sense, it was better to grow up in a Nebraska village just then than in one farther east.

In retrospect Willa Cather could see that she had never been quite so lonely or so different as she had supposed. Even in the university, crude and undiscriminating as it then was in so many important ways, there was a delight in originality, a welcome for promise, that would not probably have come in a more conventional institution committed to the usual stupid academic routines. From the beginning of her time there instructors and students saw and valued what was distinctive in her writing and in her personality; so did some people in the town—editors, clubwomen, exiles from Eastern cities, who stayed in Lincoln bewailing its rigidities but drawn to its vigor and daring.

As she matured, Willa Cather became the kind of artist to whom the past was important. She did not care to start from nothing—she wanted to start from the point art had reached in the sequence of great experiments, the chain of explorations, which make up tradition. Nor was her attachment to tradition any longer narrowly æsthetic. Art, she knew, was a flowering of fine personalities, and to their flowering the atmosphere of a fine society had brought much of the beauty and the strength. It began to appear to her that her art had been kept poor, and her personality clipped, by inadequacies in the society in which she had grown up. It was a society without a real past, and without much consciousness of what past it had.

In 1912 she made her first of many journeys to the Southwest. There she found a Western land with a past, with an interweaving of traditions complex, highly colored, and yet austere. The region began to press into her fiction, in the references to Mexico in *O Pioneers!*, in the long account of Thea's coming of age during her months in and near the canyon of the Cliff-Dwellers in *The Song of the Lark*, in the speculations about Coronado's expedition in a crucial scene of *My Ántonia*, in Tom Outland's record of his discovery of the Cliff-Dweller settlements in *The Professor's House*, and finally in the whole conception of *Death Comes for the Archbishop*. The persistence and the diversity of the references to the Southwest suggest—what is indeed the truth—that the discovery of this region was the principal emotional experience of Willa Cather's mature life. Not all the passages about the Southwest flowed from her stay there in 1912. She returned as often as she could, and when she came she remained for months. In that region she found a landscape with a beauty that was at once austere and spectacular, a proper setting for great emotions and great achievements; she found also a history of successive creations—the creation of the Cliff-Dwellers' villages, the establishment of another religion and civilization by the Spanish friars, and its re-creation by the French missionaries of the nineteenth century. In the Southwest the making of a society, a civilization, always went hand in hand with the making of beauty. Willa Cather found the artifacts of the Cliff-Dwellers as purely beautiful as any that remained from the old civilizations. With the creation of beautiful objects went appreciation of others that were old. The heavy bell that was the treasure of the Church of San Miguel at Santa Fe had been cast in Spain centuries before the discovery of America, and it was in the Southwest because someone had cared enough for its silvery tone to have it brought by cart all the thousands of miles from Mexico City across some of the most difficult country in the world. Nothing could be more unlike the early days in Nebraska than a story told in the prelude to *Death Comes for the Archbishop*. A Franciscan friar had begged a painting from one of the great collectors of Spain; the nobleman, thinking the friar would prefer a sentimental daub, had courteously bidden him choose which of his treasures the friar preferred; the choice fell on an El Greco, and somewhere in the Southwest that picture found its place. The preachers in Webster County would have chosen the daub. In the Southwest, layer upon layer of the past was visible, and each layer was an inexhaustible stim-

ulus to the admirer of the pioneer and the admirer of art.
All that Nebraska meant and all that mind meant were
here reconciled in a synthesis for which no praise, no gratitude could be sufficient.

The effects of her discovery of the Southwest were complicated by her response to the First World War and its
aftermath. Like many other American artists of her time
she had a cult of France, and from the beginning she was
attached to the cause of the Allies. The one saving element in the war was, in her opinion, that all the Americans
she knew responded to it not as a matter involving dollars
and cents, but in terms of emotions and ideas. Especially
after the United States entered the war, what she heard
and saw persuaded her that the heavy materialism that
overlaid American life, both on the prairies and in the large
Eastern cities, had not crushed, though it had hampered
and obscured, the life of the spirit, those forces within individuals which protect them from becoming mere economic units. The aftermath of the war depressed her as
nothing had before: the heavy materialism had won out
after all, it was the one genuine victor. She had never disliked the sight of a great railway-maker traveling in a special train and having the tracks cleared for his regal progress. He was a creator, and these accompaniments to his
life were merely his due. The 1920's seemed to her the period not of great creative men of business, but of their lack-
eys, their secretaries, managers, lawyers, vice-presidents:
these men were wholly uncreative, they exacted huge sums
merely for keeping the wheels turning, spent them grossly,
and nevertheless were commonly accepted as model prod-
ucts of the American way of life. In *One of Ours*, and in

A Lost Lady, studying Nebraska in the decade before the war, she showed how uncreative, mercenary, odious men kept control once they had won it, and what they did to those who were finer than themselves; in *The Professor's House* she showed the hollowness of any pretensions they might make to interest in art or mind. She was now painfully disillusioned with the world about her, and for the first time suffered from a sense of being severed from it.

Her new anxieties coincided with middle life, and the very title and the substance of *A Lost Lady* suggested Willa Cather's sense of being adrift in a world with which she no longer felt in harmony. Her next three novels are a search for the meaning of this disharmony; they also may be regarded as the protest of one who has lived intensely and heartily against the advancing years. Her exploration led her to a deeper consideration than hitherto of the role of religion, its relation to art, to the mind, and to civilization. She had been brought up a Baptist; she had accepted this faith as she had accepted much else that being a member of her family had brought to her (and much as Thea accepts the Methodism of her family). It was not until after the First World War, when she was nearing her fiftieth year, that religion, in a broad sense, came to play a more significant role in her art. In 1922, with her father and mother, she was confirmed in the Protestant Episcopal Church. In part this was because this Church, more recently established in Nebraska, had won a distinct following in Red Cloud and obtained the adherence of her family; she had always maintained close links with her home and she wanted to share to the full the participation of her kin in the institutions of the town. In part it was an emo-

tional response to religion, more keenly felt than before—
although readers of *O Pioneers!* will recall the early pleasure she expressed in the color and ritual of the French
Catholic settlement and her account of the cavalcade of
forty French boys to meet the Bishop's carriage.

It would be a mistake to say that her entrance into the
Episcopal Church brought her repose, and it is doubtful
whether she expected it would. Her association with that
Church shows only one of the directions in which she was
seeking a solution and the repose a solution would bring.
In the Episcopal Church there was no strain on the relation between religion and art, or on the relation between
religion and civilization. The great prophet for Willa
Cather's grandmothers had been John Bunyan; she never
lost her feeling for his books, and never seemed to tire of
reading *The Pilgrim's Progress*, about which many tender
memories clustered; she had read also John Henry New-
man. His name brings up powerfully the other great value
Willa Cather found in the Episcopal Church; it was one
of the great historic churches, and like all historic institutions that continue alive and faithful to their origins, it set
a high value upon the past. So, of course, as she knew, did
the Roman Catholic Church, for which she had such sympathetic insight that a great many of her readers, some of
them Roman Catholics, supposed that she had become a
member of that Church. The Episcopal Church was the
historic church of America, and notably of Virginia, and it
was natural she should turn to a church that appreciated
and was of the past. . . .

EDITOR'S FOREWORD

The introduction that Edward Killoran Brown was writing
to his critical biography of Willa Cather breaks off at this
point. He had written to me in October 1950: "I may be
close to the end by spring." In March 1951 he wrote: "I
feel a bit written out with the Willa Cather and am taking
a few weeks on odd jobs." A month later he was dead, in
his forty-sixth year, and at a time when his life seemed to
loom before him rich with the fulfilment of early promise—
with a host of literary tasks remaining to be carried out and
this one all but completed.

I have heard it said that the cruelest losses are those of
the young, who are asked to yield so many of their years
before they have had them. Certainly they are no less cruel
when they strike in the prime of life, in the midst of creation and achievement, when the false starts and wrong
turns, the trials and errors of youth, are behind and an accretion of wisdom and experience is being brought into
fullest play. In the case of E. K. Brown, professor of English Literature at the University of Chicago, who had devoted almost a quarter of a century to teaching and writing, the loss seemed deeply cruel and wasteful; in the class,
as in the study, he was in the very process of reaping the
harvest of a rich life here and abroad that had practiced a
close and exacting scholarly experience and discipline.

Fashioned in the schools of his native Canada, which
maintained Old World traditions of scholarship and whose
liberal-arts faculties even today are dedicated not to preparing young men to be competitors in a competitive society but to giving them wide cultural sympathies and in-

terests, he had pursued his studies at the Sorbonne during
the late 1920's. It was there that I first met him. When he
arrived in Europe he possessed much more than a smatter-
ing of the Romance languages. He spoke French with admirable fluency, and a well-marked copy of Dante showed
how assiduously he had cultivated Italian. We sat together
on occasions in the classes of the venerable Émile Legouis,
the French Chaucerian. I can see Legouis still, noble-
browed and white-bearded, declaiming Chaucer in an
English lightly touched with Gallic accents that rendered
the Gallic in Chaucer admirably vocal. We listened to
Louis Cazamian, Brown's principal master in Paris, ex-
pound the English humorists with subtlety and psychological insight, and to Charles Cestre of the pointed beard
and New England manner, incumbent of the chair of
American Literature and Civilization, who presided over
textual analysis of Edwin Arlington Robinson's poems at a
time when the poet had not begun to be given his full due
in the United States. Or we sat before Fernand Balden-
sperger (he looked then like a patrician painted by Rem-
brandt), to whom all American students seemed to flock,
as he expounded foreign influences in Balzac and gave us
for the first time a full appreciation of the values inherent
in the study of comparative literature. Or we might make
our way across the cobbled street to the Collège de France,
where in some unventilated room Joseph Bédier, Gaston
Paris's successor, was still lecturing on the *chansons de
geste,* and Paul Hazard could be heard in the sugared cadences he brilliantly cultivated, demonstrating how Pope's
Essay on Man spread over the Continent to have strange
offspring in Madrid or Muscovy. Or, as was natural in a

great seat of medievalism, we listened to Étienne Gilson and marveled at the clarity with which he took us over the difficult paths of faith and reason, under the illumination of the *Summa* of St. Thomas.

It seemed right and proper that we should have come across the ocean to the Sorbonne to complete our education in our own literature, for a great school of English and American studies existed there, set amid opportunities for the study of other literatures, illuminated by many fine European minds that had transcended national insularity to grasp universal ideas and the universality of the creative impulse. I invoke these memories to suggest the background that furnished the mind of E. K. Brown and equipped him for his vocation.

From the first he had dedicated himself to literary study and to teaching. He had many of the qualities of Willa Cather's Professor St. Peter, and not the least of these was a capacity alike for communicating ideas to young students and unraveling the works of the mind. He was an authority first and foremost in nineteenth-century literature in England and in France, as his painstaking study of Matthew Arnold (1948) and his earlier examination of the textual variants in Arnold's prose (1935) had shown. He had begun with an interest in criticism and poetry but increasingly, during the 1930's, he turned to the study of the great and capacious novel form which has harbored so much of the life of three centuries. We lunched almost daily during those Parisian days in a little *crémerie* on the boulevard Saint-Michel where E. K. was particularly fond of their *omelette au confiture,* and on that pleasant *terrasse* we talked much of Flaubert and James, of Joyce and Proust, of form, of architecture, of what Miss Cather came to describe as the novel *démeublé;* and in due course Brown took his doctorate—the *doctorat-ès-lettres* which is conferred by the French national ministry of education as distinct from that given by the university, and which is the degree sought by Frenchmen desiring to hold a chair in the institutions of higher learning. Brown wrote two theses, the minor on Arnold's texts, and the major on Edith Wharton's novels, which had interested him because of their craftsmanship and the moral values they reflected. But even before the completion of the book on Mrs. Wharton he had begun to read an American novelist he could admire even more. He read and reread the works of Willa Cather with an ever growing interest. His thumbed and worn copies of the novels are marked and underlined with the signs of his close perusal; and at the end of some of them he jotted down the dates of his rereadings. There is a characteristic expression of his firm belief in the value of rereading in the first of his Alexander lectures, *Rhythm in the Novel*, delivered in Toronto little more than a year before the end:

One of the most illuminating remarks I remember was overheard at a public examination for the licentiate in English at the Sorbonne. The examiner was Émile Legouis. He asked a young man for his impression of education at English and American universities. The student replied that what had impressed him most was the amount of reading expected and accomplished. "Yes," said Legouis, "yes, they read, read, read." He was silent for a full minute. "It would appear," he mused, "that they find something magical in reading."

And Brown added his own comment that "there is nothing magical in reading: it is in rereading that some magic may lie."

Although he had read every novel of Willa Cather's several times, Brown reread them all once and some of them twice while he was writing this book; its pages show how close he always was to his texts. How he came to write this biography he has related in his uncompleted introduction. The story he could not tell was how, face to face with death, knowing that his years were to be shortened, he continued to write—and to write admirably—in the supreme belief that man must pursue his appointed task to the end. Like "Neighbour Rosicky" he had his intimation. There may have been moments of deep inner suffering, of fear before the unknown; but outwardly this was not visible. Scholars, by nature, are not addicted to heroic attitudes; they have none of the swagger of men of action or the boundless physical energy of indefatigable adventurers. The quiet corner, the book, an adequate supply of paper, a well-filled inkpot or convenient typewriter, a pipe or a cigarette and they can conquer worlds. But this doesn't mean that they lack the stuff of heroism. Edward Brown was made of such stuff: he did not allow the supreme warning to discourage him from writing the book he had planned. At his desk the work grew methodically and without a flagging of purpose or style; there was never any divergence from the high critical standards he had always set for himself and there is no trace of hurry in the manuscript. He wrote with all the craft and subtlety—and urbanity—he possessed, catching Willa Cather's "vision of essences" and noting all the little details—how for instance she had mis-quoted Longfellow's translation from the Anglo-Saxon:

> *For thee was a house built*
> *Ere thou wast born,*
> *For thee was a mould meant*
> *Ere thou of mother camest*

—lines that must have come to have a particular poignancy for him, as they do for us, in the light of what he knew might happen.

He began writing this book in the winter of 1949. Early in 1950 he had several warning bouts of illness, yet by Christmas of that year most of his chapters had been set down and some of them revised. There was additional work done during January and February 1951 and he apparently at that time completed the next to the last chapter. Only the Pittsburgh years and the final years were left unwritten; but detailed notes remained which, together with his well-marked books, have simplified my task. I have also added certain passages to the study of *Death Comes for the Archbishop*, as the notes disclosed Brown had intended to enlarge this chapter. In a number of instances I have grafted into the text, and into the conclusion, certain sentences and paragraphs from Brown's article on Miss Cather which appeared in the *Yale Review* in 1946. With these exceptions, the book follows the text set down by Brown as his widow found it among his papers and as she transmitted it to me for editing and completion.

It is not clear to what extent E. K. Brown intended to explain to his readers some of the problems he encountered in the writing of this biography. He had never met Willa Cather and remembered her only from having seen her aboard a ship in which they made the same crossing from France. The book was to be an account of Miss Cather's life, as he said, but only as it illuminated the art. Miss Cather believed intensely in the artist's right to a private life; her will contains an unqualified prohibition of the publication "in any form whatsoever of the whole, or any part of any letter or letters written by me." This may be regarded, in a very real sense, as a loss to the corpus of her writings, for Miss Cather gave freely of herself in her correspondence, and her letters are touched with the cadence, as with the radiance, of her style; they reflect also, as letters can, the directness and generosity and charm of the personality, its courage and steadfastness. To understand the art of Willa Cather, however, is to understand why she decided that her letters should not be published. She belonged to the addicted "revisionists" of art, and since she could not have the re-editing of her correspondence—moreover, since that correspondence was unrelated to her work except perhaps as furnishing occasional marginal comments on it—she imposed the testamentary restrictions. E. K. Brown was able, however, to read many of her letters and to assimilate the information they contained. His logical course was to use the process to which Boswell alludes —that is, to "melt down" his materials—and this is perhaps what Willa Cather intended. George F. Whicher has expressed the belief that as a result of the novelist's restrictions upon her personal papers "even a judicious examination of her career" is made difficult "if not impossible." He added that we must "resign ourselves to the probability that the critical study of her works cannot be supported by any but superficial understanding of her personality."

Professor Brown has demonstrated, it seems to me, that this need not be so. By the use of the time-honored *témoignage* in the manner of Boswell, and in particular that offered him by Miss Edith Lewis, Miss Cather's friend of many years, who has been virtually a collaborator in the work, by ranging freely into the Virginia background of Willa Cather's childhood, by his visits to Pittsburgh, to Red Cloud and Lincoln, E. K. Brown was enabled to gather up old threads, talk with old friends and with relatives, examine old houses, study the landscape and the scene; and having already saturated himself with the work —that work which Miss Cather chiseled from her life—he arrived at a striking and one might venture to say enduring critical portrait. Willa Cather was so recently in our midst that the portrait has still the aspect of contemporaneity. If he has painted a good portrait, all future material that will be uncovered about Miss Cather's life will heighten the likeness and the coloring, but will not change the countenance he has set down. This is not the commemorative biography of which Lytton Strachey wrote, more funeral oration than life; nor is it a paper figure, as so many biographies are, fashioned out of documents alone. It is the life of a great American novelist of the first half of the twentieth century seen through the windows of her work and through the eyes of those who knew her. It will be read also as the act of courage of a scholar for whom, like Willa Cather's protagonists, only death could be defeat—and even it was to be challenged to the last.

New York City   LEON EDEL

Contents

PART ONE

1

From Virginia to the Divide

1873–1883

IN AN INTERVIEW that is often quoted, Willa Cather said in 1921—just before the publication of *One of Ours*—that the "years from eight to fifteen are the formative period in a writer's life, when he unconsciously gathers basic material. He may acquire a great many interesting and vivid impressions in his mature years but his thematic material he acquires under fifteen years of age. Other writers will tell you this. Lord Dunsany once told me that he believed he had never used any basic material he had acquired after his fifteenth year." It is a remarkable statement. What is most remarkable is not the obvious thing, the minimizing of the experiences of maturity, but the dismissal of the experiences of early childhood. The traces of the "years from eight to fifteen," roughly the years she had in Webster County, Nebraska, are almost everywhere in Willa Cather's fiction; but the traces of her early years in Virginia are few and faint. She left Virginia when she was nine, and until she wrote the last of her novels, *Sapphira and the Slave Girl*, the first nine years of her life gave her neither a subject nor a theme. There is an uncollected early short story, "A Night at Greenway Court," set at Lord Fairfax's great house a few miles to the southeast of Winchester; but this is only a routine cloak-and-sword piece written when Willa Cather was under the spell of *The Prisoner of Zenda*. Virginia is a somewhat unsubstantial standard of reference in the early chapters of *My Ántonia*, and, disguised as Tennessee, a more substantial standard in "Old Mrs. Harris." Not only does Virginia count for little; its fiction does not offer an important record of early childhood translated into Western terms. The novels are full of interesting adolescents, boys as often as girls, presented with a finely sympathetic understanding, seen very convincingly from within, and these adolescents are often devoted to younger children; but there is very little sense or feeling of what it means to be a young child.

The first nine years were passed in a society of extraordinary stability. Dorothy Canfield, who knew her well during her formative years, does not exaggerate when she says that Willa Cather "was born and lived for what is traditionally the period which most influences personality in a state which had the tradition of continuity and stability as far as they could exist in this country, and in a class which more than any other is always stubbornly devoted to the old ways of doing things." Continuity and stability were values that Willa Cather cherished, and the older she grew, the more she cherished them. It is easy to believe that they owed something of their hold upon her to the ways of life in the rural Virginia of her childhood; but except in *Sapphira* she never cared to link these values in her fiction with the first world she could remember. Edith Lewis, her friend of four decades, has said:

Her Virginia life was one of great richness, tranquil and ordered and serene. With its freedom from all tension and nervous strain, it may have helped to give her that deep store of vitality which underlay her work. When her family . . . moved west, she felt the break cruelly. But in later years she believed that for her the move was fortunate. Even as a little girl she felt something smothering in the polite, rigid social conventions of that Southern society—something factitious and unreal. If one fell in with those sentimental attitudes, those euphuisms that went with good manners, one lost all touch with reality, with truth of experience. If one resisted them, one became a social rebel. She told once of an old judge who came to call . . . and who began stroking her curls and talking to her in the playful platitudes one addressed to little girls—and of how she horrified her mother by breaking out suddenly: "I's a dang'ous nigger, I is!" It was an attempt to break through the smooth, unreal conventions about little girls—the only way that occurred to her at the moment.

Neither the antebellum South, of which her grandparents and parents often spoke, nor the South in reconstruction which she had known as a child became a temple of her imagination. In the years when she was writing critical papers and reviews she scarcely ever chose a Southern subject or concerned herself with a Southern writer. Her Virginian childhood is a prelude to her years of experience and preparation, not a part of them.

Willa Cather was born in the house of her grandmother, Rachel Elizabeth Boak, in the Back Creek Valley, a little more than ten miles to the west of Winchester, in the Northern Neck of Virginia. Cathers had farmed among the hills of this region, near what was to become the border with West Virginia, since the latter part of the eighteenth century.

The clearest figure among the older generations of the
family is James, who was Willa's great-grandfather, and a
son of Jasper, who is believed to have emigrated from
Ireland. According to manuscript family records, Jasper
Cather was at Fort Redstone in western Pennsylvania in
the early 1750's; in 1773 his name appears on a tax list of
Farquhar County in that state; by 1786 he had come to
the countryside west of Winchester and in that year married Sarah Moore in Frederick County. James, one of the
seven children of this marriage, was born in 1795 in his father's farmhouse on Flint Ridge only a few miles from the
birthplace of Willa. The historian of the Shenandoah Valley, T. K. Cartmell, knew him well. "Mr. Cather," he says,
"was largely above the average farmer in intellect. Possessed with rare physical strength and wonderful energy,
these qualities gave him an advantage over weaker men.
Always informed on the current topics of the day, his con-
versational abilities were admirable. Young men were always benefited by having him as a friend." One of the
young men who felt the benefit profoundly was a son-in-
law, John Purcell, who welcomed every errand that took
him to the farmhouse on Flint Ridge—nowhere else in the
district was there such talk, amusing, thoughtful, informed,
alive. James Cather's grandson, Charles, who was Willa's
father, admired him to the end of his days and appears to
have taken him as his model in character and manner.
James makes a fleeting appearance in *Sapphira and the
Slave Girl*, where "his talk had a flavour of old-fashioned
courtesy." The fine strong quality of the man appears in
his photograph: a broad brow, benignant eyes, resolute

mouth, the set of head and shoulders expressing both firmness and ease.

Of his seven children the one who appears to have inherited the most liberal share of his intellectual energy, his power of speech, his happy unresented dominion over others, was his daughter Sidney. Born in 1828, she was married at nineteen to Mahlon Gore, who had come west from Loudoun County to buy a farm in northwestern Frederick. Fourteen years later Mrs. Gore was left a widow with the farm on the northwestern turnpike, three sons, and a load of unsuspected debt. She saw her opportunity in the reputation of the district as a health resort: sick people flocked there from Eastern and Southern cities, often in such pathetic weakness that they died on the trains, in the railway station at Winchester, in the carriages that took them over the rough twisting roads. Mrs. Gore was at various times postmistress and schoolteacher and farmer, but she was above all manager of the resort called Valley Home, her own house, expanded again and again until for some years it is said to have had as many as fifty rooms. Valley Home is only a couple of hundred yards to the west of Willa Cather's birthplace. It is still a charming house, almost at the center of the little village that is now called Gore because Sidney Gore was for more than a generation its natural and admitted chief. From "its shady front porch behind blooming honeysuckle vines" it looks out as it did in Sapphira's day, over the valley to the south and west and to the heights beyond.

Like many other farmers in the Northern Neck James Cather opposed secession. No dogmatic Unionist, a friend

indeed of Henry Clay, who stayed at his house, he nevertheless believed that the special interests of the South
could be assured without war, and without the threat of
war. Frederick County was not to an important degree a
slaveholding neighborhood. The land did not lend itself
to the peculiar institution—much of it, like the Back Creek
district, was hilly, rocky, and sandy. "Here there were no
large, rich farms," Willa Cather says in *Sapphira*, "for the
blacks to work, as there were in Loudoun County. Many
field-hands were not needed." Few of the farmers had capital; even before the War between the States most of them
were chronically hard up. Many were recently arrived
from Germany or Ireland—there were more Germans and
Irish in the valley of Virginia than in any other part of the
dominion; others, like Rachel Boak's family, the Seiberts,
had come from Pennsylvania. James Cather had twice represented the county in the Virginia House of Delegates;
and he was speaking for the opinion that prevailed in western Frederick when as its representative at the secession
convention he opposed a violent solution. He appears to
have thought with another citizen of Frederick County,
Robert Y. Conrad, who declared: "Our present difficulties
could have been satisfactorily solved within the Union, but
for the premature movements of the States farther south.
If no attempt at coercion is made, the best course Virginia
can take is to remain peaceably in the Union." That was
Mrs. Gore's opinion; and it was her father's.

In the War between the States Winchester is said to
have changed hands at least sixty-eight times. The great
valley was crucial to both sides. Stonewall Jackson, who
did most of his fighting in or near it, believed that "if this

valley is lost, Virginia is lost"; while the valley was held,
lower Pennsylvania was in constant peril. The valley, as
one who fought in Jackson's army has said, "with its detached mountain chains and ranges" was "one of the most
remarkable fields for military operations in the country."
The main actions were contested from north to south or
from south to north, and the Back Creek district was
slightly west of the stubborn fighting. But the highway
from Winchester to Romney, on which the settlement lay,
sometimes saw an entire army; it was along this road that,
early in the war, a Confederate force moved at highest
speed in an attempt to surprise Lew Wallace.

Again and again bands of marauders, little knots of
wounded men, solitary stragglers, passed in front of Valley Home. A group of trigger-happy Union soldiers shot
down an elderly neighbor almost in Mrs. Gore's sight. The
murder, license, and destruction she saw and the deaths of
friends and neighbors fighting in the armies of the Confederacy slowly hardened her heart against the Northern
cause; but as late as Gettysburg she could still be horrified and angry at reports of Southern looting and burning
and worse across the Pennsylvania border. Her son How-
ard Gore has said: "She reasoned deeply and dispassion-
ately about every topic that came under her observation
and it is quite safe to venture the belief that her judgment
called for a continuation of the Union while her heart was
enlisted under the flag with a single star."

The journals of this remarkable woman are emphatic,
and sometimes eloquent, on the trials she underwent in so
exposed a place with no man to protect her or her house.
It is clear that she did not need a defender: the simplicity

of her character, her manifest kindness, and something
that survived in her of James Cather's instinctive domi-
nance of those around him gave her a safety no husband or
brother could have assured. The face in her photographs is
extraordinarily winning—it is an intelligent and determined
face, the eyes suggesting also an intense inner life and the
most active kind of sympathy. Looking at it one can understand how Mrs. Gore hated the institution of slavery,
how she recoiled from the fact of war, how she lodged, fed,
and tended the wounded of both armies with the unques-
tioning devotion of an evangelical Christian, and how she
gave improving lectures to those whose conduct displeased
her.

Her journals show that she was an evangelical Christian. Before she was out of her girlhood she experienced
conversion, the great event of her life. Her first independent act, the first about which she did not consult her father, was to abandon the moderate Presbyterianism pro-
fessed by the Cather family as by most of the Scotch-Irish
people in the valley, and to become a Baptist. In her new
faith she was followed somewhat tardily by her husband,
and zealously by one of her brothers, William A. Cather,
Willa's grandfather.

William A. Cather married Emily Anne Caroline Smith,
also of the Back Creek district, on March 31, 1846. Caroline's father had a tavern known for its good fare and
cleanliness far along the turnpike. Her mother, Ann Ellis,
was a pattern of pioneer virtues. G. P. Cather, Willa's uncle, writes of her: "Her great and wonderful physique was
fortified with perfect health, great strength, powerful endurance and unsurpassed industry, which carried with

them a practical knowledge of the work in her line of duty. She would take the wool as it came from the sheep's back, card it, spin it, weave it into cloth, and make it into clothes; and weave it into nice bed clothes and blankets. She would take flax and hackle it, spin it, weave it into linen, and make it into clothes, tablecloths, towels, bedticks and thread. She was a good tidy housekeeper, and a grand good cook. She was scrupulously honest, despised a liar and detested a lazy person, kind to the poor and merciful to the unfortunate. . . . Let us give her credit for much of the good that is in us, and if by chance there should be something wrong about us let us say there is no Ann Ellis about that." Her daughter Caroline greatly resembled her. Caroline appears in her late middle age as the grandmother of Jim Burden in *My Ántonia*. At fifty-five she was still "quick-footed and energetic in all her movements. Her voice was high and rather shrill, and she often spoke with an anxious inflection, for she was exceedingly desirous that everything should go with due order and decorum. Her laugh too was high, and perhaps a little strident, but there was a lively intelligence in it." She was—like her mother—the passage ends, "a strong woman of unusual endurance." She was an ardent Baptist, a reader of the Bible, *The Pilgrim's Progress*, and of such religious tracts as *The Tinker's Blind Daughter*.

William too was strong, and of unusual endurance. Among the family photographs his is the only formidable face, the face of a zealot with cold fiery eyes. In later life he was to prove his strength on a Nebraska farm, but he had proved it much earlier: he was the only member of the family to give unreserved adherence to the Union

cause throughout the War between the States, and as mar-
shal after the war had ended. His Unionist belief was
shared by his wife and his young sons, and a strong bond
with his mother-in-law. He was ostracized by some of his
sisters and brothers; but it was not in his nature to be
deterred.

In 1851 William Cather settled on a farm a mile or so to
the east of Valley Home. The property was known as the
Willowshade Farm. At first it consisted of one hundred
and thirty acres; but by 1863 it had more than doubled,
and extended to three hundred and four acres, one rood,
twenty-eight poles, "a tract of land situated in Frederick
County, about 10 miles from Winchester, lying on both
sides of the North Western Turnpike and on the East
banks of Back Creek." On this farm, a large one for that
time and place, William Cather built the large and solid
house in which Willa lived as a child. The house at Willowshade, the scene of the epilogue in *Sapphira*, is on the
north side of the turnpike just where it takes a sharp bend
and the village of Gore comes into sight. It rests at the foot
of a gentle slope that begins to rise steeply a little behind
the house. Willowshade is a red brick house of three full
stories; it has a broad front in which large single windows
are evenly spaced, each of them with twelve "lights"; and
to the rear there is a brick extension of two stories. A few
trees now stand between it and the highway; but in the
last century it was indeed shaded by willows, and there
was a somewhat formal front garden, and thick shrubbery.
The house gives an impression of indestructible solidity;
but the moldings, and the woodwork of the entrance lack
the fineness as well as the elaboration that give to the old

houses in the best streets of Winchester so graceful a
charm. Willowshade has something of the pioneer roughness about it. Across the turnpike, limiting the view of the
lower rooms, is a steep, almost perpendicular hill, the first
in the series of "high hills which shut the winter sun . . .
early" from the family at the Mill House in the closing
pages of *Sapphira*. To the southwest, beyond the fields of
the Back Creek settlement, rise the much higher heavily
wooded hills and mountains that the miller's wife in *Sapphira* liked to gaze at in the late afternoons of her last
winter.

Not much of the farm could be cultivated. It is chiefly
hills, and rocks, and woods. Raising sheep for the Baltimore market was William Cather's main concern as a
farmer; and in looking after them he soon had help from
his sons.

Charles Fectigue Cather, Willa's father, was born in
1848; his unusual middle name honored his uncle Joseph
Fectigue Smith, a doctor who lived in Back Creek Valley
and served in the Union army. On December 5, 1872, he
married Virginia, the daughter of William Lee Boak and
Rachel Elizabeth Seibert. Charles Cather's appearance as
a young man is caught up in the description of Mr. Tem-
pleton, the husband in "Old Mrs. Harris," one of the *Obscure Destinies*, with "his boyish, eager-to-please manner,
his fair complexion and blue eyes and young face." Charles
Cather had the courtesy and the gift of speech that marked
his grandfather, his equitable mind and patience at work
or in dealing with persons, but no great part of his energy.
Virginia Boak, two years younger than her husband, was
always to have more than enough energy for two. A hand-

some imperious woman, with a strong will and a strong nature, she was without effort a ruling personality. She had a great power, one who knew her well remembers, for caring about things, everything—whether the coffee was hot, whether a neighbor's child was ill, whether it was a pleasant day for a picnic or a pleasant evening for a dance at Winchester or along the highway to the west, at Capon Springs. She cared greedily for pleasure, but the simplest kinds of pleasure sufficed. She could make an ordinary social call an occasion, and read the most commonplace attention as a fragrant tribute. In the generation following the war, the young couples in rural Frederick, as in so many parts of the South, "were poor and extravagant and jolly. They were much given to picnics and camp meetings in summer, sleighing parties and dancing parties in winter." The war had impoverished a district that had never been rich, and had obscured, if not effaced, many social distinctions and assumptions. In this part of the Northern Neck Willa Cather could not recall any sense of melancholy or embitterment: people had always made do with what they had; now they made do with much less, and were happy.

At first the Charles Cathers lived with Mrs. Boak. William Lee Boak was not a native of the Back Creek district. He was born in Berkeley County in 1805 and married Rachel Elizabeth Seibert of the Back Creek district on May 6, 1830, when she was but fourteen years old. He had a career of some distinction far from Frederick County. He was a justice of the Berkeley County Court; three times a member of the Virginia House of Delegates; and in his later years an official of the Department of the Interior, resident in Washington. He died at his home there on November 2, 1854. Mrs. Boak returned to the Back Creek district, with a family of five—three sons born soon after the marriage, and two daughters much younger. Her father presented her with a house in the village.

Mrs. Boak is still remembered in the valley as a vigorous practical woman, always busy, always efficient, with a talent for being unobtrusively agreeable and helpful. Many of her traits are to be seen in Rachel Blake, the early-widowed daughter of the miller in *Sapphira*. She had Rachel's head and features, the "set of the head, enduring yet determined, the broad, highly coloured face, the fleshy nose, anchored deeply at the nostrils . . . grave dark eyes, too, set back under a broad forehead." She had a special aptness in caring for the sick. Like old Mrs. Harris, "many a time she had gone into a house where five or six children were all down with scarlet fever or diphtheria, and done what she could. Many a child and many a woman she had laid out and got ready for the grave. In her primitive community the undertaker made the coffin,—he did nothing more."

The Boaks had relations in the deep South. Cousins from Louisiana visited them in the Back Creek district. The three sons grew up strongly attached to the Southern cause. One of them died before he was twenty; the two others fought in the army of the Confederacy, and one was killed, William Lee Boak, to whose memory Willa Cather addressed a poem, "The Namesake," in 1902. Their sister Virginia shared their attachment, and to the end of her life cherished her brother's sword, and the Confederate flag. It was by her means that the breach between

William Cather and some of his kinfolk and neighbors was finally repaired. Not long after her marriage she gave a large party, driving about the valley to issue her invitations and make sure they were accepted. The record of the Boak attachment to the Confederacy was so excellent that people who shared the Boak views did not care to decline the invitation. Probably the passage of years had made the ostracism of William Cather somewhat absurd, and it was highly inconvenient. At any rate, when the estranged kinfolk and neighbors met him at his daughter-in-law's party, the open quarrel ended.

Meanwhile one of William Cather's sons, George, had married a girl from the North and decided to settle in Nebraska. The climate of Virginia was thought to be perilous to those with weak lungs; at least one of William Cather's daughters was ill with tuberculosis, and other women in the family were threatened. The dry bracing air of Nebraska was an inducement; another was the prospect of living in a Republican state. George Cather took up land in the northwest part of Webster County in 1873. William Cather paid his son a long visit in 1874–5, and in 1877 acquired a farm two or three miles from George's, leaving to Charles the care of the farm at Willowshade. It would be wrong to suppose that William's main reason for emigration was the hostility of neighbors. It would not have been in his character to run from opposition: he was not a man who would, in a phrase of the region, let others "hate him out." No doubt he felt he would be happier in a Republican state; no doubt he wished to do the best he could for the health of sisters and daughters; another reason was the need he felt, as he grew older, to farm where land was

level. The hills and vales of Back Creek were an increasing
tax on his strength; but his zeal as a farmer was at its
height.

II

Willa Cather was born on December 7, 1873,[1] and named
after a sister of her father's who died young. All through

---

[1] During the 1870's births in Frederick County were reported by the
tax collectors. Roscoe Boak Cather, Willa Cather's brother, is registered
with the birth date of June 24, 1877. E. K. Brown confirmed by a search
of the records that Willa Cather's name does not appear. In many current
works of reference the birth date is given as December 6, 1876, a date
incompatible with the registered date of her brother's birth. Brown was
told that Miss Cather began to give 1876 as the year of her birth when
she was on the staff of *McClure's Magazine* and that she did so because
S. S. McClure advised her to subtract two or three years from her age.
Who's Who from 1909 to 1919 gives Miss Cather's birth year as 1875
and from 1920 to her death as 1876. Brown was able finally to determine
the date from a letter written by Willa Cather's father to his brother,
George P. Cather, in Nebraska. It is dated January 22, 1874. "Jennie and
I were at town today . . . the first time she has been out. . . . We left
the baby at home with its Grandma; she said it did not cry once while we
were gone. She grows very fast, and is just as good as she is pretty. She is
not old enough yet to have that picture taken. We call her 'Willie' after
our little sister." There is extant also a letter to George P. Cather of February 1, 1874 from a former schoolmate in Back Creek, who writes:
"Charley and Jennie are getting along splendid. Charley don't get to
Church till it is half out on account of having to rock the babe to sleep—
that's the way of the world." This confirms the birth year as 1873. It is
interesting to note that Lesley Fergusson, the young teacher in "The
Best Years," the last story Willa Cather completed, made a change in her
age: in the high-school records she added two years because "I didn't
want to be the class baby, and I hoped I could get a school soon and help
out at home." The compunction Lesley felt when she learned she had a
school suggests that Willa Cather was not quite at ease about the harmless
deception. On the other hand she could treat the same question with high
good humor, as in the case of Doña Olivares of *Death Comes for the
Archbishop,* who was born, like Willa Cather, in the South where "no
birth records were kept; there was no document to prove the age of
Isabella Olivares, and she could not be persuaded to admit her true age."
How she is persuaded to give a reasonable if not entirely exact age is one
of the moments of high comedy in the novel.—L. E.

her childhood and youth she was usually called "Willie," and she liked to think of her name as a bond with her grandfather William Cather and her maternal grand-father William Lee Boak, as well as with her mother's brother, William Lee Boak, Jr. Three more children were born to Charles Cather and his wife before they left for Nebraska: Roscoe Boak Cather was born at Willowshade June 24, 1877; next were Douglass, born in 1880, and Jessica, born in 1881.

The household at Willowshade was full of bustling and many-colored life. The Virginian virtue of hospitality was in force there: cousins came for a meal and stayed for a month. There were always, in the phrase of "Old Mrs. Harris," "plenty of helpers." The hills were "full of solitary old women or women but slightly attached to some house-hold, who were glad to come . . . for good food and a warm bed, and the little present . . . slipped into their carpet-sack when they went away." When one of the chil-dren was ill, old Mary Ann Anderson was sent for because she was so kind, tactful, and understanding with a boy or girl obliged to stay in bed. It was almost worth the suffer-ings of croup, Willa Cather felt, to be able to count on Mary Ann's delightful coddling. The original of Aunt Till, the colored housekeeper at the miller's in *Sapphira*, was a woman of great firmness of character who used to live at Willowshade for weeks at a time, sometimes because she was needed, sometimes merely because she cared to stay.

Edmond de Goncourt remarks in *Chérie* that when one tries to recall one's childhood, it resembles a great empty space in which four or five little happenings start up with a sort of photographic clarity. For Willa Cather one of

these happenings was a ride in a steamboat when she was
not much more than a year old. She always remembered
the terror with which she clutched her mother as she was
carried aboard. The happening that in retrospect seemed
most dramatic and most suggestive was the meeting described in the epilogue to *Sapphira*. A story had been repeated again and again to Willa Cather as a part of the
district lore—of the flight of a beautiful young mulatto
slave, the daughter of the woman from whom Aunt Till
was drawn. Now this girl was to return after a quarter century of being away from the valley. Her meeting with her
mother took place in Mrs. Cather's room at Willowshade,
where Willa Cather lay in bed convalescing; it took place
there because Mrs. Cather, knowing how much it would
mean to the child to look on, arranged that it should. About
this meeting between a woman who was now grown old
and her daughter, who had passed into a prosperous and
alien middle age, Willa Cather's ideas concerning the institution of slavery and other kinds of oppressive relationship often gathered.

Another incident in which her imagination had its part
depended on her memory of a passage in *Peter Parley's
Universal History*, a work from which Mrs. Boak often
read to her. When she was four or five, one way to assure
her being quiet and immobile for a long time was to reverse a chair, place it on another, and set the child on the
upper chair. This became her chariot, and she would sit
upon it in complete silence, listening to an imaginary slave
who was repeating to her at intervals: "Cato, thou art but
man!" Willa Cather's absorption in this private situation
may have suggested to her father and mother that she was

perhaps a remarkable personality; they never forgot the
picture of the child guiding her chariot and listening to the
attendant spirit.

The farm was as pleasant to Willa Cather as the roomy,
cheerful house. She did not attend a school—her Grandmother Boak taught her. Mrs. Boak had gone to a good
school in Baltimore, she had read much and carefully, and
she had an alert mind. Much of the day, in all seasons,
however, the girl spent out in the fields with her father.
She liked to help herd the sheep, and shared his affection
for his favorite shepherd dog, Vic, for whom he made little
leather shoes to save her feet from the sharp rocks. He
would often carry her on his shoulder, like the grandfather
in her poem "The Swedish Mother," which is rich in memories of Willowshade:

> *We go big field, 'way up on hill,*
> *Ten times high like our windmill.*
> *One time your grandpa leave me wait*
> *While he call sheep down. By de gate*
> *I sit still till night come dark;*
> *Rabbits run an' strange dogs bark,*
> *Old owl hoot, an' your modder cry,*
> *She been so 'fraid big bear come by.*
> *Last, 'way off, she hear de sheep,*
> *Li'l' bells ring and li'l' lambs bleat.*
> *Then all sheep come over de hills,*
> *Big white dust, an' old dog Nils.*[2]

She had rabbit traps in distant spots in the woods, and
when she revisited Willowshade about twelve years after

---

[2] Willa Cather omitted the last two lines here quoted, when she revised the poem for the collected edition of her works.

the family had left for Nebraska, the first thing she did was to walk straight to where she had left them, and find them intact.

A hundred yards or so to the west along the road to the village was Back Creek, a sluggish stream except in spring, crossed then by an old suspension bridge. She liked to hang on this bridge and sing: "I stood on the bridge at midnight," though that was scarcely the time she chose. Less than a mile to the southwest was the mill of the Seiberts, where Mrs. Boak had grown up, and there were few things that gave Willa Cather so much pleasure as to talk with the miller in his cool dark mill, or watch the great wooden wheel turning hour by hour.

With Margie Anderson, a young girl who had come to Willowshade as nursemaid and general help, she would go as far as Timber Ridge to visit Margie's mother, Mary Ann, the Mrs. Ringer of *Sapphira*, who "was born interested," had a gift for telling stories, and a homely wisdom about people. She knew the histories of all the families in the region, rich and poor, and all the dramatic events that had become legends among the country people. Her talk was full of wit and fire, it was shot through with the vivid native idiom; and the stories she told, Willa Cather remembered all her life, as she remembered the drives along the mountain roads when she accompanied Mrs. Boak on errands of mercy or medicine, or her mother on visits to cousins, neighbors, or dependents.

The Virginia years ended in 1883, when Charles Cather was persuaded to join his parents and his brother in Nebraska. In February of that year the Willowshade property was sold for six thousand dollars. Most of the furnishings were auctioned. Even Vic, the shepherd dog, was given to a farmer who lived near by. Parting with almost everything that she knew and cared for made this a time of heartbreak for Willa Cather. There was a climax of sorrow when, just as the family was about to board a train—at that time there was a railroad running through the Back Creek settlement—Vic tore herself free and came running across the fields, dragging her broken chain.

2

Red Cloud:
the Wild Land

1884–1890

THE DESTINATION OF the Cathers was the farm of
Willa's grandfather in Webster County, Nebraska. Webster County is in the southern tier, and about halfway
across the state. In 1884 it still had the aspect and character of the frontier. The first settlement within its boundaries had been made only fourteen years before. In the summer of 1870 Silas Garber, a captain in the Northern armies
in the War between the States, had led a handful of associates and dependents overland southwest from Omaha.
The pioneers at once saw that the land in the southern
part of Webster County was the best and built their first
stockades at Guide Rock in its southeastern corner, and at
Red Cloud, some ten miles farther to the west.

Red Cloud was named after a famous and friendly Sioux
chief. By the time the Cathers arrived in the county, it was
a bustling and promising town, with a population about
one half of its present two thousand. It had grown on a
slight rise a mile or so to the north of the shallow, broad,
and sandy Republican River, which at this point flows
only a few miles to the north of the Kansas line. Much of
the surrounding countryside had been settled, and here
and there tracts were in pasture or under cultivation. The
town had its stores and hotels, its smithy and mill, its news-

papers and banks. A brick opera house, soon to be a magnet for Willa Cather, stood beside a brick bank. A school
had been opened the year after settlement began—many of
the newcomers were from New England—and soon after a
Methodist church. In 1879 the Republican Valley Railroad had been extended south from Hastings to serve Red
Cloud and continued to the west on the present line from
St. Joseph to Denver. Soon afterward the eastward line to
St. Joseph and Kansas City was completed.

The Virginia colony, in which Cathers were the leaders,
had taken up land to the northwest of Red Cloud, close to
the western border of the county; and long before 1884
they had a post office called, significantly, Catherton. Into
other townships Europeans were flocking, as into almost
every region in the state. "Nebraska," it was said in a proc-
lamation from the state department of immigration, "is the
last agricultural state in America offering cheap and good
homesteads to the landless. . . . Nebraska is the only remaining state wholly and richly agricultural and pastoral
where millions of acres are almost donated to the brave pioneers of the world by the generous government of America." Men and women of almost every European national-
ity were trying to make cornfields where there had been
for centuries a sweep of high, rough, shaggy red grass, the
"colour of wine-stains." To the north of Catherton there
was a settlement of French Canadians holding apart from
their neighbors. Spotted across the northern and central
tiers of the county were colonies of Germans, Bohemians,
Swedes, Danes, and Swiss. All but the Swiss were within
a morning's ride of Catherton; and all but the Swiss have
important roles in Willa Cather's fiction. In the richer

southern parts of the county, near the river, where the cottonwoods grew more luxuriantly, there were families of native American stock.

Charles F. Cather, though he continued to own a large farm and added steadily to his holdings, remained on the land for little more than a year; but his eleven-year-old daughter made an extraordinarily full use of the time. A merchant in Red Cloud who met her during her first years in the state described her to his daughter as "a young curiosity shop." It was the best kind of curiosity, the omnivorous artist's, that took her out delivering mail on horseback, with a pretext for entering many a lonely sod farmhouse in which few native Americans ever cared to set foot. In her essay on Nebraska, written more than twenty-five years after she had left for the East, Willa Cather was still impatient of the incuriosity of her family and other native groups.

Unfortunately, their American neighbors were seldom openminded enough to understand the Europeans, or to profit by their older traditions. Our settlers from New England, cautious and convinced of their own superiority, kept themselves isolated as much as possible from foreign influences. The incomers from the South—from Missouri, Kentucky, the two Virginias—were provincial and utterly without curiosity. They were kind neighbors—lent a hand to help a Swede when he was sick or in trouble. But I am quite sure that Knut Hamsun might have worked a year for any of our Southern farmers, and his employer would never have discovered that there was anything unusual about the Norwegian. A New England settler might have noticed that his chore-boy had a kind of intelligence, but he would have distrusted and stonily disregarded it. If the daughter of a shiftless West Virginia mountaineer married the nephew of a professor at the University of Upsala, the native family felt disgraced by such an alliance.

Willa Cather's own kin conformed to the Southern pattern. Like the grandparents of Jim Burden in *My Ántonia* they were kind to luckless neighbors and sought to encourage those who despaired; but neither Bohemian nor Scandinavian aroused their curiosity or taught them anything about the nature of man or of this prairie country in which European and Eastern American were at first equally alien.

The Bohemians at once drew Willa Cather. It was in the first of her years in Nebraska that she met and admired the girl from whose character and appearance she drew Ántonia Shimerda, and the old man who suggested to her Anton Rosicky. In the Bohemian settlements there were families that had come to America for political and ethical reasons, and some of the older men had the impress of a high European culture. But Willa Cather did not require that for her interest to stir. Simpler men like Rosicky were enough. In a leading editorial devoted to the story that centers in him, Anton Rosicky was described in the *Omaha World-Herald* as "the very stuff of which Nebraska was builded . . . the love of the land . . . combined with hard work . . . and a great spirit, and the will to take a beating and do battle again." In foreign-born men and women of this stripe Willa Cather found the most interesting people in her new home.

The old farmwomen, Bohemian and Scandinavian, moved her imagination. In a long story that she did not care to collect, "The Bohemian Girl," she presents the grandmothers gathered at a barn-raising in the northwest part of Webster County. It is the fullest of many such pictures in her fiction:

The older women, having assured themselves that there were twenty kinds of cake, not counting cookies, and three dozen fat pies, repaired to the corner behind the pile of watermelons, put on their white aprons, and fell to their knitting and fancywork. They were a fine company of old women, and a Dutch painter would have loved to find them there together, where the sun made bright patches on the floor and sent long quivering shafts of gold through the dusky shade up among the rafters. There were fat, rosy old women who looked hot in their best black dresses; spare alert old women with brown, dark-veined hands; and several of almost heroic frame, not less massive than old Mrs. Ericson herself. Few of them wore glasses, and old Mrs. Svendsen, a Danish woman, who was quite bald, wore the only cap among them. Mrs. Oleson, who had twelve big grandchildren, could still show two braids of yellow hair as thick as her own wrists. Among all these grandmothers there were more brown heads than white. They all had a pleased, prosperous air, as if they were more than satisfied with themselves and with life.

Nils, the sensitive and traveled narrator, asks his brother's wife:

Aren't they the Old Guard? I've just counted thirty hands. I guess they've wrung many a chicken's neck and warmed many a boy's jacket for him in their time.

As he spoke,

He fell into amazement when he thought of the Herculean labors those fifteen pairs of hands had performed: of the cows they had milked, the butter they had made, the gardens they had planted, the children and grandchildren they had tended, the brooms they had worn out, the mountains of food they had cooked. It made him dizzy.

As a young girl Willa Cather felt the vigor and energy in these old women from Europe; it was later, when she came out from Red Cloud to stay with her aunts, that she saw something that in her maturity she set even higher than vigor or energy—endurance.

When she was a girl, as in her later years, she cared as much about places as about persons. The high plains between the valley of the Republican and the valley of the Platte are not conventionally beautiful. In winter they are as dreary as a desert. "The variegated fields," Willa Cather wrote in *O Pioneers!* "are all one colour now; the pastures, the stubble, the roads, the sky are the same leaden grey. The hedgerows and trees are scarcely perceptible against the bare earth, whose slaty hue they have taken on. The ground is frozen so hard that it bruises the foot to walk in the roads or in the ploughed fields. It is like an iron country, and the spirit is oppressed by its rigour and melancholy. One could easily believe that in that dead landscape the germs of life and fruitfulness were extinct forever." "In the cold light," she wrote elsewhere, "even the fresh snow looked grey, and the frozen weeds sticking up through it." In all seasons, the Divide (as the high plains between the Republican and the Blue and between the Blue and the Platte are often called) was "one of the loneliest countries in the world."

If it was lonely, it was spacious; and even when Willa Cather was a little girl she was pleased with broad vistas and turned to places where her privacy was secure. In the more hospitable seasons the high plains had a vigorous beauty to which she responded with joy. The red grass, the rustling corn (Naples-yellow as she later learned to call its color in the end of summer), the sunflowers and ironweed along the soft dirt roads, skies "bright and shadowless, hard as enamel," were strange to a girl from Virginia, but delightful. The warm southwest wind that blew with the beginning of spring was another exhilarating discovery. "There were none of the signs of spring for which I used to watch in Virginia," Willa Cather wrote in *My Ántonia*, "no budding woods or blooming gardens. There was only—spring itself; the throb of it, the light restlessness, the vital essence of it everywhere; in the sky, in the swift clouds, in the pale sunshine, and in the warm, high wind—rising suddenly, sinking suddenly, impulsive and playful like a big puppy that pawed you and then lay down to be petted. If I had been tossed down blindfold on that red prairie, I should have known that it was spring." In the heat of summer Willa Cather "used to love to drift along the pale-yellow cornfields, looking for the damp spots one sometimes found at their edges, where the smartweed soon turned a rich copper colour and the narrow brown leaves hung curled like cocoons about the swollen joints of the stem." Trees led a precarious life on the Divide, and Willa Cather "used to feel anxious about them, and visit them as if they were persons."

The stay in the Virginia colony, so rich in impressions that were to pour out in novels and tales, ended sometime in 1885, when Charles F. Cather, who was not born to be a farmer on the prairie, opened an office in Red Cloud where he dealt in loans and mortgages on farm property. He leased a house, which remained the family's home un-

til long after Willa Cather left Nebraska for the East. This
house is at the southwest corner of Cedar Street and Third
Avenue, one short block from the main street. It is a long,
narrow frame house, painted white, one and a half stories
high. Something of the rooms downstairs and the life that
went on in them has been recorded in "Old Mrs. Harris,"
the longest of the stories in *Obscure Destinies*. The Cathers' was a crowded household: to the four children they
brought with them from Virginia three were added in Nebraska—James, Jack, and Elsie; Mrs. Boak continued to
live with them; and Margie Anderson continued to be their
servant until her death well on in this century. In the back
rooms there was the confusion that numbers always bring
unless the mistress of the house is an adroit manager of detail, and Mrs. Cather was never that, though her firm will,
supported by her rawhide whip, arrested disorder when
it became a tumult. The parlor was always a pleasant
room. "The hard-coal burner threw out a warm red glow.
A faded respectable Brussels carpet covered the floor, and
an old-fashioned wooden clock ticked on the walnut book-
case. There were a few easy chairs, and no hideous orna-
ments about." For Willa Cather the attic with its bare rafters was the most important part of the house. Her memory
of it is in the description of Thea Kronborg's attic room
and in one of the last of her writings, "The Best Years,"
the one Nebraska story in *The Old Beauty and Others*.

"Upstairs" was a story in itself, a secret romance. No caller
or neighbour had ever been allowed to go up there. All the
children loved it—it was their very own world where there
were no older people poking about to spoil things. And it was
unique—not at all like other people's upstairs chambers. . . .

Lesley and the boys liked space, not tight cubbyholes. Their upstairs was a long attic which ran the whole length of the house, from the front door downstairs to the kitchen at the back. Its great charm was that it was unlined. No plaster, no beaver-board lining; just the roof shingles, supported by long, unplaned, splintery rafters that sloped from the sharp roof-peak down to the floor of the attic. Bracing these long roof rafters were cross rafters on which one could hang things—a little personal washing, a curtain for tableaux, a rope swing. . . .

In this spacious undivided loft were two brick chimneys, go-ing up in neat little stair-steps from the plank floor to the shin-gle roof—and out of it to the stars! The chimneys were of red, unglazed brick, with lines of white mortar to hold them to-gether.

The children's beds stood side by side; and on a winter night, with hot bricks at their feet, while the snow sifted in through cracks in the shingles and sprinkled their faces and the covers, and through the single small window at the end of the loft "the white light from the snow and the half-strangled moon" shone on the floor, the children had some of their happiest moments. Willa Cather regretted a change that her mother insisted on as the girl grew older. "Her mother had said she must have a room of her own. So a carpenter brought sheathing and 'lined' the end of the long loft—the end over the kitchen." The little room was "very like a snug wooden box"; but she could "leave her door open into the long loft, where the wood was brown and the chimneys red and the weather always so close to one." The loft was no common bedroom—she thought of it as a feudal hall and associated it with lines in Grimm's *Fairy Tales*.

In the Virginia colony Willa Cather had been taught by
her grandmother Mrs. Boak and others in the family. In
Red Cloud she began to attend school and had extraordinary fortune in her teachers. With three of them, all people of remarkable gifts, she remained in touch for many
years, and one was an intimate friend for life. Mrs. Eva J.
Case, who is still recalled in Red Cloud as a teacher of
literature and foreign languages and a woman of great
charm, was one of Willa Cather's first teachers. It was
probably with her that Willa Cather read *Paradise Lost*,
one of her first literary experiences. Mrs. Case later was Superintendent of Public Instruction for Webster County,
and something of her nature and her work is recorded in
the character of Miss Knightly in "The Best Years." Mrs.
Case had a remarkable perception of the moral and intellectual flaws in the town's way of life and was an ally in
Willa Cather's efforts to find an environment in which her
mind could grow more freely. The other teachers to whom
Willa Cather was specially drawn were Mr. and Mrs. A. K.
Goudy, and it was an agreeable coincidence that when she
was graduated from the Red Cloud high school in June
1890, the two signatures on her diploma were theirs, Mr.
Goudy as county superintendent, Mrs. Goudy as principal.
The Goudys moved to Lincoln in 1891, when Mr. Goudy
became state superintendent, and Willa Cather was much
in their company and confidence during the years when
she was a student at the University of Nebraska. She admired Mr. Goudy's union of quietness with force, and until
Mrs. Goudy died, in 1930, she was one of Willa Cather's
intimates.

From gifted people in the town Willa Cather learned

more than her teachers could tell her. Not far from the Cather house lived Mrs. Charles Wiener, a brilliant Frenchwoman, married to one of the merchants of Red Cloud. The Wieners spoke French and German and had collected a library extraordinary both in size and in quality. They soon gave Willa Cather the run of it and of their house. What the privilege meant to her she has recorded in "Old Mrs. Harris," where the Wieners were the models for the Rosens. Willa Cather began to read French and to wish that she could read German; and she began to inform herself about life in France and Germany and in Europe generally. On hot afternoons, when her attic retreat was stifling, she would go over to the Wieners. "She would take a sofa pillow and lie down on the soft carpet and look up at the pictures in the dusky room [the shades were drawn], and feel a happy, pleasant excitement from the heat and glare outside and the deep shadow and quiet within." Mrs. Wiener's house exemplified a kind of culture she had not known, and at once recognized as akin to her spirit. In this household she also found intellectual encouragement: Mrs. Wiener was among the first to appreciate what a remarkable mind Willa Cather had and to urge her to hard work.

A German music teacher from whom she drew Wunsch in *The Song of the Lark* was another source of information about European life and culture. Willa Cather was no Thea Kronborg: if she delighted in listening to music and in talking about it, she had no interest in learning to play or to sing. The old music teacher used to ask the mother of another and more docile pupil what he should do with "that Cather girl," for he could find no argument that

would induce her to practice as she must if she would become even a mediocre musician. Wisely he decided that he
would give her her head, overlook what she could not or
would not do, and spend his time with her playing or talking about great music and musicians, or about the life and
culture he had known in European cities.

William Ducker, "Uncle Billy" to so many children in
Red Cloud at the time when Willa Cather knew him, was
the first to make Greek and Latin literature come alive
for her. Of English birth, he had come to Waukegan, Illinois, when he was eighteen to join older brothers who had
a store there. His formal education was slight, but he had
a passion for learning and a love for poetry seldom found
together. His brothers allowed him a good deal of leisure,
and much of this he gave to reading ancient writers, particularly the poets. When he was fifty he came to Red
Cloud with members of his family, who opened a store in
which he might sometimes be found leaning over a counter
with the *Iliad* or the *Æneid* or the *Odes* of Anacreon lying
open before him. The schools of Red Cloud did not satisfy
him; and he gave his own children lessons in the classics
and other subjects to supplement the meager official schedule. He too found something remarkable in Willa Cather,
and he supervised her reading as closely as if she were a
daughter. After she had begun to study at the University
of Nebraska, she continued to read Latin and Greek with
Mr. Ducker in the vacations; and she contrasted his passion for poetry with the somewhat arid scholarship she
found in the classical instructors in Lincoln. Ducker's sudden death in the terrible drought-ridden summer of 1893
was one of her first deep griefs. Willa Cather had just left

his house one afternoon when she was suddenly sum-
moned by one of his children who came running after her.
Mr. Ducker was dead when she reached him. He lay on
the couch with the *Iliad* open on the floor beside him.
"There are always dreamers on the frontier," she wrote in
O Pioneers! He was one of the most memorable.

The pleasure that Willa Cather found in the company of
older people, and the readiness with which they accepted
her, appear very sharply in "Two Friends," the story with
which *Obscure Destinies* closes. The two middle-aged men
—one of them was the merchant Mr. Miner—pass the early
part of their evenings together; it is the only time they see
each other. In colder months they sit in the store that one
of them owns; on any night that is warm enough they draw
two chairs out on the broad sidewalk. They allow the narrator of the story, from the time she was ten years old, to
sit within hearing of their wide-ranging talk and to make
what she can of it. A whole evening's discussion might
pivot on a scientific novelty, a play, a reminiscence of the
older and better West, or the life-history of a remarkable
farm family in this or a neighboring county.

I liked to listen to those two because theirs was the only
"conversation" one could hear about the streets. The older men
talked of nothing but politics and their business, and the very
young men's talk was entirely what they called "josh"; very
personal, supposed to be funny, and really not funny at all. It
was scarcely speech, but noises, snorts, giggles, yawns, sneezes,
with a few abbreviated words and slang expressions which
stood for a hundred things. The original Indians of the Kansas
plains had more to do with articulate speech than had our
promising young men.

It is a revealing passage. There was scarcely a man or a
woman in Red Cloud who had any "conversation," who
knew anything worth hearing and could tell something of
it, whom Willa Cather did not frequent. Doctors, lawyers,
clergy, men of affairs, she listened to them all; and when
there was a woman such as Mrs. Miner, whom she drew
as Mrs. Harling, Ántonia's employer, Willa Cather never
tired of eliciting her experience of life and the conclusions
she had drawn from it.

Just beyond the southeastern edge of the town, in a
house much larger and much more grandly furnished than
any in Red Cloud, lived the most famous man in Webster
County, the leader in the first settlement at Guide Rock
and Red Cloud, Silas Garber. In 1873 he had been elected
to the state legislature to represent Webster and adjacent
counties; and in 1875 he became Governor of Nebraska.
(He passed, said a local paper, the *Nation*, "in three years
from a 'dug-out' on yonder bank to the Capitol at Lincoln,
from the organization of Webster County to the reorgan-
ization of the State of Nebraska.") In 1879 he was thrown
from a carriage and suffered injuries that condemned him
to an inactive life. Silas Garber and his wife, a Southern
woman of extraordinary charm and color, took little part
in the life of the town; but he had broadly scattered in-
vestments in land and was the principal power in a local
bank. Presidents of railroads, politicians from Lincoln, and
other notables stayed at the Garber house. It was the center of a larger kind of life than any other that Willa Cather
knew. She was often in it, and as she came to know Governor Garber and to hear the story of his life, he symbolized for her the ideal pioneer. Red Cloud and Webster

County were passing into another phase, in which Silas Garber was a relic of a bolder past, full of a promise that was not to be realized. From him she drew Captain Forrester in *A Lost Lady*, who "looked like the pictures of Grover Cleveland" and whose "clumsy dignity covered a deep nature, and a conscience that had never been juggled with."

The cemetery of Red Cloud lies at the southwest of the town on a wind-swept height from which the ground drops sharply to the south and the west. The tombstones are conventional and most of them small; but at the center of the cemetery rests a rugged reddish granite boulder of massive size with the name and dates of Silas Garber. The boulder would stir the imagination of a casual visitor: it has a place in *A Lost Lady*. Captain Forrester, ailing like Governor Garber, and like him impoverished in his last years, sits for hours in his garden by "a red block of Colorado sandstone, set on a granite boulder in the midst of the gravel space around which the roses grew." The red block was a sun-dial; and block and boulder were removed to mark the captain's grave. Governor Garber was the largest personality to come within Willa Cather's view when she was a girl. In her own generation she found no one with his stamp, and she never resigned herself to the disappearance of the generation of the founders. "The Old West had been settled by dreamers, great-hearted adventurers who were unpractical to the point of magnificence; a courteous brotherhood, strong in attack but weak in defence, who could conquer but could not hold."

II

Persons were the most important aspect of the town to Willa Cather in her girlhood. But they were not her sole resource. The opera house was a magical place, and the actors and actresses who played there were an enchantment. "Half a dozen times during each winter, a travelling stock company settled down at the local hotel and thrilled and entertained us for a week." As soon as posters began to appear "on the side of a barn, on the lumberyard fence, in the 'plate-glass' windows of drug stores," the children on their way home from school would pause and study them, choosing which plays or operas they would ask to see, and debating whether their parents would allow them to go only on the first and last nights or whether they might hope to attend every other night during the company's all too brief stay. The company usually arrived on the evening train from the east; and the children would walk the mile to the station—along a sidewalk that crossed the fields—often drawing younger brothers and sisters on sleds. The actors and actresses seemed like creatures from another planet. "If by any chance one of the show ladies carried a little dog with a blanket on, that simply doubled our pleasure." Everything the company did during their stay at the hotel evoked curious and favorable comment. They were almost as much a show as the plays and operas they performed, such plays as *The Corsican Brothers, Damon and Pythias, The Count of Monte Cristo,* such operas as *The Mikado, The Chimes of Normandy, The Bohemian Girl.*

This last was, in memory at least, the one that most affected Willa Cather; it found a way into more than one of her stories.

The companies were not of the first order, but when "old Frank Lindon in a frilled shirt and a velvet coat blazing with diamonds, stood in the drawing room of Madame Danglars and revealed his identity to Madame de Morcerf, his faithless Mercedes, when she cowered and made excuses, and he took out a jewelled snuff-box with a much powdered hand, raised his eyebrows, permitted his lip to curl, and said softly and bitterly—'a fidelity of six months,' then we children were not in the opera house at Red Cloud, we were in Madame Danglars' salon in Paris." In a nostalgic letter to the *Omaha World-Herald*, written as long afterward as 1929, Willa Cather recalled the effect of the old operas and plays and affirmed that they were one of the great imaginative elements in her youth. No movie, she thought, not even a Chaplin comedy, could do for a later generation what the plain old opera house with its scratch companies of beginners and veterans had done for hers.

Books of many kinds mattered to her, even more than the operas and the plays. She was interested in the history of the Western plains and the Mississippi Valley; and in Parkman's volume on La Salle and in his *Oregon Trail* she found aspects of this described in a prose that delighted her. The main paths of English fiction in the nineteenth century were another resort—George Eliot, Hardy, Stevenson, and Kipling in especial. She had already begun to take what proved to be a passing pleasure in Tennyson— the Tennyson of the *Idylls*—and in Byron's narratives. *Sar-*

tor Resartus and *The French Revolution* were to exercise
an influence the most decisive of all.

There was also the river. The Republican has often
changed its course and there is no trace above water of
the pirate headquarters on a large sandy island in which
Willa Cather, her two brothers next in age, Roscoe and
Douglass, and many friends spent pleasant summer days.
Stevenson, Mark Twain, and many a humbler source combined with the misshapen roots of trees, the odd configu-
rations of sand and the grotesque contours of the island to
make of this retreat a place of high childish romance.
Much of what the river and the island meant to her is recorded in an early story, "The Treasure of Far Island":

> Of all the possessions of their childhood's Wonderland, Far
> Island had been dearest. . . . Long before they had set foot
> upon it the island was the goal of their loftiest ambitions and
> most delightful imaginings. . . . They had even decided that
> a race of kindly dwarfs must inhabit it and had built up a civ-
> ilization and historic annals for these imaginary inhabitants,
> surrounding the sand bar with all the mystery and enchant-
> ment which was attributed to certain islands of the sea by the
> mariners of Greece.

It was Willa Cather who gave imaginative names to the
several parts of the long sandy island—and to many other
places of adolescent resort: the Silvery Beaches, the Utter-
most Desert, the Salt Marshes, the Huge Fallen Tree.
"The Treasure of Far Island" was later to be remolded into
a different tale, a little masterpiece, "The Enchanted
Bluff." The hold the memory of river and isle had upon
Willa Cather's imagination as a place where her childhood
was eternally enshrined may be judged by the dedicatory

lines she inscribed in the first edition of her poems, to her
brothers, in which she remembered the "Odysseys of summer mornings" and the "starry wonder-tales of nights in
April. . . ."

> *Of the three who lay and planned at moonrise,*
> *On an island in a western river*
> *Of the conquest of the world together.*

Another kind of romance entered into the children's explorations of the countryside when they learned at school
about Coronado's expedition in quest of the seven golden
cities. The orthodox view was that Coronado had not
come as far north as the Nebraska line; but there were
many in the state then, and there are some now, who believed that he had traveled along the Republican River.
The children had no doubt that he had done so; they were
convinced that the great captain had paused within sight
of their citadel. The debate concerning Coronado was the
first link in the long chain that was to bind Willa Cather
to the Southwestern country and the Spanish explorers
and missionaries.

Opera house and river island were invitations to her imagination. So were the European families she always saw
when she visited her aunts Mrs. G. P. Cather and Mrs. An-
drews in Catherton township, and on the streets of Red
Cloud, where on many evenings there were more farmers
than townsfolk.

The town as she knew it in the 1880's has been described
in *The Song of the Lark* with the name of Moonstone. Approached from the river, it began with the red Burlington
"depot" and the settlement that had grown up about it—

a roundhouse, a restaurant or two, and some modest houses. A boardwalk and dirt road led north across the fields and up a hill close to the Catholic church and the cemetery. It rose past some small houses until on a slightly higher rise it reached the main part of Red Cloud, where there was an occasional house of two full stories, and on the main street an impressive expanse of brick. To the west of the main street lived the important and more or less wealthy, the Cathers among them; to the east, on streets that have altered little in half a century, "the humbler citizens, the people who voted but did not run for office." Those who lived to the west had the usual indifference to the homes and ways of the respectable poor; but Willa Cather preferred the eastern streets when she took one of the younger children for a walk or for a ride in carriage or express wagon. She had a strong pleasure in the unpretending simplicity—old women washing clothes in back yards, men sitting at front doors smoking a pipe. In the quiet streets there were few of the elms and pines that dragged out a somewhat precarious life in front of the larger houses to the west. Instead the cottonwood, one of her great pleasures, "had its way and spread in luxuriance."

III

Among many of the poorer people her curiosity was not disliked, but in both east and west there were some families stirred to disapprove, after the fashion of a small town anywhere, of a young girl who was obtrusively unconventional. Much of the disapproval centered in one peculiar pursuit, which began with the arrival of the personal belongings of an uncle who had died not long after he became a doctor. The presence of medical instruments in the household strengthened her already lively interest in zoology, a pursuit that fascinated Mr. Ducker about as much as epic poetry. She had more than a passing wish to become a doctor, and she understood that she could not progress in zoological science unless she performed experiments on animals. Her medical interest extended beyond the usual terminus of a physician's care and curiosity to include embalming.

The echo of the conflict between the young experimenter and the stuffily correct townsfolk is clearly to be heard in the remarkable high-school commencement address that Willa Cather, aged sixteen, delivered in the opera house on June 5, 1890. Her topic was "Superstition versus Investigation." These forces, she declared, had contended for mastery since the dawn of history. "The ancient orientals," she continued in language that must have been all too clear to the conservatives in her audience, "were highly civilized people, but were dreamers and theorists who delved into the mystic and metaphysical, leaving the more practical questions unanswered, and were subject to the evils of tyranny and priestcraft. Those sacred books of the east we today regard as half-divine; we are not apt to think as we read those magnificent flights of metaphor that the masses of people who read and believed them knew nothing of figures. It is the confounding of the literal and the figurative that has made atheists and fanatics throughout the ages." After an allusion to Carlyle, who was for more than twenty years to be her special modern prophet, she contrasted the Greeks with the ancient Hebrews. "The Greeks lacking the intense religious fervor of the Orient entertained broader views. Their standard of manhood was one of practical worth. They allowed no superstition, religious, political or social, to stand between them and the truth, and suffered exile, imprisonment and death for the right of opinion and investigation." In the Middle Ages, superstition regained the mastery. "All the great minds were crushed for men were still ruled by the iron scepter of fear and it was essential that they should remain ignorant. Superstition has ever been the curse of the church and until she can acknowledge that since her principles are true, no scientific truth can contradict them, she will never realize her full strength." Superstition sustained a major defeat from Francis Bacon. "In the Elizabethan age, a book was written asserting that nature is the only teacher, that no man's mind is broad enough to invent a theory to hold nature, for she is the universe. With the publication of the *Novum Organum* came a revolution in thought, scientists ceased theorizing and began experimenting. Thus we went painfully back to nature, weary and disgusted with our artificial knowledge, hungering for that which is meat, thirsting for that which is drink, longing for the things that are. She has given us the universe in answer."

Against this vast background Willa Cather began to deal with the issue on which she had offended local opinion:

It is the most sacred right of man to investigate; we paid dearly for it in Eden; we have been shedding our heart's blood for it ever since. It is ours; we have bought it with a price.

Scientific investigation is the hope of our age, as it must precede all progress; and yet upon every hand we hear the objections to its pursuit. The boy who spends his time among the stones and flowers is a trifler, and if he tries with bungling at-

tempt to pierce the mystery of animal life he is cruel. Of course
if he becomes a great anatomist or a brilliant naturalist, his
cruelties are forgotten or forgiven him; the world is very cautious, but it is generally safe to admire a man who has succeeded. We do not withhold from a few great scientists the
right of the hospital, the post mortem or experimenting with
animal life, but we are prone to think the right of experimenting with life too sacred a thing to be placed in hands of inexperienced persons. Nevertheless, if we bar our novices from
advancement, whence shall come our experts?

But to test the question by comparison, would all the life destroyed in experimenting from the beginning of the world until
today be as an atom to the life saved by that one grand discovery for which Harvey sacrificed his practice and his reputation, the circulation of the blood? There is no selfishness in this.
It came from a higher motive than the desire for personal gain,
for it too often brings destitution instead. Of this we have a
grand example in the broken-down care-worn old man who has
just returned from the heart of the Dark Continent. But perhaps you still say that I evade the question, has any one a right
to destroy life for scientific purposes? Ah, why does life live
upon death throughout the universe?

Investigators have styled fanatics those who seek to probe
into the mysteries of the unknowable. This is unreasonable.
The most aspiring philosopher never hoped to do more than
state the problem, he never dreamed of solving it. Newton did
not say how or why every particle of matter in the universe attracted every other particle of matter in the universe. He simply said it was so. We can only judge these abstract forces by
their effect. Our intellectual swords may cut away a thousand
petty spiderwebs woven by superstition across the mind of man
but before the veil of the "Sanctum Sanctorum" we stand con-
founded, our blades glance and turn and shatter upon the eter-

nal adamant. Microscopic eyes have followed matter to the molecule and fallen blinded. Imagination has gone a step farther and grasped the atom. There, with a towering height above and yawning death below even this grows sick at soul. For over six thousand years we have shaken fact and fancy in the dice box together and breathlessly awaited the result. But the dice of God are always loaded, and there are two sides which never fall upward, the alpha and omega. Perhaps when we make our final cast with dark old death we may shape them better.

This discourse, which like Jim Burden's "stated with fervor a great many things" the speaker "had lately discovered," is still remembered as a startling dissonant note in a conventional program. Among the flowers and the evergreens, with a festoon bearing the legend "1890," a male quartet and a female duet had rendered appropriate music and song. There were three graduates. A boy developed the theme of "Self-Advertising," with which "he was thoroughly conversant"; and his counsels "if followed generally would be a great boon to those men who think that advertising doesn't pay." Another boy, the son of a rich money-lender, addressed himself to the topic "New Times Demand New Measures and New Men," proving "what close application to study in early childhood will do for those who improve the opportunity." We are in the world of Bayliss Wheeler in *One of Ours,* and of Ivy Peters in *A Lost Lady.* "They would drink up the mirage, dispel the morning freshness, root out the great brooding spirit of freedom, the generous, easy life of the great land-holders. The space, the colour, the princely carelessness of the pioneer they would destroy and çut up into profitable bits, as the match factory splinters the primeval forest. All the way from the Missouri to the mountains this generation of shrewd young men, trained to petty economies by hard times, would do exactly what Ivy Peters had done when he drained the Forrester marsh." Between the addresses of the two boys and Willa Cather's there was an interlude of music and song. Then came the "masterpiece of oratory," with "its line of thought well carved out," in which Willa Cather linked her defiance of local currents of opinion with the history of genius and of heresy.

Willa Cather was already beginning to feel that the conventionalism of Red Cloud was a denial of life itself, a network of caution, evasion and negation. In a chapter of *My Ántonia* which was much resented in the town she recalls that the girls refrained from exercise as from something inelegant if not indecent, and "stayed indoors in winter because of the cold, and in summer because of the heat." Even when they danced, their bodies seemed not to move inside their clothes—"their muscles seemed to ask but one thing—not to be disturbed." What kind of life would they have in comparison with the sturdy pioneers who had founded the town? "The Black Hawk boys looked forward to marrying Black Hawk girls, and living in a brand-new little house with best chairs that must not be sat upon, and hand-painted china that must not be used." Willa Cather had no intention of taking the mold that was prepared for her generation. She offered a challenge that was much more obtrusive than her preoccupation with zoological experiments. In her high-school days she wore her hair shingled, shorter than many of the boys. Her clothes and hats were also boyish: a starched shirt, a tie, and a hat almost like a boy's. She did not care to be called Willa; many of her friends used Willie, but to this she preferred Will or Billie; and it gave her a particular satisfaction when a perceptive, appreciative person would call her Dr. Will.

A young girl who dressed like a boy, preferred the conversation of unusual older men to most of the pleasures sought by the other boys and girls of the town, and was reputed to hold dangerous opinions about religion as well as to enjoy cutting up animals, was an alien creature in what she was to call a "bitter, dead little Western town." About her, as about Jim Burden, circulated the whisper that there was "something queer" and unsound in so complete a rebel. Willa Cather was under the spell of the Nebraska countryside, and she was under the spell of philosophy, science, history, and the arts. The town was not a place where either spell could work. In 1890 she made a choice between the two kinds of interest which were to divide her being for the rest of her life, and it is recorded with modifications in "Old Mrs. Harris": she went to Lincoln to complete her preparation for the University of Nebraska.

3

Lincoln: the Striving Years

1891–1895

WILLA CATHER ARRIVED in Lincoln at the end of the summer of 1890. She still wore her hair very short and straight, her hats and clothes were boyish, and in more important ways she was determined to obey what she thought to be the law of her individual nature. She came expecting to encounter teachers as speculative as William Ducker and as responsive to beauty in literature; as civilized as Mrs. Wiener; and above all with a store of scientific knowledge far beyond that in any mind in Red Cloud.

A full year was to pass before she could become a student in the University of Nebraska. Like many of the smaller institutions in the state the high school at Red Cloud did not offer adequate preparation for a university course. It was especially weak in scientific instruction. The Latin School, a preparatory academy with a two-year program, had been established at Lincoln primarily to enable students from other parts of the state to make up their deficiencies. Willa Cather was enrolled in the senior year, or "Second Prep." Members of the university faculty taught most of the courses, and their teaching has been remembered as effective and stimulating. William Linn Westermann recalls that while the "preparatory" class in Greek was waiting for the instructor to begin the first les-

son the door opened and a head appeared, with short hair
and a straw hat; a deep masculine voice inquired whether
this was where the class in elementary Greek was meeting;
a boy nodded that it was; and as the newcomer opened
the door wide and revealed a girl's figure and skirts, the
entire class burst into laughter. Willa Cather, unruffled,
quietly took her place.

Willa Cather's instructor in English, Professor Ebenezer
Hunt, who was soon to say to her: "Life is one damned
grind, Cather," was alert for signs of originality in writing.
Late in the winter he assigned a long theme on the topic:
"The personal characteristics of Thomas Paine as judged
from his writings." There was alarm among some of Hunt's
friends and colleagues. The "filthy little atheist," as a President of the United States was to call him, was an inap-
propriate theme for the speculations, or studies, of preparatory students in pious Lincoln. Hunt yielded to advice,
and scoring out "Paine," he substituted "Carlyle." Members of the class recall that on the day when Hunt returned the themes, he wrote on the blackboard a sentence
from one of them, Willa Cather's: "Like the lone survivor
of some extinct species, the last of the mammoths, tortured
and harassed beyond all endurance by the smaller though
perhaps more perfectly organized offspring of the world's
maturer years, this great Titan, the son of her passionate
youth, a youth of volcanoes and earthquakes and great un-
systematized forces, rushed off into the desert to suffer
alone." This sentence, surviving in yellowed notes at Lincoln, and still repeated when classmates meet at street
corners, reveals much more about Willa Cather than about
Thomas Carlyle. So does the rest of the theme: there is

scarcely a mention of his "personal characteristics." Like the essential parts of the graduation address of the preceding spring this paper is intensely emotional; but here the emotion is almost unrestrained, though far from the ebullience of Carlyle. In a deeper likeness to the graduating address, the theme expresses Willa Cather's sense of being at variance, even at war, with the world surrounding her and pressing upon her. In what Hunt shrewdly took to be the key sentence she has translated into general terms her individual problem—that of nonconformity in a small town —which later was to be retranslated into the larger sense of tragedy in the supersession of the heroic pioneer generation of Nebraska by the neat petty generation of Ivy Peters and Bayliss Wheeler.

Hunt was so pleased by the theme that without consulting its author he arranged for its appearance in the local paper, the *State Journal,* where it was published on March 1, 1891. A note on the editorial page drew attention to "Some Personal Characteristics of Thomas Carlyle" as the work of a student at the university, "a young girl sixteen years of age who comes from Webster County." "A careful reading," Charles H. Gere, the editor, declared, "will convince any student of literature that it is a remarkable production, reflecting not a little credit on the author and the university."

Thirty years afterward the appearance of her theme in print at that time seemed to Willa Cather to have been a decisive event. She had come to Lincoln intending to take a chiefly scientific course, and later to specialize in medicine. The sight of her work in print, and no doubt the commendation it drew, had an effect upon her which she could only describe as "hypnotic." Henceforth it was clear that her aim must be to write. Miss Mariel Gere, a classmate and lifelong friend, who followed a scientific program, cannot recall among "numberless discussions of various topics" from 1891 to 1895 any that touched on science. She does not believe that Willa Cather retained "any interest in science worth mentioning."

The courses Willa Cather attended in her four years at the University of Nebraska were primarily literary. In her first and second years her principal studies were in classics and in English. The records of the university do not include her grades. It is clear that her ability continued to be recognized in the department of English: in each of these years she was permitted to substitute advanced courses in literature for the courses normally required. Her interest and competence in Greek are shown by her election in her second year of a course in the Greek lyric; and she was prone to quote Greek on unlikely occasions. If there are no records of her grades, her contemporaries recall her in those years as working very long hours, and distinguishing herself in both the linguistic and the literary courses that constituted most of her program.

She had no intention of becoming a scholar, and some of the courses she took seemed to her pedantic and sterile. What she desired from the classics was the experience of great literature and the knowledge of great civilization. In the classical courses at Nebraska, as at most universities, there was altogether too much gerund-grinding, too much about *hoti* and the enclitic *de*. The great initiation promised for the truly elect was into the mysterious classifications of Sanskrit verbs. Even the classicist from whom she learned most, James T. Lees, was notable for precision rather than insight. What she had hoped the teachings of the classics would give in terms of literature and civilization she has shown in *My Ántonia* in her rendering of Jim Burden's response to the inspired teaching of Gaston Cleric, an imagined figure, superior to any of Willa Cather's instructors.

He could bring the drama of antique life before one out of the shadows—white figures against blue backgrounds. I shall never forget his face as it looked one night when he told me about the solitary day he spent among the sea temples at Paestum: the soft wind blowing through the roofless columns, the birds flying low over the flowering marsh grasses, the changing lights on the silver, cloud-hung mountains. . . . I remember vividly another evening, when something led us to talk of Dante's veneration for Virgil. Cleric went through canto after canto of the "Commedia," repeating the discourse between Dante and his "sweet teacher," while his cigarette burned itself out unheeded between his long fingers. I can hear him now, speaking the lines of the poet Statius, who spoke for Dante: *"I was famous on earth with the name which endures longest and honours most. The seeds of my ardour were the sparks from that divine flame whereby more than a thousand have kindled; I speak of the 'Aeneid,' mother to me and nurse to me in poetry."*

The words from the twenty-first canto of the *Purgatorio* are very close to Charles Eliot Norton's translation. The sort of teaching that Willa Cather desired she might have had if Norton's favorite pupil, George Edward Woodberry, had found Lincoln and the University of Nebraska agreeable to his temper and his aims. In 1882, after three years as professor of English, he was engaged in such spirited controversy with the chancellor that both parties were encouraged, if not required, to leave the institution. In the year that Willa Cather arrived in Lincoln, Woodberry became professor of comparative literature at Columbia, and his course on the Epic was exactly what Willa Cather longed for, and indeed required—a study of ideas, personalities, and forms conducted by a man to whom all three were living realities.

His successor at the University of Nebraska was a man of very different stamp, and Willa Cather's aversion from his approach to literature became an important fact in the history of her mind and art. Lucius A. Sherman, a graduate of Yale, had taught in an Eastern school for a few years before coming to Nebraska in 1882 as head of the department of English. His interest was about as wholly literary as Woodberry's; but, as his books make very plain, it was not the ideas, the personalities, and the forms, but the laws he could frame that really interested Sherman. He made an exhaustive study of sounds as expressions of emotion. "The vowel of pain," he wrote in his *Elements of Literature and Composition*, is ō, and its best supporting sounds are *g* hard, *r*, and *w*, with the vowel accompaniments of *uo, au, a̤, u,* and *oi*." He devised elaborate diagrams for the analysis of words, in which such a term as *bicycle* was judged by two tests, "ideals of the beautiful" and "ideals of the true." The ideals of the beautiful he described as "adornment," "symmetry," "pleasure," and "form"; the ideals of the true as "construction" and "reliability." "A bicycle," he opined, "is not a thing of beauty, although every effort has been made, in its construction, to secure symmetry and comfort for the eye. After the sen-

sation of the outline, and of the lacquer and polish, we recognize the proportion, and the finish of the instrument, and
begin to be conscious of the pleasure of the motion it invites." The bicycle satisfies more nearly the tests of "construction" and "reliability": it is indeed notable for "its
staunchness and safety." Sherman worked out similar tests
for more complex kinds of form in art, for the organization of incident and the revelation of character. He delighted in long sets of minute questions. About the mother
of Coriolanus he inquired, Miss Olivia Pound remembers,
in one seemingly interminable test: "What did the noble
matron Volumnia say then?" Willa Cather's answer ran:
"The noble matron Volumnia then said 'Bow-wow.'" She
had many courses with Sherman, but this was her essential judgment of his mechanical approach to literature.
When a younger member of the Cather family enrolled
more than a decade later in a course of Sherman's, Willa
Cather telegraphed to insist on cancellation. It gave her
great pleasure when, during her years in Pittsburgh, she
met Ian Maclaren newly returned from Lincoln and conversation with Sherman, to find that he dismissed Sherman's analysis of his own work in terms of "effects of degree" and "effects of tone" as fantastic and sterile, as well
as comic.

Sherman's systematic studies seem silly enough; but
there is scarcely a chapter in any of his books that does
not have a valuable perception. The perceptions are not
wholly independent of his systems. His weakness was that
he could not discern when his systems led him into the
rigidities of pedantry; he lacked to a startling degree what
Matthew Arnold called literary tact. Unfortunately Willa

Cather rejected him entire. Forever after she was suspicious of complicated or systematic literary analysis. In general, criticism, as she practiced it, was but purely personal response, unsupported by argument and occasionally veering into fantasy.

This was the kind of criticism she wrote in "Shakespeare and Hamlet," a remarkable paper prepared when she was a student in Sherman's class in Shakespeare, a course for juniors to which she was admitted in her freshman year. The paper was printed in the *State Journal*, in the Sunday issues of November 1 and 8, 1891. Her method appears in her account of Shakespeare's interest in the material:

> I don't think Shakespeare had any definite purpose even in writing Hamlet. It was not like him to write a play that should be a puzzle for all time to come. He probably read the legend, felt sorry for the young prince, and as an expression of his sympathy wrote about him. He probably had no intention of giving the drama any more of himself than he gave to any other of his plays. The Danish prince had nothing in common with him except that both were misunderstood. He gradually grew into the play as he wrote it, without any special reason. Perhaps outside matters bore more heavily upon him than usual. It may be his feeling and individuality were wrought up intensely and crept into the play which he happened to be writing.

This has the genuine mark of Willa Cather. It is the kind of explanation that she often gave in later years for her own interest in subjects, and for the way in which she had dealt with the subjects once they had demanded expression.

II

At the beginning of her sophomore year, in the fall of 1892, Willa Cather became one of the editors of the undergraduate literary periodical, the *Hesperian*, and shortly afterward its mainstay. One of her associates remarked years later: "The truth is the *Hesperian* was Willa practically. . . . The rest of us looked wise and did nothing. The sheet would have been rolled into a scroll and gone *thither* if Willa had not worked like a nigger." Willa Cather contributed verse, criticism, dialogues, satirical sketches of students, and, above all, stories. It is the stories that matter.

Her first published story had appeared six months earlier, on May 21, 1892, in a Boston literary weekly called the *Mahogany Tree*. It was probably submitted on Willa Cather's behalf by her English instructor, Herbert Bates, a young New Englander and a Harvard graduate who held the faith of his teacher, Barrett Wendell, on the importance of courses in composition. In her mature years Willa Cather believed that Bates had stimulated her to publish stories in the magazines before she had the command of her craft; but the encouragement he gave her, if it may have been somewhat uncritical, helped a great deal more than it hurt. The brief tale published in the Boston magazine—it is little more than a sketch—was titled "Peter" and it is the episode that will become the suicide of Mr. Shimerda in *My Ántonia*. Indeed, Peter Sadelack differs from the amateur fiddler Shimerda only in being more of a professional musician who is also strongly addicted to drink. Their longing for the past is the same. Peter lives in his memories and these are of his days as second violin in the big Prague theater where he "wore a dress coat every evening and there were always parties after the play." He had watched the great Rachel and heard Liszt perform when the Countess d'Agoult sat in the stage box and threw white lilies at the master. But now in the bleak Western winter he makes his irrevocable decision:

. . . He took Antone's shot-gun down from its peg, and loaded it by the moonlight which streamed in through the door. He sat down on the dirt floor, and leaned back against the dirt wall. He heard the wolves howling in the distance, and the night wind screaming as it swept over the snow. Near him he heard the regular breathing of the horses in the dark. . . . He held his fiddle under his chin a moment, where it had lain so often, then put it across his knee and broke it through the middle. He pulled off his old boot, held the gun between his knees with the muzzle against his forehead, and pressed the trigger with his toe.

This is sufficiently remarkable narrative for a young college student.

Willa Cather republished the story in the *Hesperian*, where it appeared in the issue of November 24, 1892. Before that she had published another tale in the college magazine; probably both had served first as compositions for Herbert Bates's class. "Lou the Prophet" in the October 15 number, is an outcome of her life on the Divide; in substance and attitude, though not in art, it is akin to the presentation of Ivar in *O Pioneers!* or the two aloof Russian farmers in the first book of *My Ántonia*. A young Danish farmer, Lou works with a peasant's laboriousness until his spirit is broken by the desertion of the girl he expected

to marry, and by the death of his mother. He develops a
religious mania, buries himself in solitude, broken only by
the sympathetic company of young boys, and at the end
rushes away across the prairie to avoid the police who have
come to remove him to an asylum. The last scene is as
melodramatic in its own way as the sentence quoted from
the theme on Carlyle. But there are passages that might
appear in any of the Nebraska novels without disharmony.
The descriptive touches are often precise and striking in
a manner that is a rough anticipation of *O Pioneers!*
"When the moon came up, he sighed restlessly and tore
the buffalo pea flowers with his bare toes." The phrase is
not satisfactory; but like many of the unsatisfactory phrases
in *Endymion,* and for the same reason, it is full of promise. Willa Cather's lifelong attachment to the very old and
the very young appears in the opening reflection: "Among
the northern people who emigrate to the great west
only the children and the old people ever long much for
the lands they have left over the water." The figures of Mr.
Shimerda and Ántonia are distinctly on the horizon.

Another story, "The Clemency of the Court," appearing
a year later, October 26, 1893, is more elaborate. It is
about Serge Povolitchky, a Russian who grew up as an
orphan on a farm in the western part of Nebraska; he
was even more of a solitary than Lou, since the only creature ever to show him affection was a farm dog. When out
of mere passing bad temper the farmer splits the dog's
head with a hatchet, Serge, now a young man, kills him
"even as the man had struck the dog." (This episode
emerged later in *Death Comes for the Archbishop,* trans-
formed into the story of a man and his rooster bred for

cockfighting.) Condemned to imprisonment for life, he is set to factory tasks that he cannot perform. After a long stay in a dark cell, during which he is "roped up" tight against a wall night and day, he dies, alone. The grimness of this story is without relief except for the quiet treatment of the emotion the Russian feels for the dog, and for rare notations of the prairie landscape, with its buffalo grass, wild roses, and "a little marshy pool, grown up in cat-tails and reeds." The extension of meaning beyond a horrifying individual case comes through an ironic treatment of the idea of the State. The old Russian woman on whose farm Serge spent his childhood had heard in a Fourth of July oration of a beneficent power in America to which there was no parallel in Europe: here there was a benevolent State, and all were her beloved children. In Serge's starved inward life the idea of the maternal State became an obscure but powerful consolation. "About his trial Serge remembered very little, except that they had taken him to the courthouse and he had not found the State." Even in prison he trusted serenely that "the State would come some day and explain, and take him to herself." As he strangled he was still expecting the arrival of his savior the State. Many of the elements in Willa Cather's novels about Nebraska are already present: there is the deep concern over the plight of the foreign-born in a society that requires them to conform and has no generosity of spirit, no perception of their troubled frame of mind; there is the sympathy with people rooted in the land to whom confinement and city labors are intolerable; and there is the governing emotion of so much she was to write already governing here—an alarm and dislike at the pressure of a community on a personality which, like Lou's, is essentially at variance with it and has a central core the community will never rightly value.

Whatever the false notes in these stories, written before Willa Cather was twenty, they point forward to the substance of her first great novels, and to an element in the attitude with which she would always view the American community.

During her last two years at the university Willa Cather's interest in her studies declined. Exact scholarship, represented in a conventional way in the professors of Greek and Latin, and with peculiar personal additions in L. A. Sherman, irked her more and more. She was eager to explore authors who had special value for her personal life, and for the practice of fiction and poetry. She is remembered in Lincoln as a devotee of Flaubert, and of *Madame Bovary* in particular: she often carried a copy of that novel. In the sketch "A Chance Meeting," written in the early 1930's, she speaks of Flaubert as one in whom and near whom "lay most of one's mental past." From Flaubert she passed to Mérimée, to whom she came, as so many American undergraduates have come, by way of *Colomba*. She felt a close, lasting and at first sight rather surprising, affinity with his mind and his art, with his critical writings as much as with his fiction. She also read Maupassant and Ibsen, and the *Dame aux Camélias* of Dumas *fils*. Her enduring pleasure in Stevenson began in these years, encouraged perhaps by Bates, who was strongly drawn to him— to the stylist even more than to the creator of character, teller of tales, and commentator on life. She bought Stevenson's complete works, the first large set she acquired,

paying for it at the rate of a dollar a month. At the time of
her death the "Stevenson" occupied a shelf conveniently
accessible to casual reading in the living-room of her apartment. Like the rest of the reading that was important to
her as an undergraduate, it was important to the end.

She was active in one of the undergraduate literary societies, the Union, which was at that time more intellectu-
ally disposed than its principal rival, the Palladian. She edited the senior yearbook or annual of 1894, *The Sombrero*.
Dramatics interested her, and she was especially effective
in comic and in masculine roles, though she had ceased to
wear strikingly masculine clothes and had let her hair
grow and even submitted to having it curl. Her recitation
of "Curfew Shall Not Ring Tonight" was a hilarious success she was called on to repeat.

<h2 style="text-align:center">III</h2>

She was often in the houses of interesting Lincoln families. Among her principal friends were Louise and Olivia
Pound, the sisters of Roscoe and daughters of Judge Stephen M. Pound, and Mariel and Frances, the daughters
of Charles H. Gere of the *State Journal*. Sarah B. Harris, editor of the Lincoln *Courier*, and Mrs. Gere were
no less important to her: she was drawn to these older
women much as she had been drawn to Mrs. Miner in Red
Cloud. She was especially devoted to Mrs. Emma Tyndale
Westermann, the mother of six young men, students or recent graduates, and the center of a circle of young people
attracted to her by the richness and warmth of her nature
and the range of her culture. Mrs. Westermann's brother,
Dr. Julius Tyndale, had recently come west from New

York, seeking a drier climate. He was a man of great personal and intellectual force, and as keenly interested in music and letters as in medicine and science generally. With him she formed the same kind of association she had enjoyed with the gifted, experienced men in Red Cloud. His stories about the literary and musical world of the east coast and his opinions about contemporary movements in the arts became an important element in her growth.

The Westermanns occupied a large and striking house on S Street near Sixteenth, on the edge of the campus. (It had been occupied during Willa Cather's earlier years in Lincoln by the chancellor of the university, James H. Canfield.) A studio had been added, and it is this room Willa Cather describes in the sixth chapter of *One of Ours*, "all windows on three sides above the wainscoting." This and all the other details about the house, William Linn Westermann declares, have been recaptured in that novel with a precision of visual memory startling in its sureness. The bust of Byron, the portrait of Napoleon were recalled, one may suppose, because the quality in the family life of the Westermanns, so intense, and so deeply marked by European culture, had meant so much to the young girl from Webster County. The Westermanns represented in these years in a more developed form the same values she had found in the Wieners, whose house was recalled with equal fullness in "Old Mrs. Harris."

Willa Cather's relation with the family of James H. Canfield was just as intimate. Dorothy Canfield was several years younger than Willa Cather—she was in primary school when Willa Cather came to Lincoln—but a son, James Canfield, was in Willa Cather's class. Dorothy Can-

field Fisher describes the response to Willa Cather by the
members of the family: "It was through what my parents
and my brother who was in her class thought of Willa that
I saw her, I think, as I look back on those years—my father
an impassioned educator, always a flame of hope and eager, forward-looking, when some student showed rare
gifts; and my erratic highly talented artist-mother rejoic-
ing in any young person who spelled Art with a capital, as
Willa certainly did. And my brother, a lively, tennis-play-
ing, dancing, extremely social-minded party-loving undergraduate." Mrs. Canfield's cult of art, nourished by her
association with French artists and her broad reading in
French literature, was important to Willa Cather—it
strengthened her in the æsthetic attitude she was forming
in her years at Lincoln. Before long the two novelists-to-be
had found each other. A short story on a football game,
submitted in a competition for a prize of ten dollars and
published in *The Sombrero*, was the fruit of a collaboration between Dorothy Canfield and Willa Cather. It is un-
characteristic of either. It is indeed the least promising of
all Willa Cather's juvenilia.

In the 1890's students at the University of Nebraska
lived in various parts of the town—"where we could and as
we could," Willa Cather says in *My Ántonia*. There were
no dormitories and few fraternities or sororities. Willa
Cather's room was not far from the central business district, and remained bare and austere, more like a boy's
than a girl's. She spent much more time at her desk than
most students cared to do, but in the evenings she would
very often go out for long talks in the houses of her friends,
and usually would return on foot and alone through the si-

lent streets as late as one or two o'clock. Lincoln might be the state capital and a vigorous commercial town; to her it was as manageable and familiar as Red Cloud.

Her later years at the university fell in one of the most difficult periods in the history of the state. Its "rapid industrial development," as she says in her essay on Nebraska, "was arrested in the years 1893–1897 by a succession of crop failures and by the financial depression which spread over the whole country at that time—the depression which produced the People's Party and the Free Silver agitation." The first Nebraska district was represented in Congress from 1891 to 1895 by a Lincoln lawyer who made the issues of Populism and free silver plain across the state before he became the Democratic candidate for the Presidency in 1896. There are echoes of William Jennings Bryan in Willa Cather's fiction: the issues that he dramatized appear movingly in "Two Friends" and to a lesser extent in "The Best Years." Willa Cather's own family suffered heavily in the years of agricultural failure. Charles F. Cather had acquired a great deal of land in Webster County, and much of it was heavily mortgaged. A large farm that he had under cultivation was abandoned. A bank with which he had dealings failed. He was in desperate straits to keep the land and to meet the expenses of a large family, even though Roscoe and Douglass, the next in age to Willa, taught school and helped to the utmost.

IV

A chance to help came to her in the autumn of 1893. Willa Cather enrolled for a course in journalism with Will Owen Jones, the managing editor of the *State Journal,* who for a few years gave special instruction at the university. She was invited to become a regular contributor to the Sunday issues of the *State Journal* at a dollar a column, and the prodigious number of columns she filled gave her literary earnings sufficient to meet many of her expenses.

In the contributions to the *State Journal* it is possible to follow many of Willa Cather's early enthusiasms, and to discover her artistic aims. C. H. Gere and Will Owen Jones left her free: she could say what she would and say it as she would. In later years she was grateful for the privilege of "stepping as high as she cared to" in her rhetoric, and thus working out a rhetorical vein which was so rich that otherwise she might never have come to the end of it. A slight smile, stopping short of the sarcastic, was all she had to endure when she had been particularly outrageous or Corinthian.

The most explicit statement of her conception of art is this:

The further the world advances the more it becomes evident that an author's only safe course is to cling to the skirts of his art, forsaking all others, and keep unto her as long as they two shall live. An artist should not be vexed by human hobbies or human follies: he should be able to lift himself into the clear firmament of creation where the world is not. He should be among men but not of them, in the world but not of the world. Other men may think and believe and argue, but he must create.

The stress upon the sufficiency and separateness of the artist's function appears again in a review of Paul Bourget's volume of impressions of America:

It is rather a pity that Paul Bourget should have written *Outre Mer*, thoroughly creditable book that it is. . . . Mr. Bourget is a novelist, and should not content himself with being an essayist, there are far too many of them in the world already. . . . When God has made a man a creator, it is a mistake for him to turn critic. It is rather an insult to God, and certainly a very great wrong to man.

Perhaps the writer of these lines addressed them more to herself than to Paul Bourget; but if she believed that she should be about her creative business, she could reflect that at twenty she was not ripe for the kind of fiction she cared to write:

A man cannot write a novel before he has grown a mustache. . . . O for the good old days of Thackeray and Dickens when a man did not dare to write a novel before he was thirty. . . . A man must live and know and labor and endure before he can write a book that purports to tell of life.

At least one of the columnist's examples was dubious; when Dickens reached thirty he had behind him the *Pickwick Papers*, *Oliver Twist*, *Nicholas Nickleby*, *The Old Curiosity Shop*, and *Barnaby Rudge*. But Dickens is not a writer that a novelist beginning his craft in the 1890's would be likely to study. He was never to be an enthusiasm or a model with Willa Cather.

Her most pungent articles were reviews of plays. In an interview that appeared in the *State Journal* on February 3, 1895, Gustave Frohman remarked: "Lincoln newspapers are noted for their honesty in dramatic matters, and it is the best advertisement of intelligence and refinement that a town can have. I have heard of it from professionals and

non-professionals all along the road, and poor companies
begin to tremble long before they get here. That kind of
respect is worth something." From an impresario this was
a generous way of putting a good face upon a characteristic histrionic malaise. By "Lincoln newspapers" Frohman
really meant Willa Cather's columns in the *State Journal.*
A retrospective editorial appearing in that paper on November 1, 1921, and probably written by Will Owen Jones,
leaves an impression that not all the theatrical visitors to
Lincoln took her criticisms so urbanely. "Many an actor
of national reputation wondered on coming to Lincoln
what would appear next morning from the pen of the
meat-ax young girl of whom all of them had heard. Miss
Cather did not stand in awe of the greatest actors, but set
each one in his place with all the authority of a veteran
metropolitan critic." It has been said that a *State Journal*
reporter who presented a pass at a theater in Chicago was
contumeliously refused admission to the play, which was
one that Willa Cather had excoriated.

How pointed her criticism could be appears in a comment on the acting of Lillian Lewis:

She will next year stage a magnificent spectacular production of *Cymbeline*, in which she will play Imogen. When one
knows Lillian, her nose and her emotions, one hopes they dug
Shakespeare's grave very deep.

She could be equally pointed in a comment on a playwright. In a review of *Lady Windermere's Fan*, published
on June 5, 1894, almost a year before the first trial of Oscar Wilde, Willa Cather remarked:

Mr. Wilde is afraid to be coarse, so he is insinuating. . . .
He does not attempt to apotheosize filth, he plays with it because he likes it when it is pretty. . . . To hear Mr. Wilde, on
[motherhood] is like hearing one of the very little Satans phi-
losophizing on Calvary.

It is the slashing passages that are most vividly and long
remembered in a dramatic critic. But Willa Cather's best
reviews in the *State Journal* are admirably balanced. There
is for instance an estimate of Julia Marlowe. Marlowe
seemed to Willa Cather to carry grace, delicacy, and
beauty to perfection. It was a distinguished æsthetic pleasure to see her move and hear her speak. "A sort of warm
rich delight will hover about us for days." But for all the
fascination, there was a reach beyond Marlowe, a reach
she never attempted. "She lives too beautifully to live very
hard, dies too gracefully to die very effectively." The reservation about Marlowe is generalized in a way that re-
lates Willa Cather's critical principles to her own early
attempts in fiction:

After all the supreme virtue in art is soul, perhaps it is the
only thing which gives art the right to be. The greatest art in
acting is not to please and charm and delight, but to move and
thrill; not to play a part daintily and delightfully, but with
power and passion. All prettiness for its own sake is trivial. No
matter how dainty, how refined, how spirituelle, it is still a
thing of the sense only.

The insistence on the grave, hard core of all great art is
often repeated in the dramatic reviews. She found this
core in Clara Morris's rendering of Camille:

Camille is an awful play. Clara Morris plays only awful plays.
Her realism is terrible and relentless. It is her art and mission

to see all that is terrible and painful and unexplained in life. It is a dark and gloomy work that has been laid upon more geniuses than one.

In her own fashion, in the stories of Lou and Serge Povolitchky, Willa Cather had written awful works. Some of the readers of the *Hesperian* found the stories "morbid" and "brutal"; they were instead "painful" and "relentless," the product of a mind that was already committed to a work which, though it was seldom dark and gloomy, had its dark depths and gloomy passages. The spirit of Carlyle was still her spirit; what she has to say about books is much nearer to his kind of judgment than to that of the critics who in the 1890's had authority and disciples—Matthew Arnold, for instance, or Henry James, or the impressionists native and foreign. It is not known when Willa Cather first discovered Tolstoy, but it could be predicted that when she did, *War and Peace* and *Anna Karenina* would be among the chief literary experiences in her life, as indeed they were. Already, however, her primary care for the grave, hard core of art went along with a delight in exquisite form; and she would not easily be content unless she found both the hard core and the perfect form. Her period of apprenticeship would inevitably be a long one.

V

In June 1895 she was graduated. Like many another artist she had had her struggles with mathematics; not until the end of her senior year had she succeeded, and then only by special instruction, in removing her deficiency in the first-year course in that discipline.

The year 1895–6 was spent at home in Red Cloud. It was a year of recovery and preparation. Willa Cather left Lincoln very tired, much more tired than she knew. Her first three years had been a time of most assiduous study, in which she rose as early as a farmer on the Divide and went to bed long after midnight. In the last two years she kept the same exhausting hours, though not so many of them went to reading for her courses. Much of her time was given to writing for the *Journal*, and during the dramatic season to haunting the theaters; much went to writing done for her own satisfaction or experiment. These were the years in which she began to discover what art meant, and the process of discovery was attended with great emotional excitement and disturbance. Her mind and spirit now required a fallow season.

Red Cloud was at the bottom of its depressed period. Charles Cather kept afloat only because he had become the representative in south-central Nebraska of R. E. Moore, one of the most successful financiers in the state, whose headquarters was at Lincoln. The father had begun to spend more of his time in Lincoln than he did at home; and Willa Cather's presence in the house on Cedar Street, and often in her father's local office, allowed Mrs. Cather to accompany her husband to Lincoln. She gave her father some help in his work, which at this time had to do mainly with land-titles and mortgages. It was some reassurance to feel that she was partly paying her way when the family was short of money. She tried to pick up the threads of her friendships, but some of the older friends were dead, others had moved away, and among those of her own age she could not overcome the feeling she at-

tributed forty years later to Lucy Gayheart, that "she was
not there in the old way . . . scarcely herself at all . . .
trying to feel and behave like someone she no longer was;
as children go on playing the old games to please their
elders, after they have ceased to be children at heart." She
believed that her family and friends, who had heard so
much of her writing at Lincoln for undergraduate magazines and for the *State Journal*, were expecting her to make
some dazzling success, to place stories in some popular
journal or bring out a brilliant novel. She was writing
stories, but they seemed jejune and superficial—how, she
wondered, could they seem otherwise, coming from one
who had seen so little of the world? If only she might
travel, as Stephen Crane had done, and quickly accumu-
late a knowledge of cities and men; but first there were
debts to pay, some of them incurred in helping actresses
she had met in Lincoln to some tawdry pleasure, paste
jewelry, or champagne. During the winter of 1896 Herbert
Bates resigned from the University of Nebraska and rec-
ommended that she be named in his place. Her age and
her sex were, she knew, against her; and she also knew
that Lucius Sherman had a low opinion of her abilities.
She enlisted friends in Lincoln in support of her application, but she was not surprised when it was unsuccessful.
She was able to make a number of visits to Lincoln during
the year—the *State Journal* was always ready to supply
free transportation—but, just as Claude Wheeler in *One of
Ours* found the trips he took to Lincoln after he had
dropped out of college ended with acute depression when
he was once more at home, Willa Cather felt that the few
days she could spend among stimulating people like the

Geres and the Westermanns served mainly to make her months at a stretch in Red Cloud a greater trial.

By one of her visits to Lincoln, however, she was able to make her escape not only from Red Cloud but from Nebraska. Once when she was visiting the Geres she met Charles Axtell, a Pittsburgh businessman, with his wife and daughter. Axtell appears to have been struck by her experience as a journalist—no doubt Charles Gere spoke golden words of her—and late in the spring of 1896 he offered her a position in the editorial office of a "family" magazine he was founding, the Pittsburgh *Home Monthly*. Before the end of June Willa Cather was in Pittsburgh.

4

Pittsburgh: the Bright Medusa

1896–1901

WILLA CATHER HAD had a foretaste of the world beyond the prairies during the spring of 1895 after her graduation. To mark the end of her college years she traveled to Chicago for a week of opera—an expedition arranged with the sympathetic aid of Dr. Tyndale. Like Thea Kronborg, she boarded the train in elaborate attire, more feminine than she allowed herself to wear in her everyday life in Lincoln, and before the week was out she was surfeited with music, dazzled by the glittering audiences, and exhausted by her tramping of Chicago's streets. The successive evenings at the opera were to find their way many years later into a dramatic portion of Lucy Gayheart's adventure in Chicago.

Perhaps more significant for Willa Cather's future was the arrival in Lincoln, also during that spring, of "the first man of letters I had ever met in the flesh." He was scarce a man, barely twenty-four, just two years older than she was. He seemed to come out of nowhere. But he brought a glimpse of distant things and the aura of struggle and fame. The author of *The Red Badge of Courage* walked one day into the office of the managing editor of the *Journal*, where Willa Cather happened to be. He was slender and narrow-chested and wore shabby gray; his soft felt hat

was low over his eyes. He had on a flannel shirt and a
"slovenly apology" for a necktie. His shoes were dusty,
worn about the toes, badly run over at the heel. Only his
gloves contradicted his general shabbiness, and when he
took them off to search his pockets for his credentials,
Willa Cather noticed that his hands were singularly fine,
"long, white and delicately shaped, with thin nervous
fingers."

Stephen Crane was on his way to Mexico. He wanted to
get rid of his cough and to try to do some work there. He
was waiting in Lincoln for some money to catch up with
him. In the ensuing days Willa Cather repeatedly sought
to draw from him his literary opinions and an account of
how he practiced his craft. She asked him about Maupassant. His unhelpful rejoinder was "Oh, you're Moping, are
you?" as he buried himself in the little volume of Poe he
always had with him. Then, one hot evening, sitting on
the ledge of the window in the newspaper office, Stephen
Crane finally—

Quite without invitation on my part . . . began to talk, began
to curse his trade from the first throb of creative desire in a boy
to the finished work of the master. The night was oppressively
warm; one of those dry winds that are the curse of that country was blowing up from Kansas. The white, western moonlight threw sharp, blue shadows below us. The streets were silent at that hour, and we could hear the gurgle of the fountain
in the Post Office square across the street, and the twang of
banjos from the lower veranda of the Hotel Lincoln, where the
colored waiters were serenading the guests. The drop lights in
the office were dull under their green shades, and the telegraph
sounder clicked faintly in the next room. In all his long tirade,

Crane never raised his voice; he spoke slowly and monoto-nously and even calmly, but I have never known so bitter a heart in any man as he revealed to me that night. It was an ar-raignment of the wages of life, an invocation to the ministers of hate.

Crane spoke of how he led a double life: he wrote the matter that pleased himself slowly and with care; he dashed off anything he could sell. "He declared," Willa Cather remembered, "that his imagination was hide-bound; it was there, but it pulled hard. After he got a no-tion for a story, months passed before he could get any sort of personal contact with it, or feel any potency to handle it." And then he pronounced these words, of the greatest significance for the future art of Willa Cather: "The detail of a thing has to filter through my blood, and then it comes out like a native product, but it takes for-ever." The young-old Stephen Crane did not have for-ever. But Willa Cather was to have many years in which to ponder and cherish these words.

II

Willa Cather threw herself into her Pittsburgh life with all the young ardor she possessed. The Eastern city meant what Chicago was to mean to Thea Kronborg and Lucy Gayheart, "the freedom to spend one's youth as one pleased"—freedom to live according to one's measure of life, a degree of economic security, access to the arts, lib-eration from the ceaselessly active tongues in Red Cloud that had given her an acute sense of being an outcast among her own people. Yet Willa Cather was soon to discover that the price of her new-found freedom was long and unremunerative hours in an office and printing shop which could not be reconciled with the art she wished to practice. When the young narrator in *My Mortal Enemy* is asked why she does not turn to journalism, and is warned that teaching is a cul-de-sac in which generous people use themselves up, she replies with a vehemence that eloquently proclaims the author's feeling: "I hate journalism. I know what I want to do, and I'll work my way out yet, if only you'll give me time." It took Willa Cather a rounded decade to work her way out of journalism and teaching in Pittsburgh.

She spent the first few days after her arrival as the guest of her employer. The Axtells seemed to Willa Cather rigorously and comically puritan; in her room there were three Bibles and a shelf full of novels of the Reverend E. P. Roe. If the Axtells had known of her belief in artistic creation as the first of the values, she was sure they would not have had her under their roof; she thought they suspected her of Bohemianism, for shortly before she arrived they had sent their daughter, whom she described as the "Puritan Maid," to stay with relatives at a safe distance. In this household she discovered what was characteristic of one side of Pittsburgh: an alliance between business and an unpleasant religious formalism. "Presbyterianism of that day," Elizabeth Moorhead has observed in writing of the city, "offered little encouragement to any sort of artistic activity. Physical comfort was admissible, yes—the good Presbyterian was by no means an ascetic—but duty was the law of life. Aesthetic impulse too often led to a dangerous laxity." Willa Cather was to make the same obser-

vations in a much more mordant way in an article she
wrote for the Lincoln *Courier* in the autumn of 1897 on the
Pittsburgh horse show. "Of course the most sensible beings
present were down in the horse stalls. They were not Presbyterians, nor were they covered with diamonds, and everything they did was in good taste. . . . There is no getting away from a Presbyterian environment, no getting
around it, or behind it or above it."

To this environment the *Home Monthly* was dedicated
—to "more than half a million firesides" within a hundred
miles of downtown Pittsburgh. It offered "entertainment
for the idle hour . . . pure and clean in tone" and pur-
veyed by "the best story writers in the country." There
were departments devoted to floriculture, fashions, the
nursery, Christian endeavor; articles on cycling for pleasure, Angora cats, Harriet Beecher Stowe, and the care of
the children's teeth. The stories offering the "entertainment for the idle hour" in the first number—issued in August 1896—were "A Modern Elaine," a stereotype of moderate realism (an English boy of gentle manners and
refined character becomes a farm laborer in America, the
farmer's daughter is charmed, and so on); "The Lovely
Malincourt," a romantic stereotype (noble families, virtu-
ous lovers separated by a cruel worldly mother, one of
them dying of despair and reviving when the mother re-
lents, etc.). A third story, "Tommy the Unsentimental" by
Willa Cather, as its title suggests, is a revolt against the
stereotype. It is not a revolt against Barrie, who was a
lifelong admiration of Willa Cather's (the admiration was
returned—for more than twenty years Barrie asked her to
autograph her books for him); it is a revolt against the

conception of the young girl which ruled the magazines
and most of the national thinking at the turn of the century. Willa Cather is writing, as in the grim stories in the
Hesperian, about her own corner of Nebraska. Her heroine is a sketch of herself:

Needless to say, Tommy was not a boy, though her keen gray
eyes and wide forehead were scarcely girlish, and she had the
lank figure of a half-grown lad. Her real name was Theodosia,
but during Thomas Shirley's frequent absences from the bank
she had attended to his business and correspondence signing
herself "T. Shirley" until everyone in Southdown called her
"Tommy." That blunt sort of familiarity is not unfrequent in
the West, and is meant well enough. People rather expect some
business ability in a girl there, and they respect it immensely.

Tommy is in love with a feckless and effeminate cashier
in her father's bank, "the only foolish man" she knew; the
other men she cared for were among her father's middle-
aged or elderly friends, "who had seen a good deal of the
world and were very proud and fond of Tommy." A touch
in the drawing of Tommy's relationship with them must
have been passed when Axtell was nodding; it must, indeed, have startled subscribers at a thousand firesides:

She played whist and billiards with them, and made their
cocktails for them, not scorning to take one herself occasionally. Indeed Tommy's cocktails were things of fame in Southdown, and the professional compounders of drinks always
bowed respectfully to her as though acknowledging a powerful rival.

No evil fate overtakes her because of pursuits so abhorrent
to the Presbyterians of Pittsburgh and western Pennsylvania. Tommy dispatches the cashier to his Eastern girl,

who is his true mate; she remains to the end a sharply
drawn portrait, framed to excellent effect by brief realizations of the Nebraska landscape. If "Tommy the Unsentimental" was one of the stories Willa Cather wrote and was
unhappy about during the year at Red Cloud, the move to
Pittsburgh may have been a mistake. Not until she wrote
"The Sculptor's Funeral" did she achieve anything better
—and that remarkable story lay nine years ahead.

She found, indeed, little time for writing fiction. The
Home Monthly made great demands on her, and Willa
Cather was soon managing editor of the journal in everything but name, with only a stenographer to help her. She
read manuscripts and proof, presided over the make-up in
the hot composing-room until all hours of the night, and
wrote articles and small fillers for gaps in the dummy. She
learned to discipline herself and, what was hardest of all,
to keep still and do what she was told. She wrote her Nebraska friends that she had never worked so hard and so
consistently in all her life. While there was a certain rel-
ish in some phases of her work, and a very real sense of
achievement, she found the journal's conventionality and
parochialism increasingly stifling. She made a virtue of
the drudgery, however; it was a question of maintaining
her as yet uncertain foothold in the East; and it was a
question of demonstrating to the doubters back home that
she could "win out."

III

In Pittsburgh Willa Cather rode to work on her bicycle
from her boarding-house in Craig Street to the *Home
Monthly* office at Pennsylvania and Eighth Street. She

said the only excitement she allowed herself was her daily
race with the tram; however, everything at first was rather
exciting. She enjoyed the coal-smeared aspect of the city,
its hills and rivers and the flaring skies and plumes of gas
flame ("the very incandescence of human energy") that
reflected the spectacular sources of Pittsburgh's wealth.
Early in her stay she visited, with a group that included
her Lincoln friends George W. Gerwig and Dorothy Canfield, the great Homestead steel mills, where they saw
fountains of flame and the workers moving like ants in a
clanging inferno. She was to catch the city's rhythm and
tone and the "legends of the iron kings" in one of her best-
known stories, "Paul's Case," in which she drew on many
elements of her life in Pittsburgh. Unlike the Western silver kings in Colorado and Nevada, whose conception of
art was the building of palatial and grotesque homes with
ornate bathrooms, the iron kings were endowing museums
and concert halls and turning grimy Pittsburgh into one of
America's centers of culture; steel and oil, coal and gas
were transmuted into vast fortunes, and the overflow of
this money became painting and music, literature and opera. The iron kings had blasted their way deeply into that
earth whose surface on the frontier was being tamed by
quite another type of pioneer. Willa Cather had a profound admiration for both.

This, then, was the dichotomy of Pittsburgh: out of
its ugliness and slums, its industrial smoke and flame
sprang the beautiful things that were the breath of life to
Willa Cather. And her own life there had the same dichotomy. "It was at the theatre and at Carnegie Hall that Paul
really lived; the rest was but a sleep and a forgetting."

Willa Cather's work and the lonely drabness of most of the boarding-houses in which she lived were things to run away from, and the avenues of escape were there: in the newly inaugurated Carnegie Institute with its library, its art gallery, and its concert hall. In the library she could have more books than had ever been available to her on the prairie and she could meet librarians such as the sensitive and discerning May Willard, who was to become a lifelong friend. At Carnegie Hall she could hear Victor Herbert conduct the symphony orchestra and like young Paul feel that some hilarious spirit in her was freed by the first sigh of the instruments, "something that struggled there like the Genius in the bottle found by the Arab fisherman." Paul felt "a sudden zest of life; the lights danced before his eyes and the concert hall blazed into unimaginable splendour." Something of that splendor touched the artists and composers she began to meet, among them Ethelbert Nevin, whose dazzling success and whose kindness to Willa Cather made him one of the heroes of her early Pittsburgh days, so that to her Red Cloud and Lincoln friends she evoked him as a young prince or a king, almost a fairy-tale figure, who lived with a devoted wife in a beautiful suburban home named Vineacre, where he entertained the girl from the prairie, treating her with a generous and disarming gallantry that endeared him to her. The author of "The Rosary" dedicated a song to Willa Cather and showed her warm friendship and an appreciation of her talents that she never forgot. Like Crane, he was to die young, and many years later Willa Cather put her recollections of him into the story "Uncle Valentine," where Vineacre is barely disguised as Greenacre.

The flight from ugliness and monotony to things of
beauty and enchantment led Willa Cather to the Pittsburgh stock company, where every week a new play enabled her to cross that "boundary line beyond which
dreams came true and lost illusions live on, forever young."
Here too she found a loyal and devoted friend in one of
the artists. Lizzie Hudson Collier was the leading lady,
and this meant that her audiences would find her there on
the stage every week in a new role, with the same warmth,
charm, and dignity that had made her almost a legendary
institution in Pittsburgh. Dorothy Canfield Fisher remembers her as "singularly decent and straight-fibred." For
Willa Cather the stage-door leading to Mrs. Collier's dressing-room was "the actual portal of Romance"; she was
an increasingly frequent visitor there, and an attentive
watcher from the wings of the way in which the theater's
"lost illusions" were created. Memories of those evenings,
as so much of the emotion of those days, are to be found
in "Paul's Case." When Paul went to visit his young friend
backstage at the stock company and crossed its portal,
"the moment he inhaled the gassy, painty, dusty odour
behind the scenes, he breathed like a prisoner set free, and
felt within him the possibility of doing or saying splendid,
brilliant, poetic things. The moment the cracked orchestra
beat out the overture from 'Martha,' or jerked at the ser-
enade from 'Rigoletto,' all stupid and ugly things slid from
him, and his senses were deliciously, yet delicately fired."

Perhaps it was because, in Paul's world, the natural nearly always wore the guise of ugliness, that a certain element of arti-
ficiality seemed to him necessary in beauty. Perhaps it was
because his experience of life elsewhere was so full of Sabbath-

school picnics, petty economies, wholesome advice as to how
to succeed in life, and the unescapable odours of cooking, that
he found this existence so alluring, these smartly-clad men and
women so attractive, that he was so moved by these starry ap-
ple orchards that bloomed perennially under the limelight.

The table of contents of the *Home Monthly* and the boarding-houses are in this paragraph.

This harder side of Willa Cather's Pittsburgh life was
not so readily apparent to those who had an opportunity
of seeing only what might be called its softer side—that
side which she recounted to her friends in animated letters
or which was visible to Dorothy Canfield, who occasionally stopped off in Pittsburgh and stayed with her college
friend. For her young visitor she provided concerts, the
glamour of her celebrated friends, after-theater suppers,
and access to the friendly houses in which she herself was
often a guest—the homes of George Gerwig or Edwin Hat-
field Anderson, the chief librarian at the Carnegie, or the
European-like home of George Seibel, where music and
pfeffernüsse were somehow mingled and where she went
regularly to improve her French. Seibel too was a librarian. "She came once or twice a week to read the French
classics," he remembers, "and always helped to trim our
Christmas tree as long as she lived in Pittsburgh." She had
known the Gerwigs during her *Sombrero* days in Lincoln
and at their home met a number of persons who became
good friends during her Pittsburgh days, including Preston Farrar, head of the English department at Allegheny
High School, where she was later to teach.

IV

Willa Cather resigned from the *Home Monthly* during the
summer of 1897 while she was vacationing in Red Cloud.
The journal was to change hands at the end of its first
year and this seemed the appropriate moment to withdraw
gracefully. Her resignation did not mean that she was
abruptly burning her valued Pittsburgh bridges. As far
back as the previous January she had investigated the possibility of finding work on one of the city's dailies. Before
the summer's end a telegram arrived offering her a position with the *Daily Leader*, the largest evening paper in
Pennsylvania, at a salary of seventy-five dollars a month.

During the four years Willa Cather worked for the
Pittsburgh *Leader* her principal task was the editing and
rewriting of telegraphic news as well as copy-reading and
headline-writing. This was drudgery of a different sort
from that of the *Home Monthly*, but here, at least, she had
no disagreeable editorial responsibilities and did not have
to write what she considered to be quite simply "trash." At
times the tedium of the telegraph desk was relieved by
the interest of the news—as when she handled the story of
the bottling up of Cervera's fleet in Santiago Harbor during the Spanish-American War—but even the excitement
of headlines and newsflashes can pall, and it did for Willa
Cather once the novelty wore off.

The *Leader*, however, gave her a sense of permanence
and security she had never enjoyed at the *Home Monthly*,
and presently she was able to resume the writing of dramatic criticism, which had been the form of journalism
she had enjoyed most in Lincoln. It was still marginal to

her routine duties but offered a welcome relief from them.
Her first drama notices appeared early in the autumn of
1897 signed "Sibert"—a variant of her grandmother's name
which she later adopted as a middle name, only to drop it
in 1920 to become again simply Willa Cather. Dramatic
criticism for her was still often the wielding of a sharp
hatchet rather than of an urbane pen: she could still describe a play as "awful" or "terrible." What she lacked in
finesse, however, she made up in vigor and conviction; and
she never lacked the capacity to formulate and frame her
strong opinions with complete clarity and often with
charm, as when she characterized the miscasting of Julia
Marlowe in a melodrama as "trying to force the notes of a
'cello from a violin" or when she dismissed Cora Tanner as
an actress who could "shed more pearly tears to the minute and still remain more perfectly calm than any other
woman on the stage—or off it."

One suspects on reading Willa Cather's metropolitan
drama reviews that her emotions often ran away with her
critical sense at a performance and that her interests more
often lay in the players than in the play. She believed the
drama's laws to be inflexible, in common with many nineteenth-century critics: "the demands of the drama are rigidly exacting, and chief and foremost among them is this—
that the chief persons of the play shall be identified with
some great purpose or strong passion." Her association
with Mrs. Collier gave her a sense of being in possession
of the practical side of the theater as well as understanding the histrionic temperament. It was this saturation with
the theater frontstage and back that led her two years later
to the preparation of what she hoped would be her first

book. She had been writing a series of open letters to living actors, the soliloquies of a critic offering praise and
blame (and tending to pontificate at moments rather
freely). Nothing could be calculated to touch—and hurt—
the special vanity of the stage-folk more than to have gra-
tuitous counsel offered them on how to play their roles;
and perhaps for this reason publishers did not warm to the
book that Willa Cather tentatively spoke of as *The Player
Letters.* A few of these letters appeared as separate articles in the Nebraska newspapers, and we can discover the
writer's intention in the directness of her communication
to Joseph Jefferson:

The enormous financial success of *Rip Van Winkle* checked
your career gloriously, but finally your ambition went to sleep
with Rip upon the mountain top, and though thirty years have
passed, it has never awakened. You have chosen the placid
waters and sheltered harbors. . . . Unlike Richard Mansfield
you have risked nothing and lost nothing. In our hearts, sir,
you reign always, the Prince of Players, best loved, most honored of them all. . . .

She might call him a Prince, but if so she was scolding
royalty; and this compound of stricture and accolade was
hardly likely to be received with favor. It was one thing to
criticize a specific performance and a specific play; it was
another to address the actors directly in terms of an un-
compromising schoolmistress talking to her pupils. The
manuscript lingered in a few publishers' offices and then
was quietly withdrawn; and from this distance the circumstance may be judged a happy one. Had the book
been published, Willa Cather's emergence in letters would
have been somewhat stormy, we suspect, and certainly

heartbreaking. As it was, she was destined to make a much more modest and indeed a happy debut.

V

It is not, however, in Willa Cather's dramatic criticism that we can obtain a coherent picture of her slowly maturing personality and of her growing confidence in her artistic future. That picture emerges rather from the series of columns she wrote, first for the Nebraska *State Journal* and then for the Lincoln *Courier*, under the rubric "The Passing Show." The column lived up to its name, and if it is not quite a diary of Willa Cather's activities in the East, it permits us to follow her to play and opera, to art gallery and horse show; whatever seized her interest—the latest book, the latest literary gossip, the life of Pittsburgh's Bohemia—was grist to her productive and lively mill. She read A. E. Housman's poems in their freshness of first appearance and promptly communicated her elation of discovery to her Western readers. She discoursed on John Philip Sousa and described a reception tendered Anthony Hope Hawkins, whose *Prisoner of Zenda,* no less than the spectacle of Richard Mansfield in the then comparatively new *Cyrano,* touched the deepest well of romanticism in Willa Cather. The young woman who had trailed wistfully after Stephen Crane now chatted informally with Rudyard Kipling (for forty-six minutes, she informed her readers with precision) and Marion Crawford, Fridtjof Nansen, and Minnie Maddern Fiske—whose performance of Tess Willa Cather saw four times in one week. And there was the first discovery by her as yet unsophisticated musical

taste of Dvořák's *New World* Symphony, which she translated promptly into a prose picture:

the Largo . . . before you stretch the empty, hungry plains of
the middle west. Limitless prairies, full of the peasantry of all
nations of Europe . . . and it seems as though from each of
those far scattered lights that at night mark the dwellings of
these people of the plains, there comes the song of a homesick
heart.

Thea Kronborg found in the same movement, during her
first evening at the symphony in Chicago, the "immeasur-
able yearning of all flat lands," and this yearning was now
being gratified in Willa Cather by such experiences. Piece-
meal in these running chronicles written for her home papers Willa Cather was setting down material that would
in time filter into her novels.

"The Passing Show" is alike a record of experience and
a revelation of Willa Cather's artistic growth. If we set
aside those portions of her columns written with an eye to
her Western audience, we have a substantial quantity of
lively reflection on the arts and the personalities who practice them, and a consistent effort to define—and to refine—
her critical views. The element of hero-worship is strong.
Willa Cather never overcame it. But mingled with much
biographical matter concerning the personalities of the
artists, we find discussions of realism in the novel, critical
evaluation of dramatic and lyric poetry, and frequent consideration of the art of the actor and the playwright. She
praises Zola and admires his young American disciple
Frank Norris; her literary interests reflect her reading of
the French novelists, but also show the closeness with

which she followed the new English writers and drama-
tists. If the columns reflect in part Willa Cather's playgoing
and her nights in Carnegie Hall, they provide also a
glimpse into her extensive raids on the shelves of the Carnegie Library.

Most important for the future of Willa Cather's novels
were the nights in Carnegie Hall and at the opera. She
heard the great voices of the era—Melba and Nordica,
Schumann-Heink, Sembrich, Calvé, Campanari, the de
Reszkes. They interested her not only as musicians but as
figures who had acquired their artistry by long discipline
and tenacity of purpose, and who had finally, like her own
heroines later—Thea, or Cressida Garnet, or Kitty Ayrshire
—conquered. Concerts and opera were a ritual, occasions
for dressing up, for brilliant gatherings, for discussions during intermissions; they possessed a dramatic quality of
their own—applause and curtain calls, artistic triumphs
and artistic failures. Willa Cather liked the artist's "inde-
finable air of achievement"—but the time was to come
when it would be defined and was, in her longest novel, a
study of the growth and development of a great singer.

VI

During her years on the *Leader* Willa Cather wrote very
little fiction. The process of day-to-day living, the round of
plays and celebrities, the act of absorbing experience, pre-
empted all her energies. Moreover, she had begun to range
out from Pittsburgh, traveling to New York to see Broad-
way plays—and one summer to act as guest drama critic
for the New York *Sun*—and in the spring of 1898 paying a
protracted visit to Washington. Here she obtained that

glimpse of bureaucracy and the routinized life of the civil servants of which she wrote with a biting pen in her story of Tom Outland. During one of her visits to New York she had lunch with Helena Modjeska, whom she judged one of the greatest actresses of the time, and this experience too was to be translated into fiction. It forms a dramatic scene in *My Mortal Enemy*.

These forays beyond Pittsburgh, and her immersion in the life of art, only made her work on the telegraph desk seem increasingly oppressive and mechanical. Her imagination soared from the city room, beyond the prosaic literalness and perishable content of the daily newspaper, and there began a process by which she sought gradually to disengage herself from the pressure it imposed upon her. The Pittsburgh directory of 1900 still listed her as reporter for the *Leader*, but during that year she undertook no tasks outside her regular routine and there are no signed articles by her. She devoted her free time instead to writing for a short-lived periodical, the *Library*, founded by a wealthy Pittsburgh citizen who dispersed a legacy of twenty thousand dollars to foster literary talent. When the money was spent, the journal suspended publication. The *Library*'s twenty-six numbers contain some two dozen items by Willa Cather—reportage, poetry, stories. Much of the reportage, including her reminiscences of Stephen Crane, is under the pseudonym of Henry Nicklemann; the literary material, however, with the exception of one tale, carries her own name. She reprinted one story of 1896 from the *Nebraska Literary Magazine*, "A Night at Greenway Court," and she wrote one tale, "The Sentimentality of William Tavener," in the vein of the early *Hesperian*

pieces; save for a few descriptive touches, it showed that
Willa Cather had made little progress in the writing of fiction during her first three years in Pittsburgh. Nevertheless what she did write, in this return to imaginative prose,
was beginning to find favor with editors. Not only the *Library* was publishing her during the new year of the new
century. In addition to verses placed in the *Critic*, the *Cri-
terion*, and *McClure's*, there was a story in *Cosmopolitan*
and an illustrated article in the *Ladies' Home Journal*. It
was this ever increasing acceptance of her work that demonstrated to Willa Cather that she could ultimately hope
to free herself completely from the demands of newspaper
work. She could not yet be sure of her capacity to earn a
livelihood as a free lance, and after a long trip to the West
she was led to a decision that marked a turning-point in
her life. She applied for a position in the Pittsburgh school
system. Aided by Mr. Gerwig's connection with the Allegheny Central Board, she received a post in the Central
High School as a teacher of English and Latin at an annual
salary of $650. This was three hundred dollars a year less
than what the *Leader* paid her; but in reality she had
never worked the year round at the newspaper, taking
leave of absence regularly to spend her summers at home.
Consequently her earnings in both positions were roughly
the same and quite sufficient for her modest needs.

Willa Cather taught at Central High during 1901–2, and
from 1903 to 1906 at Allegheny High, where she was given
the post vacated by her friend Preston Farrar, who left to
pursue further studies. In 1902 her salary was advanced to
$750, and by 1906, when she resigned, it had increased
to $1,300. Her first year in school convinced her that the

step had been wise. Newspaper work had drained her energy, strained her eyesight, and kept her from her own
writing. Now she taught only three or four hours a day and
had a theme-reader to assist her. She took her duties as
teacher seriously, however, and believed that she succeeded better at teaching than in anything else she had
ever done before she became a writer. Her work, moreover, was recognized and appreciated. One of her students, who was later to become a teacher himself and a
distinguished critic, has recorded his recollections of this
time:

I first knew her [writes Norman Foerster] during my two years,
1902–04, at the Central High School in Pittsburgh. This was a
regular academic high school—with ancient history, for example, as a freshman requirement—in distinction from the Commercial High School a mile or so away. The Central High
School building was a dismal, grimy structure on a bluff looking down on the Union Station. The darkness of fog and smoke
in fall and winter, the dirt of the squalid streets that led up to
it, must have made Willa Cather feel that the great plains and
skies of Nebraska were very far away—as they were. Miss
Cather was my freshman teacher only. . . . Her voice was
deeper than is usual; she spoke without excitement; her manner was quiet, reposeful, suggesting reserves of energy and
richness of personality. Her teaching seemed natural and human, but without contagious sparks. . . . She liked some of
my own themes. I remember one, which I believe I still have,
on my memory of the dreamy summer time while I lay in bed
during a blizzard that beat against the windows. On her advice I submitted it to the High School Journal where it appeared, to my great delight, with my name in print for the first
time. . . . What could I do but respect and admire her? This

attitude was heightened in my second year (when I no longer
had her as a teacher) by the publication of her *April Twilights.* I thought it wonderful of her to write a book. . . .

Willa Cather thus turned her back forever on journalism. Edith Lewis says that "it never gave her any pleasure
to remember her newspaper work." Perhaps for this reason it never figured in her novels. It was not a part of her
life she could draw upon in recapturing the past; indeed, it
did not seem worth recapture. Journalism had been a
means to an end. It could never be for Willa Cather an end
in itself.

5

Troll Garden, Goblin Market

1902–1905

THE DECADE Willa Cather spent in Pittsburgh—from her twenty-third to her thirty-third year—fell evenly into two periods devoted to the two careers; she was a newspaperwoman for five of these years and a teacher for the remaining five. As if to establish, also, a difference between the unsettled, exacting journalism and the settled life of the classroom, the second half of the decade was marked by a change from boarding-house life to residence in a sedate mansion, in Pittsburgh's finest section, where Willa Cather found herself surrounded by the luxuries she had craved when young and a warm friendship that was devoted to providing her with an environment helpful to creative writing.

Willa Cather met Isabelle McClung in Lizzie Collier's dressing-room backstage at the stock company apparently in 1901, and it took very little time for the two to become close friends. Isabelle McClung was the daughter of a conservative Pittsburgh judge, a strict and upright Calvinist of considerable dignity and affluence, who lived with his wife, son, and two daughters in a large house at 1180 Murray Hill Avenue. She had revolted early against the rather rigid pattern of life in her home and gravitated toward the arts. She did not care for the society in which it was thought fit the daughter of a judge should move; she preferred the company of players, singers, writers. She shared Willa Cather's passion for music and the stage. And she was an avid reader. Elizabeth Moorhead, who has written of Willa Cather's life in Murray Hill Avenue in *These Too Were Here*, thought Isabelle McClung "the most beautiful girl I had ever seen . . . large of mind and heart, entirely frank and simple with natural dignity of manner. Not an artist in the sense of producing, she could identify herself wholly with the artist's efforts and aims. She had an infallible instinct for all the arts. She never mistook the second-best for the best. She became for Willa Cather what every writer needs most, the helping friend."

Isabelle McClung proposed to Willa Cather that she leave her boarding-house and come to live in the McClung mansion. Dorothy Canfield Fisher remembers:

The McClungs had a great rich house, with plenty of servants, conducted in the lavish style of half a century ago. Isabelle was simply devoted to Willa always, and was sweet, warm-hearted and sincere—as well as very beautiful, at least I used to think her so, in a sumptuous sort of way. There was a good deal of stately entertaining carried on in the McClung house too, the many-coursed dinners of the most formal kind, which seemed picturesque (and they really were) to Willa.

For Willa Cather the invitation must have been a welcome one. It meant release from boarding-house life and greater freedom to write in ideal surroundings. In a sense she was achieving a childhood dream and reliving a childhood experience; there had always been in Red Cloud the other house, the house where there were books and pictures and cultivated manners—that of the Wieners—which had later been translated into the Westermann home in Lincoln. The McClung residence was the Wiener or Westermann house many times more spacious and elegant. Isabelle McClung offered Willa Cather a quiet room at the back of the house; it had, like the study in *The Professor's House*, been the sewing-room. Here she could work in peace, looking down over garden and trees to the Monongahela and the hills beyond. It is of this that she wrote when she dedicated *The Song of the Lark*:

To
Isabelle McClung

> *On uplands,*
> *At morning,*
> *The world was young, the winds were free;*
> *A garden fair,*
> *In that blue desert air,*
> *Its guest invited me to be.*[1]

Judge McClung's house stood high on the top of a hilly street, on a little ridge with steps leading to a front porch banked with honeysuckle.

Isabelle McClung's parents at first wondered at the propriety of having Willa Cather come to reside in the household, though they welcomed her as their daughter's friend. The daughter promptly threatened to leave home if she could not have her way; her parents yielded and Willa Cather settled in Murray Hill Avenue as a temporary guest. She remained there, at Isabelle McClung's urging, during the rest of her Pittsburgh stay. Life for her now became even-paced and less driven; she could spend precious

[1] Willa Cather retained the dedication but eliminated these lines in the collected edition of her works.

hours in her room writing in a more sustained fashion than hitherto. Elizabeth Moorhead, who called at Murray Hill Avenue after the publication of "Paul's Case," and became a friend of both Willa Cather and Isabelle McClung, says that evening after evening the two young women would forsake the McClung family group and spend their time reading Tolstoy, Turgenev, Balzac, and Flaubert. This was the way Willa Cather appeared to her when she first called at the house:

Short, rather stocky in build, she had a marked directness of aspect. You saw at once that here was a person who couldn't easily be diverted from her chosen course. "Pretty" would indeed be a trivial word to describe a face that showed so much strength of character as hers, yet she was distinctly good-looking, with a clear rosy skin, eyes of light grey and hair a dark brown brushed back from a low forehead—an odd and charming contrast in color. They were observant eyes, nothing escaped them. . . . She looked me straight in the face as she greeted me, and I felt her absolute frankness and honesty. She would never say anything she didn't mean. . . .

To the years in Murray Hill Avenue belong the poems that constituted Willa Cather's first book and the tales that were incorporated in her first volume of prose fiction, *The Troll Garden.*

II

Before Willa Cather published her first two books she had to undergo one further experience; she had to discover the world that lay beyond the Eastern seaboard, beyond the Atlantic. Her first journey to Europe was made with Isabelle McClung during the summer of 1902 when she had

completed her first year of teaching. To go to the sources
from which much in America was derived, to discover
links with a distant past, made the journey a time of exciting intellectual and æsthetic discovery. In England it
was not only the present that interested her—and she saw
it with the open eyes of a newcomer in its ugliness as well
as its beauty—it was the evidence that still remained of the
Imperial Rome of her Latin excursions with Mr. Ducker in
Red Cloud. So in France later she discovered the sources
from which sprang not only New France but the missions
of the Southwest. In later years Willa Cather was to say
that it takes the right kind of American to go to France—
one with character and depth and a passion for the things
that lie deep behind French history and French art. In a
sense she was describing the qualifications of Claude
Wheeler, her hero in *One of Ours,* and indeed her own.
Grounded deeply in American soil, the novels of Willa
Cather nevertheless are attached also by visible threads
to roots in the Old World. The journey of 1902 was a landmark in the formation of the novelist.

It is possible to follow Willa Cather's European itinerary
in the series of vivid letters which she contributed to the
State Journal during her travels. She sailed with her companion in June. Presently they were in Chester, where
three decades earlier another American novelist, Henry
James, had begun his English tour recorded in *Transatlantic Sketches.* We catch the note of Willa Cather's mood
from the first as she and Isabelle spent half of a June day
"in utter solitude" at the foot of Chester's reconstructed
tower: "The rains and winds of a thousand years have
given the masonry of the tower a white clean-washed look,

like the cobble-stones of the street after a shower." The solitude is complete, the swallows nest serenely in the embrasures and loopholes, past and present merge in a timeless synthesis.

Speedily the journey becomes a pilgrimage to literary scenes, to the graves of the great. Under the impulse of Willa Cather's admiration for A. E. Housman there was a lively and enthusiastic trip through Shropshire, and later, as we shall see, a call on the poet himself. But Willa Cather did not confine herself to the arts in her European reportage; her journalistic training enabled her to gather information rapidly and translate it into readable narrative; thus, at this point, she reported to her fellow Nebraskans in a lively and circumstantial manner on English canals, boats, crews. In London they stayed in a comfortable little hotel in King Street off Cheapside and Willa Cather's transition from the world of castles and romance and the English countryside to the sharp Hogarthian picture was complete:

. . . the living city and not the dead one has kept us here, and the hard garish ugly mask of the immediate present drags one's attention quite away from the long past it covers. If the street life . . . is in any city more gloomy, more ugly, more grimy, more cruel than in London, I certainly don't care to see it. . . . Of all the shoddy foreigners one encounters there are none so depressing as the London shoddy. We have spent morning after morning on High Holborn or the Strand watching this never ending procession of men in top-hats, shabby boots, ragged collars; they invariably have a flower in their button-hole, a briar pipe between their teeth, and an out-of-the-fight look in the eyes that ranges from utter listlessness to sullen defi-

ance. . . . But very few of these night birds are fond of water
and next to gin they are enamoured of life; of these muddy
skies and leaky night skies, of their own bench along the em-
bankment, of the favorite neighbor they beat or chew or claw,
of the sting of cheap gin in empty stomachs and the exciting
game of chess they play with the police back and forth across
the marble squares.

Willa Cather observed the London shop girl: "She wears
flowers and paste jewels but she seldom bathes, never has
enough hair pins and considers tooth brushes necessary
only for members of the royal family"; and the flower girl:
"We have nothing at all at home to correspond with her.
Her voice is harder than her gin-sodden face, it cuts you
like a whip lash as she shouts 'Rowses! Rowses! penny a
bunch!' " *Rowses! Rowses!* The cry was to be remembered
and despite its whiplash was to acquire a romantic con-
notation for Willa Cather as the theme for a poem:

> *Roses of London, perfumed with a thousand years . . .*
> *Roses of London town, red till the summer is done. . . .*

Joined by Dorothy Canfield, Willa Cather and Isabelle
McClung traveled to Paris at the Bank Holiday in August.
They took the overnight boat from Newhaven to Dieppe.
"Certainly so small a body of water as the English Channel
never separated two worlds so different." In the dawn they
had their first glimpse of the twinkling lights of France.
Presently they were breakfasting at a Dieppe hotel, and on
its stone terrace Willa Cather caught the glare of the sun
on white rock and yellow sand and "a little boy . . . was
flying a red and green kite, quite the most magnificent kite
I have ever seen, and it went up famously, up and up until

his string ran short and of a truth one's heart went just as high." This vision of escape from the things that bound one to earth was always to haunt Willa Cather. In "Coming, Aphrodite!" the pigeons wheeling out of the dust of Washington Square into the sky were described in the same way, and in the opening pages of *Lucy Gayheart*, from her sleigh Lucy sees the first star in the frosty sky and it "brought her heart into her throat. . . . That joy of saluting what is far above one was an eternal thing, not merely something that had happened to her ignorance and her foolish heart."

On that memorable day Willa Cather saw from the doorway through which she entered France the play of light and color, the reach of something for the sky, even though but a child's kite, and warm impressions flooded upon her, lighting up France for all the years to come. They proceeded to Rouen with its many associations of Flaubert. Willa Cather's report was sharply personal: "Late in the day we arrived at Rouen, the well-fed, self-satisfied town built upon the hills beside the Seine, the town where Gustave Flaubert was born and worked and which he so sharply satirized and bitterly cursed in his letters to his friends in Paris. In France it seems that a town will forgive the man who curses it if only he is great enough." She might be writing of Rouen, but she seems to have thought of Red Cloud. "The Sculptor's Funeral" was already in her pen.

They viewed the Flaubert monument and the bust of Flaubert's protégé, Maupassant, and continued their travels. Looking at Paris from a terrace in Montmartre, Willa Cather saw it gleaming and purple across the ribbon of the

Seine "like the city of St. John's vision or the Heavenly
City that Bunyan saw across the river." The pilgrimages
to the graves of the great continued: Heine's, which Willa
Cather found covered with forget-me-nots, Musset's, Cho-
pin's, the Balzac monument, "conspicuously ugly and de-
serted, but Balzac seems more a living fact than a dead
man of letters. He lives in every street and quarter; one
sees his people everywhere. He told the story not only of a
Paris of yesterday, but of the Paris of today or tomorrow."
To Willa Cather he seemed second only to Napoleon himself.

A visit to Barbizon caused her to reflect that creative
artists had worked there leaving "intact the beauty that
drew them there. They have built no new and shining vil-
las, introduced no tennis courts, or golf links, or electric
lights." Looking beyond the town, she translated a French
paysage into familiar terms for her readers:

The wheat fields beyond the town were quite as level as those
of the Nebraska divides. The long even stretch of yellow stubble, broken here and there by . . . Lombard poplars recalled
not a little the country about Campbell and Bladen and is certainly more familiar than anything I have seen on this side of
the Atlantic.

She was interested in discovering in the field a reaper of
American make.

In September they journeyed into the south, into the
warm land of Alphonse Daudet, where the mistral blew
"more terrible than any wind that ever came up from
Kansas." Willa Cather drank in the warmth and color of
the land and rejoiced in its people. The impressions of

Provence garnered now were ineffaceable to the last. She
rejoiced in the landscape, the history, the architecture, the
food, the wine; she stayed at the hotel in the ancient Pa-
pal city of Avignon, which Henry James had affectionately
praised in his travel writings. Willa Cather and Isabelle
McClung were the only English-speaking people in the
town; there seemed to be no other tourists and Willa
Cather enjoyed saturating herself with the life and aspect
of the place. Here on the bank of the Rhône the young
woman from the Divide had found something that
touched her more deeply than the metropolitan density of
London or the luminous quality of Paris; a life rooted in
the centuries—what she later had in mind when she spoke
of the things that lie deep behind French history and
French art. That art extended to the sense of well-being
that comes from sun and light and artfully cooked food;
it is reflected in Bishop Latour's remark when he tastes the
soup cooked by Father Vaillant: ". . . a soup like this is
not the work of one man. It is the result of a constantly refined tradition. There are nearly a thousand years of history in this soup."

A rapid trip to Nice and Monte Carlo was followed by a
return to the heart of Provence, to Arles, where Willa
Cather again could discover the Roman past:

It is with something like a sigh of relief that one quits the oppressive splendor of Monte Carlo to retrace one's steps back
into Daudet's country. I am sure I do not know why the beauty
of Monte Carlo should not satisfy more than it does. . . . I
had a continual restless feeling that there was nothing at all
real about Monte Carlo; that the sea was too blue to be wet,
the casino too white to be anything but pasteboard, and that

from their very greenness the palms must be cotton . . . nothing at all produced or manufactured there and no life at all that takes hold upon the soil or grapples with the old conditions set for a people.

In Arles she found no pasteboard. The Roman ruins had withstood the centuries; the Roman colonists had "a sort of Chicago-like vehemence in adorning their city and making it ostentatiously rich," and the great eagle with a garland in its beak mounted on a section of cornice, "the one bird more terrible in history than all the rest of the brute creatures put together," had the inscription above him: "Rome Eternal"—amid ruins! Willa Cather wondered, as she described this, whether the Latin peoples, inheritors of the Romans, "must wither before the cold wind from the north, as their mothers did long ago." It was a pity. "A life so picturesque, an art so rich and so divine, an intelligence so keen and flexible—and yet one knows that this people face toward the setting, not the rising sun." It was difficult for Willa Cather to accept anything that did not endure.

III

The visit to A. E. Housman during the English phase of the European journey deserves to be chronicled apart since Ford Madox Ford made the episode the occasion for one of his finely spun imaginative anecdotes of his late years and because it reflected some of the passion and intensity Willa Cather brought to poetry and to literary achievement during this period of her life. She had discovered Housman's poetry long before he became a celebrated figure. As early as 1900 she had written in her Nebraska column: "I wonder who and what this man Housman may be." She found his touch "as genuine as Heine's" and its quality "as unmistakable as it is rare." In writing from Ludlow to the *State Journal* she observed that anyone "who has ever read Mr. Housman's verse at all must certainly wish to live awhile among the hillside fields, the brooklands and villages which moved a modern singer to lyric expression of a simplicity, spontaneity and grace the like of which we have scarcely heard in the last hundred years." She related that she went to Shrewsbury "chiefly to get some information about Housman—and saw the old files of the little country paper where many of his lyrics first appeared as free contributions and signed *A Shropshire Lad*. There was one copy of his book in the public library, but no one knew anything in particular about him." The Western countryside was full of reminders of the poems; her original enthusiasm for them was natural enough in one for whom Stevenson's verse had so great an appeal. The Housman poems and the Housman countryside, reacting upon each other, produced an excitement that was different from any she had experienced in the work of other living poets. She determined to see the writer.

Ford Madox Ford in his *Return to Yesterday*, with that fondness for spinning stories which H. G. Wells characterized as "a copious carelessness of reminiscence," turned the story of Willa Cather's visit into a veritable saga. She and Isabelle McClung are here described not merely as curious young American women seeking out their favorite poet, but veritable emissaries sent abroad by the "Pittsburgh Shropshire Lad Club" to present a solid gold laurel wreath to Housman; Ford tells in detail of their wandering across England and their calls at innumerable parsonages in search of the writer of the lyrics. To make Ford's long story short, they ultimately discovered Housman, laid the wreath on his grand piano, and departed after he had mistaken them for American cousins.

As with all of Ford's elaborate reminiscences, there was only a germ of truth in the story and even that was not accurately recounted. What actually happened was that Willa Cather began to inquire, when she reached London, where Housman lived (he was then teaching Latin at University College). One afternoon, accompanied by both Isabelle McClung and Dorothy Canfield, she made the trip to his lodgings in Highgate. On the bus she was still wondering what he would be like. "We may find he's a blacksmith, working at his trade, or perhaps a retired officer living on half pay." This was the image his poetry had created in Willa Cather's mind. Dorothy Canfield Fisher remembers:

I think from what he turned out to be in personality that nothing would have induced him to let in three young American women, entire strangers to him, on an incense-burning trip. He came racing down the stairs full of cordiality, holding out both hands, thinking that we were three Canadian cousins whom he was expecting and whom he had never seen. It was a shock to him to find who we were, and I think if he could have managed it without actually pushing us out of the house he would have been very glad to get rid of us with no delay.

What followed was a little comedy of manners, a veritable scene out of Molière. The man envisaged by Willa Cather as a robust retired officer or a brawny blacksmith who could write immortal lyrics appeared to be more prosaic than the Browning of the London drawing-rooms. He had for the young women a reticent presence, perhaps an awkward charm, but a minimum of conversation. Shabbily dressed, as withdrawn as only Englishmen can on occasion be, he lamely, in a flat accent of conventional acceptance of an unexpected social situation, asked his visitors upstairs.

While Dorothy Canfield, who had not had a sight of Shropshire and to whom Willa Cather had not imparted the full extent of her enthusiasm, was looking at their reluctant host, the academically shabby furnishings (totally unendowed with the grand piano Ford Madox Ford later moved into the rooms), and the commonplace books on the shelves, Willa Cather and Isabelle McClung tried to convey to him what the poems had meant to them. This was not a kind of conversation that Housman found easy or even agreeable. Soon an awkward silence enveloped the group. Willa Cather in her newspaper days had met celebrities and knew how to cope with them. But how cope with this shy and seemingly aloof English professor who was not then a celebrity and seemed to be the very opposite of all his poetry suggested? As the silence grew thicker, Dorothy Canfield mentioned her work at the British Museum. Housman was interested; French drama, the study of dubious and corrupt texts, the relation between French and Latin poetry, the kinds of Latin poetry and the difficulties they offered to the research student—on topics like these Housman could be expansive and was. It was the opportunity he needed to depersonalize the situation, to lower a protective curtain between himself and his admiring guests. Indeed, nothing could persuade him to abandon the discussion, which became a dialogue between Dorothy Canfield and the poet. There was no more said about his lyrics or about himself. When the three left, Dorothy Canfield was embarrassed at having monopolized the conversation. Magnanimously Willa Cather said: "But Dorothy, you saved the day." And then on the bus-top as they rode back to the city she suddenly burst into uncontrollable sobs. They were tears of rage and of exasperation —and of disillusionment. Years later she told the anecdote with amusement and spoke of it as "my very pleasant visit with Housman," told it, indeed, once too often, to Ford one day at *McClure's*. To Carl J. Weber, of Colby College, who questioned her about the Ford version, she said that it had all happened "many years ago when I was very young and foolish and thought that if one admired a writer very much one had a perfect right to ring his doorbell. On the occasion of that uninvited call—certainly abrupt enough—Housman was not in the least rude, but very courteous and very kind. I judged he was not accustomed to such intrusions, but he certainly made every effort to make one feel at ease." And she added: "Some day I intend to write a careful and accurate account of that visit for persons who are particularly interested." Unfortunately the account was never written. Yet it had undeniably been an emotional experience. The poet Willa Cather imagined in the work seemed, perhaps, difficult to reconcile with the poet she met that day in the flesh.

IV

Willa Cather's first book was published in 1903, the year
after her return from abroad. Like the debut of many a
writer it was a slim volume of poetry. It bore the title *April
Twilights*, and most of the poems had been published in
the preceding months in magazines; the dedicatory verse
to her brothers recalled the mood of "Far Island," and the
twilights alluded to belonged to Nebraska, not to Pittsburgh. Twenty years later, when it was reissued under the
same title with thirteen additional poems, she discarded
the verse dedication and inscribed the book "To my father
for a Valentine." The poems, early and late, show Willa
Cather's verbal skill and her firm grasp of prosody. There
are echoes in them of her readings of Virgil and Horace;
there are other echoes of Rossetti, and the inevitable influence of Housman emerges in stanzas such as

> *Lads and their sweethearts lying*
> *In the cleft of the windy hill;*
> *Hearts that are hushed of their sighing,*
> *Lips that are tender and still.*[2]

We find, however, at every turn a curious poetic rigidity
and we discover the anomaly that one who could infuse a
page of prose with the cadences of poetry grew self-
conscious and artificial in the writing of verse. The reader
today can glean at best from *April Twilights* certain lines
filled with delicate music:

> *Flutes for the feathery locusts,*
> *soft as spray*

[2] From "On Media Vita." This poem was not included in the collected
edition.

and an occasional bright image. Willa Cather came closest to the contemporary idiom in "Prairie Dawn" or in the flatness of "Macon Prairie" or "Going Home":

> *How smoothly the trains run beyond the Missouri;*
> *Even in my sleep I know when I have crossed the river.*

Largely we catch from the poems those subjects and moods which will find their way into the novels. Spanish Johnny ("those were golden things he said, To his mandolin") is there; the poem "Grandmither, think not I forget" heralds "Old Mrs. Harris"; the picture of "The Swedish Mother" is painted in early pigments she will use in *O Pioneers!* or later with rich tones in *Sapphira*; and there is the general note of the elegiac, the ache of things dead and gone, the "incommunicable past," which will be struck repeatedly and in particular in *My Ántonia*. All her life was a quest for the *neiges d'antan:*

> *Where are the loves that we have loved before*
> *When once we are alone and shut the door?*

and finally that sense of time immutable, the cave-dwellers and the Rock, touched perhaps with the accent of Yeats:

> *The old volcanic mountains*
> *That slope up from the sea—*
> *They dream and dream a thousand years*
> *And watch what-is-to-be.*
>
> *What gladness shines upon them*
> *When, white as white sea-foam,*
> *To the old, old ports of Beauty*
> *A new sail comes home!*

It is when we catch in the early poems the foreshadowings of mood in the novels, or echoes of them contained in the later poems, that we can endow them with an added quality of feeling that was not originally evoked. *April Twilights* remains a part of the *œuvre* of Willa Cather largely as gleams and flashes from the mind that wrote the fiction.

V

Publication of *April Twilights* won Willa Cather a measure of recognition and a marked degree of respect from her fellow teachers and pupils. Ethel Jones Litchfield, a musician and a friend of Willa Cather's for almost half a century, remembers her at this time, when she first met her, as busy with her school work, her writing, her friends, and caught up in the web of calculated social life provided by Isabelle McClung. Yet she found time always for music and the theater and in particular liked to listen until all hours of the night to chamber-music rehearsals, in which Mrs. Litchfield, an accomplished pianist, participated with Pittsburgh's leading musicians as well as guest artists. One such guest, at a later date, was Jan Hambourg, the violinist, who was to marry Isabelle McClung and to whom Willa Cather dedicated two of her later novels. Jan Hambourg was a cultivated musician of a mixed Russian-Jewish-English background, a sensitive performer, an avid reader, particularly fond of the French novelists and a man of considerable general culture. He lived in Canada, in Toronto, where he and his brother Boris, the cellist, and their father taught music. The time was to come when Hambourg would sit for a not wholly flattering portrait as Louie Marsellus in *The Professor's House*.

Willa Cather's literary output during the three years that followed the European journey was modest. She wrote slowly and with great care and had little difficulty in placing her work in the larger magazines. She appeared in *Lippincott's*, the *New England Magazine, Scribner's, Everybody's*, and *McClure's*, and the publication of "Paul's Case" in the last in 1905 gave her a foretaste of the interest her work would arouse increasingly with an ever-growing public. In retrospect it seems fitting that she climaxed her stay in Pittsburgh by producing her first volume of short stories; when she was assembling it she did not know that it would mark the end of a decade, and indeed of a distinct period of her life; but with the appearance of *The Troll Garden* in 1905, published by McClure, Phillips & Company, Willa Cather closed a door upon her formative years and by the same token opened another upon her future.

Her first book in prose contained two groups of stories. Three of the stories, the first, the third, and the fifth, present artists in relation with persons of great wealth. Alternating with these sophisticated tales is another series, comprising the second, fourth, and sixth stories, in which an artist or a person of artistic temperament from the prairies returns to them in defeat. The collection closes with "Paul's Case," the story of a sensitive Pittsburgh youth, for which there is a subtitle: "A Study in Temperament." The book, dedicated to Isabelle McClung, carries two epigraphs. The first, facing the title page, is a quatrain from Christina Rossetti's "Goblin Market":

> *We must not look at Goblin men,*
> *We must not buy their fruits;*

> *Who knows upon what soil they fed*
> *Their hungry, thirsty roots?*

The second epigraph, on the title page, is taken from Charles Kingsley:

A fairy palace, with a fairy garden . . . inside the trolls dwell . . . working at their magic forges, making and making always things rare and strange.

When Willa Cather brought out her second collection of stories, *Youth and the Bright Medusa*, fifteen years later, she discarded the sophisticated stories of the artists living amid wealth and the troll epigraph, but retained the tales of artistic defeat in the West and the epigraph from the "Goblin Market," thus ratifying the inescapable conclusion that *The Troll Garden* consists of two interwoven themes, with "Paul's Case" as a sort of coda.

Willa Cather was under the spell of Henry James at this time and quite possibly was struck by the manner in which he always arranged his short-story collections thematically. If one were to seek a parallel to *The Troll Garden* in James, it is to be found in his volume *The Two Magics*, published while Willa Cather was in Pittsburgh, in which he juxtaposed a tale of black magic ("The Turn of the Screw") with what might be considered a tale of white magic ("Covering End")—the one baleful, filled with suggestions of nightmare and evil, the other bright, sunny, cheerful, fairy-tale-like in substance and denouement. So Willa Cather's two strands in *The Troll Garden* are the baleful and the sunny, the evil-working goblins and the industrious trolls. Her stories of artists creating "things rare and strange" amid the wealthy belong to the trolls and to that "fairy garden" which was also the "garden fair . . . On uplands" to which Isabelle McClung had invited Willa Cather. The fairy palace and the fairy garden are the preserves of art; and the trolls are artists or persons with artistic temperament. In each of the stories the trolls come into relation, and usually into conflict, with those who live outside the preserves of art or trespass upon them. The tales of the defeated artists from the prairies are tales filled with an undercurrent of malaise and a sense of nightmare: those who venture into the goblin market, that great and exciting yet treacherous world beyond the prairies, risk eating of the poisoned fruit. The goblins will "get them"—if they don't look out! The sensuous fruits of life and of luxury can be tainted with evil. Success somehow exacts an ominous price. There is always the danger of having to retrace one's steps, back, back into the open stretches. This is the equivalent of death: the stony death that lies in the deceptive stare of the Bright Medusa. The attitude toward the aspect of the prairies, toward the people who live on them and form the ideas that prevail there, is still hard.

VI

The first of the three tales of the "troll" series, "Flavia and Her Artists," is the story of the wife of a manufacturer of threshing machines. Lacking any æsthetic responses, and unaware of her lack, she collects artists and intellectuals so that from the phrases she forces from them she can make an appearance of cleverness before the rest of the world. An ironic story might have been written about Flavia's parasitic relation with her artists; and that story is in fact here, but entangled with much else. It is entangled, for instance, with the presentation of her artists—some of them persons of the first rank in performance—as sorry, stunted human beings. The crux of the story comes when a French novelist, just after he leaves the house-party, gives an interview in which Flavia's type is ridiculed; everyone who remains, except Flavia, sees the report of the interview; and her loyal husband, believing that what Monsieur Roux has said the rest of the artists think, rebukes them at his own table. "As for M. Roux," Arthur Hamilton says, "his very profession places him in that class of men whom society has never been able to accept unconditionally because it has never been able to assume that they have any ordered notion of taste. He and his ilk remain, with the mountebanks and snake charmers, people indispensable to our civilization, but wholly unreclaimed by it; people whom we receive, but whose invitations we do not accept." An ironic story might have been written also about the chasm between the artist's devotion to beauty and what is sordid and trivial in the rest of his life; there are fragments of that story here, in the crude manners of one, the simper of another, the "malicious vulgarities" of a third; but only fragments, for just where this story required definition and elaboration, in the rendering of Roux, it evaporates. There does not seem to be anything wrong with Roux except that he is candid where the laws of hospitality require silence or a lie. The center shifts from Flavia to her artists and then to her husband, not with development, but only with vacillation.

The second in the series, "The Garden Lodge," is essentially a record of an inner conflict. Caroline Noble questions whether the practical stodgy life she lives in reaction against the fecklessness of her musician father and painter brother is not a negation of life. In the rendering of Caroline's bitter, anxious mood one can feel not only Willa Cather's personal sense of the value for one's life of devotion to art, but no less, and for the first time in her writing, a sense that sustained labor, when forced upon one by ambition and determination and directed toward a nonartistic goal, threatens the very core of personality. This was an opinion that Sarah Orne Jewett was soon to preach to her; her own experience was already leading her to feel its force.

The third and most Jamesian of the tales, "The Marriage of Phaedra," tells of an artist's visit to the studio of a fellow artist after his death and his discovering there an unfinished masterpiece. He decides after talking with the late Hugh Treffinger's servant, whose name is James, to write a biography of the artist. This leads to a meeting with Treffinger's widow. As later, in "Coming, Aphrodite!" he discovers the woman understood neither the artistic aims nor the temperament of her husband. In the end she sells the great unfinished picture to a dealer in a distant land. The story is filled with Jamesian echoes, and notably of those of his tales of artists and writers which appeared during the 1890's. As in "Flavia," the author writes from a recent superficial absorption of the material. The process Stephen Crane described, the "filtering through the blood," had not occurred, had not begun to occur.

From the group, the work of an author who had been

thinking about the arts more than about anything else for
fifteen years, it is unexpectedly difficult to derive any theory, any general idea. Artists do not often appear practicing their art, or theorizing about it, and never do they
attempt either theory or practice at length; they appear in
their relations with others, usually either with nonartistic
persons or with persons who are merely appreciative. One
may safely derive the idea that artists are crucially unlike
other beings; Roux's discourtesy is an outcome of his radi-
cal honesty, his need to tell the truth whatever may fall;
Treffinger loved his wife, but he sacrificed her as he sacrificed everything else that threatened his art; the emphasis
on the unlikeness of the artist runs through all the stories.
The unlikeness often brings havoc into the lives of those
who surround the artist. The emphasis on the enriching
force of an artist's personality also runs through the stories,
and Willa Cather has made no attempt to weigh the havoc
and the enrichment in the balance: she is content to suggest that both are real, both weighty.

The most promising source for a general idea about art
is "The Marriage of Phaedra," for here one artist is seeking
to unravel the artistic method as well as the personality
of another. The narrator discovers that Treffinger was
guided toward his method and the range of his subjects by
an older painter from whom he learned as much as an
artist of genius can learn from anyone; in order to paint
his masterpiece he needed to add to what he had learned
the fruit of painful intimate experience. The clue to Treffinger's greatness as an artist is in the fusion of experience
with instruction. Simple as this formula may be, it is not
superficial. It applies generally to Willa Cather's writing—

to the few promising pieces she had done before "The Marriage of Phaedra" and to the works she was to do.

The stories in which art and the prairies are brought together were of quite another sort, as Willa Cather herself recognized when she reincorporated them into *Youth and the Bright Medusa*. These stories arise from old memories, they have the richness that long preoccupation can give. They have been filtered through the blood. In "A Wagner Matinée" the deep source is in Willa Cather's brooding over the life of an aunt for whom the years on a farm in Webster County were a form of slow suffocation to which she was almost inhumanly resigned; in "The Sculptor's Funeral" the source is in her sense of her own differentness, vulnerability, and value during her years in Red Cloud. The incidents scarcely matter, and there is no contrivance in the arrangement of them: the stories take their life and also their shape from the force and fineness of the feelings poured into them. The quality that animated those passages in "The Garden Lodge" where the theme is the woman's feelings about the crucial and irremediable mistake in her management of her life sweeps through "A Wagner Matinée" and "The Sculptor's Funeral." For "A Death in the Desert"—the title derived from Browning—one cannot say the same. It is like the other two stories about art and the prairies in the rendering of the foreground; but in the background is the world of "Flavia and Her Artists," evoked as the dying singer and the brother of the great composer she has loved talk away her last afternoons in the Colorado summer, with the same chasm between the artist's devotion to beauty and what is ugly and small in his personal life. The fall in force from the scenes in the

foreground to those in the background is always palpable.
Only in the rendering of the Western elements is there an
effect of moving authenticity or of depth.

In a very direct manner these tales are saying what
Thomas Wolfe expressed more crudely as "you can't go
home again." An image of "home" creates the tense and
emotional climax of "A Wagner Matinée." As the music in
Boston dies away and the reality of Nebraska replaces it,
the aunt sobs: " 'I don't want to go . . . I don't want to
go!' . . . For her, just outside the concert hall, lay the
black pond with the cattle-tracked bluffs; the tall, un-
painted house, with weather-curled boards, naked as a
tower; the crook-backed ash seedlings where the dish-
cloths hung to dry; the gaunt, moulting turkeys picking up
refuse about the kitchen door." [3] In "A Death in the Desert" Katharine Gaylord's fate is summed up by her brother:
". . . She got to Chicago, and then to New York, and then
to Europe, and got a taste for it all; and now she's dying
here like a rat in a hole, out of her own world, and she can't
fall back into ours." The burden of "The Sculptor's Funeral" is that even in death the artist cannot escape the
harshness and hostility of his home surroundings where he
is fated to be remembered as "queer" because he never
conformed, and because he fled to unfamiliar worlds un-
dreamed of by his family and friends. It is the town lawyer
who pronounces the strange eulogy over the sculptor's coffin: "There was only one boy ever raised in this border-
land between ruffianism and civilization who didn't come
to grief, and you hated Harvey Merrick more for winning

---

[3] This passage is quoted from the first edition. It underwent slight
verbal alteration in the collected edition.

out than you hated all the other boys who got under the wheels." One couldn't go home even in death. Or, as Lucy Gayheart was to discover, to go home was to die.

Although different in setting and material, "Paul's Case" is of a piece with these tales. It has been the most widely read of Willa Cather's short stories; for many years it was the only one she would allow to be reprinted in anthologies or textbooks. A surprising number of the aspects in her experience of Pittsburgh are gathered into "Paul's Case." Paul is a student at the Pittsburgh high school; and in the early scenes the life of the school is given in classroom vignettes and in one long disciplinary incident in which the boy is under attack from principal and staff. The neighborhood where Paul lives has the petty-bourgeois dreariness that Willa Cather had resented during her years of boarding-house living: the ugly dirty plumbing, the kitchen odors, the unbuttoned laziness of Sunday afternoons, the everlasting sameness from house to house and street to street. Into this stagnant world there seeps one romantic element, the legends of "the cash-boys who had become famous." On every stoop there were tales of the prodigies of effort by a Carnegie or a Frick, and of their costly pleasures, their Mediterranean cruises, their Venetian palaces. The practical deposit of these legends was not inspiriting to a boy like Paul: the whole duty of a boy was to qualify by hard work, miserly economy, respectable living, and the shunning of all distractions. One might almost as well have lived in the small Western town of "The Sculptor's Funeral," in Red Cloud. From the routines of home and school Paul's regular escape is to the symphonies and pictures in Carnegie Hall; and for him the great "portal of romance" is, as it was for Willa Cather, the stage entrance to the downtown theater where a stock company plays. The doors to the Schenley Hotel, where she had gone to interview so many visitors when she wrote for the *Leader,* make another such portal: Paul is drawn to them not only because they are the approach to luxury but because the singers and actors with whom he identifies himself are always passing through them. Like Willa Cather and so many others who lived in Pittsburgh, he felt the pull of New York, the wish to exchange Carnegie Hall for the Metropolitan Opera, the Schenley for the Waldorf, to feel himself in the center of "the plot of all dramas, the text of all romances, the nerve-stuff of all sensations."

The first half of the story describes Paul amid his circumstances in Pittsburgh, the second his yielding to the pull of New York, stealing a thousand dollars from his employers, buying everything one should have to mingle with the millionaires, and after his few days at the Waldorf carrying out the last phase of his plan by taking his life. In the end Paul too can't go home again; he has burned his bridges and has no wish to rebuild them. The Pittsburgh scenes are vivid beyond anything in the series of sophisticated stories, with sharp strokes from experience both of outer objects and of personal states, never multiplied in excess of what the effects demand. New York is drawn in a contrasting manner, for which there is not a parallel in any of the other stories, as a dream city, snow-covered, with a beautiful thick impressionistic haziness that suits the setting for the dreamlike climax of Paul's life.

VII

The two strands of *The Troll Garden* belong to one experience. At the end of her decade in Pittsburgh Willa Cather stood at a crossroad: there was disillusionment in the garden and danger in the marketplace. The artist from the cornfields that reached to daybreak and the corrals that reached to sunset was still searching for a path upon which to set her feet. In the houses of the rich the trolls proved to be less magical and less creative than they seemed; in the goblin world the roots of success were tainted with the poison of evil and the threat of destruction. And there was that other world to which one might have to return like Katharine Gaylord, dying, or Harvey Merrick, dead, or even young Paul, frustrated and a suicide, a boy who "got under the wheels," the world of the Philistine of which Thea Kronborg discovered that "nothing that she would ever do . . . would seem important to them, and nothing they would ever do would seem important to her." The inner texture of these stories seems to reflect strong ambiguities of feeling: a continuing resentment of the West, a continuing fear of attaining success in the world into which Willa Cather had escaped and in which, temporarily, she had found a garden sanctuary. How to make peace with these two haunting worlds—this was the problem to which Willa Cather was to address herself, and the very book that stated the problem was instrumental in offering a solution.

S. S. McClure, publisher of the magazine that bore his name, came to Pittsburgh to meet the author of *The Troll Garden*. The stories had produced a marked impression on him. He dined at Judge McClung's and talked brilliantly all evening. Then he had a talk with Willa Cather. The upshot of it was that at the end of the school year she resigned from Allegheny High and moved to New York to enter upon a new career that mingled the experience of her journalistic days with her literary talents and ambitions. She became a member of the staff of *McClure's Magazine*. There had been the sudden, unexpected leap from Red Cloud to Pittsburgh ten years earlier; and now, as she neared her middle thirties, Willa Cather made the second leap—from an obscure classroom to a post on an important national magazine. S. S. McClure, with the magic of his talk and his capacity for eloquently pyramiding grandiose plans, had swept Willa Cather into the very path for which all the years of striving in the West and the bright hard years of Pittsburgh had prepared her. The inexperienced young girl who, tense and eager, had stepped from the prairies into the smoky Eastern city a decade before was now a mature woman of thirty-two; and though she could not have known it at this singularly triumphant moment, she was entering the final and most exacting phase of her long literary apprenticeship.

6

At *McClure's*

1906–1912

WILLA CATHER CAME to *McClure's Magazine* after the worst upheaval in its never tranquil life. Ellery Sedgwick, who also came to it in 1906, speaks of the upheaval as a "revolution," in which "the most brilliant staff ever gathered by a New York periodical left Mr. McClure in a body." The sort of revolution it was shows rather precisely what it meant to work in S. S. McClure's dominion, as Willa Cather was about to do for six years; and that the secession at one time of Lincoln Steffens, Ida Tarbell, and Ray Stannard Baker did not ruin the magazine, or even endanger its strength, shows rather exactly what sort of editor-in-chief S. S. McClure was, and why to the end of her life Willa Cather admired him.

The magazine had been founded in the spring of 1893, the *annus mirabilis* for intelligent popular monthlies. The great monthly magazines of elder date such as the *Century*, the model in format for *McClure's*, sold at thirty-five cents a copy or more and were addressed to a relatively small cultivated public. *McClure's*, and its two chief competitors, *Munsey's* and the *Cosmopolitan*, sold for a time at ten cents a copy and sought twenty subscribers in towns where the *Century* had one, and one in villages of the Middle West where no one had ever heard of the *Century* or the *Atlantic* or *Harper's*. The low price was possible provided a large circulation was assured, because paper had become cheaper and because the process of photoengraving had cut the cost of illustrations. How were the new scores of thousands of subscribers to be won? Frank A. Munsey described his formula years afterward: "I began to analyze the magazines. They seemed made for anaemics, and their editors editing for themselves and not for their subscribers. Living in an artificial literary world they got out publications which woefully lacked human interest. . . . I became convinced that both the prices and the magazines were wrong for a wide circulation. If a magazine should be published at ten cents and made light, bright, and timely, it might be a different story." S. S. McClure would never have accepted "light, bright, and timely" as a sufficient formula; he wished not only to win readers, but to improve them. He would, however, have endorsed with the greatest enthusiasm the stress Munsey laid on "human interest." With his own extraordinary indifference to the past, with his excited absorption in what was here and now, he would scarcely have understood how anything could have much "human interest" if it was not timely.

It was by its "human interest" that *McClure's* had its first great impact. The *Century* was running a sober, somewhat ponderous life of Napoleon; McClure persuaded Ida Tarbell, who was deeply read in the French eighteenth century and the Napoleonic period, to produce a much more humanly interesting life. From her serial on Napoleon she went on to another on Lincoln, enriched, according to another formula that helped the magazine to capture "human interest," by a profusion of pictures, some of them never before published. Among the features in the early years of *McClure's* was a new sort of interview in which one distinguished person was queried by another distinguished person on topics of a humanly interesting kind. S. S. McClure understood the importance for circulation of lively well-wrought fiction, especially serial fiction. In his syndicate, his main venture in publishing before he founded the magazine, he had negotiated with many of the most popular English writers, and he had paid them well. He was now able to draw on their good will, and to present in *McClure's* Stevenson's *The Ebb Tide* and *St. Ives, Rupert of Hentzau*—the sequel to Anthony Hope's *The Prisoner of Zenda*—and Kipling's *Captains Courageous*. Among the short stories in the early years of the magazine were some of Stephen Crane's and Conan Doyle's; the first of David Graham Phillips's short stories appeared in it.

"Human interest" was at the core of another specialty of the magazine with which its place in the history of American periodicals is now indissolubly linked. This was the "serious article," usually written by a member of the editorial staff. "Its method," one historian has said, "is to present, without sensationalism or exaggeration, facts skilfully marshalled and sternly compressed, and let them speak for themselves." Its substance was typically a report on an outstanding problem in American life, such as the corruptive forces in the government of a city or a state, or the effect on a community of some big business, or of some social evil. Lincoln Steffens, who was for many years the managing editor, desired above all else to "put news" into the magazine. He believed that a complicated news story lost much of its value, and more of its impact, when it was told in driblets in a daily, but that "a monthly could come along, tell the whole completed story all over again, and bring out the meaning of it all with comment." McClure had set Ida Tarbell to studying the Standard Oil Company some time before Steffens came on the magazine; and it is probable that he had a clearer idea of what a "serious article" should be than Steffens brought with him after years of work on newspapers. It was like S. S. McClure to know. Miss Tarbell was allowed to work at collecting and writing her material for three years before her first article appeared; her fifteen chapters consumed five years of her time; and McClure estimated that each article had cost him two thousand dollars. Circulation rose, and he was jubilant. "To secure the accuracy that alone makes such studies of value," he said, "I had to invent a new method of magazine journalism. The fundamental weakness of modern journalism was that the highly specialized activities of civilization were very generally reported by uninformed men, and what experts had to say was seldom interesting. I decided to pay my writers for their study rather than for their copy—to put them on a salary and let them master their subjects before they wrote about them." In "Ardessa," a story that appeared in the *Century* in May 1918, and is full of lighthearted reminiscences of *McClure's*, Willa Cather remarked: "The great men of the staff were all about her, as contemplative as Buddhas, in their private offices, each meditating on the particular trust or form of vice confided to his care." In no other magazine was contemplation in private so normally linked with topics inherently practical.

Steffens soon appreciated that McClure's formula would give the magazine the news value appropriate to a monthly publication. Not only would the story be told at once, the commentary on the story would have a solidity that could not be impeached. Although many of the "serious articles" were not complete in themselves, the new method in journalism was an immediate success: the combination in them of nearly expert knowledge of the problem under review with first-rate ability in journalistic writing, both brought to bear on a subject that every reader who thought at all would care about, deserved to succeed. It did succeed; it was much imitated; and whenever it is tried in more recent times the success is as certain as it was at the beginning of the century. What McClure was doing was simply deepening the idea that possessed Joseph Pulitzer, who wrote: "I should make a paper that the judges of the Supreme Court of the United States would read with enjoyment, but I would not make a paper that only the judges of the Supreme Court and their class would read. I would make this paper without lowering the tone in the slightest degree."

Steffens and Baker studied municipal and state and finally federal government. They brought out the ties between business and politics. They linked both with the world of crime. Yet they managed their material in such a fashion that the individuals they exposed did not appear to be ogres, but simply rather limited mortals with an extreme delight in the exercise of power, or in the accumulation of money. "Human interest" is very rich in almost all their exposures. Steffens was far too cynical to become a zealot; and from the observation of many businesses and many governments he drew the conclusion that whatever spots of deepest black might disfigure a politician he was preferable to the business mind in politics, or the humorless do-gooder. So able and so imitable a builder of circulation as the "serious article" was certain to spread across the country and to leave a mark on public opinion. That mark became permanent with the application of a phrase by a President of the United States. In 1905 the *Cosmopolitan* was bought by William Randolph Hearst and, at the instance of his managing editor, David Graham Phillips wrote a series called "The Treason of the Senate." The articles had that ferocious sincerity which Phillips applied to all his analyses and comments on contemporary life. The Senate was presented as a nest of conspirators against the welfare of the democracy, in the interests of big business. The effect was too much for Theodore Roosevelt. In the spring of 1906, without naming Phillips, and by leaving his indictment general, inviting the country to extend it to the entire tribe of "serious" journalistic critics, he said:

Expose the crime, and hunt down the criminal, but remember that even in the case of crime, if it is attacked in sensational, lurid, and untruthful fashion, the attack may do more damage to the public mind than the crime itself. . . . The men with the muckrakes are often indispensable to the well-being of society but only if they know how to stop raking the muck, and to look upward to the celestial crown above them, to the crown of worthy endeavor.

Men with the muckrakes, muckrakers, muckraking—these were the words that for years after the President used the phrase—drawn from *The Pilgrim's Progress*, that favorite book of Willa Cather's grandmothers and of Willa Cather's, too—people applied to the staff of *McClure's*, and to the specialty that was more than anything else the reason for the magazine's success and fame.

No one has praised McClure's powers as an editor so highly as men who found they could not remain on his staff. McClure was what a more modern generation would call an "idea man." "He was," says Steffens, "a flower that did not sit and wait for the bees to come and take his honey and leave their seeds. He flew forth to find and rob the bees." He knew where all the bees were; no one could doubt it; but all too often he would mistake another and perfectly useless insect for the bee he desired, and his staff had to dispose of the result. He would commission a series of articles from someone whose appeal lay in his having one idea or having had one experience of note; and when the articles arrived they would often be hopelessly past mending. Or he would appoint to his staff someone who could be put to no use. By the time manuscript or appointee arrived, McClure would be far away where he could not be reached, and even if he had been reached it would have done no good. He was no longer interested in what he had done; or rather, the interest had been overlaid by so many other and newer interests that he would not fix his mind on it. He was like the editor in "Ardessa," "who went in for everything, and got tired of everything; that was why he made a good editor." Someone else was required to deal with the outcome of McClure's reckless decision. When he was away from the office—and since he hated sitting still he was usually away—he was a source of trouble. But when he was there! Writing forty years afterward, Ellery Sedgwick recalls, "The blessed quiet of those days when McClure was abroad! The dove of peace descended upon the office and every man took up his own life. Never," he adds, "in American business was there a brighter genius than McClure's for disorganization." George Kibbe Turner, who came to the magazine in the same year as Ellery Sedgwick and Willa Cather, has described to me what the office was like when McClure arrived with an idea. The publisher's sanctum was at the rear of the suite. It would take McClure nearly half the morning to get to it, pausing at each desk and explaining, exhorting, excoriating; and it would take him the rest of the morning to get out as he repeated the process from the other end. Mark Sullivan reports McClure as saying after one such morning: "I get an idea. It comes to me in the night. I lie awake until morning. I rush to the office with it—and they throw cold water on it." No wonder they did; no wonder they spent much of their time circumventing him; no wonder that when a member of the staff was at work on an article or a story and the deadline was close, a room had to be taken for him (or for her) at some remote and unlikely hotel, and always, even if the hotel were in another city, there was the fear that somehow this man of genius would discover where the writer was. Since there was nothing McClure liked more than getting on a train, he would then unearth the absentee in person. "He could raise a rumpus," says Steffens in a tone almost of awe.

It was into the dominion of this remarkable person, from whom almost an entire staff had just fled, that Willa Cather came late in 1906. In September 1905 she came to New York at McClure's invitation, and remained for a week. Between them there was an immediate liking; and in the six years Willa Cather remained in his employ there

was not a cloud on their relationship. She at once perceived that in McClure there was an element of wild genius: he was a great creator, and she thought of him much
as she thought of the large-scale men who had opened the
West. She responded to the warmth and enthusiasm with
which he advocated all his ideas, with a kindred warmth
and enthusiasm. Responding to his temperament did not
mean that she accepted each idea; but when she disapproved, as she often did, she did not pour cold water on it.
She could disapprove and yet not offend, not even discourage. In the campaign against corruption in business
and politics, which went on unabated with a new corps of
writers, she took scarcely any interest, and she did not pretend the interest she did not feel. McClure accepted her
indifference, perhaps with regret, certainly with understanding.

During her first months in New York Willa Cather lived
in an old studio building on the south side of Washington
Square (Number 60), now torn down. In a story written
long afterward, "Coming, Aphrodite!" she has captured
the feel of that building, the dirt and must and paucity of
baths, the young artists and musicians and writers who occupied most of the rooms, and the general air of a somewhat innocuous Bohemia. In that story she also records her
delight in the beauty of the square, and the interest of the
foreign populations near by. The main characters in "Coming, Aphrodite!" have dinner in "the back garden of a little French hotel on Ninth Street, long since passed away."
This was the Griffou, where she lived for a short time.
The inconvenience and drabness of her rooms in Greenwich Village were a sharp break from the ordered luxury

of Judge McClung's house, but Willa Cather does not appear to have minded. To live among other young artists, and as they lived, was, for the present, more than enough.

It was her stories and perhaps also her poems that first interested S. S. McClure in Willa Cather; but her main task during her first two years on the magazine had no relation with either. Some months before the secession of talent, McClure was excited by the possibilities he saw in a manuscript that clearly had matter of extraordinary interest but just as clearly could not be used in anything like the form in which it had come in. This was *Mary Baker G. Eddy: The Story of Her Life and History of Christian Science*, by Georgine Milmine, the wife of a newspaperman in Rochester, New York. One of the first members of the staff to work over it was Mark Sullivan, who tells in *The Education of an American* of trips he took to remote villages in New Hampshire and other parts of New England to verify the astonishing facts of Mrs. Eddy's early life. The Milmine manuscript was packed with facts, some of them so startling that careful verification was necessary at whatever cost. After a while Mark Sullivan was taken off the scent, and others were put on. When the first installment was published, in January 1907, it was accompanied by a picture that purported to present Mrs. Eddy in youth, but was in fact the likeness of one of her friends. The mistake was pointed out, and threatened to discredit the series. The chief responsibility for preparing the remainder of the long manuscript for publication was given to Willa Cather. The outcome was a series of thirteen articles (in addition to the first), appearing at intervals, the last of them in June 1908.

II

This was the outcome for *McClure's*; the important outcome for Willa Cather was quite different. It was the opportunity to live for months at a time at the old Parker
House in Boston, and then in an apartment on Chestnut
Street—months broken, it is true, by trips to the neighboring shoe towns and to a few places farther away. From the
beginning Boston meant Ferris Greenslet, whose review of
April Twilights had opened a cordial friendship, and who
was soon to introduce this "fresh-faced, broad-browed
plain-speaking young woman, standing her ground with a
singular solidity," to Houghton Mifflin Company. It came
to mean Mrs. James T. Fields and Sarah Orne Jewett.

It was not Ferris Greenslet but Mrs. Louis D. Brandeis
who introduced Willa Cather to these women who were to
leave so strong a mark on her life and art. From the beginning of their acquaintance Willa Cather admired and liked
both the Brandeises. Louis Brandeis was among the few
persons who seemed to her to have an intuitive understanding of her art, so sure that she was safe in allowing it
to influence her. She shared with the Brandeises many enthusiasms in literature and music, and she was pleased
with their way of responding to life. Mrs. Brandeis, she
thought, was an ideal wife for a great man, extremely
handsome, extremely intelligent, extremely perceptive,
very much at home in the world and yet very much superior to it.

Late in the winter of 1908 Mrs. Brandeis took Willa
Cather to call at 148 Charles Street, the house where
Mrs. James T. Fields had been living for over fifty years,

the first twenty-five with her husband, who had died in
1881. He had been a publisher of the *Atlantic* as a member of the house of Ticknor and Fields, later Fields, Os-
good & Co., a firm that had dealt generously with English
authors in the bad days of piracy. The house on Charles
Street had been the American home of Charles Dickens;
in one of its upper rooms, scarcely changed since he had
slept in it, Thackeray had written a part of *Henry Esmond.*
Dr. Holmes had been a neighbor and had dropped in at
all hours; another neighbor had been Thomas Bailey Al-
drich, whose life Ferris Greenslet was writing while Willa
Cather was in Boston. Longfellow and Lowell had come
over from Cambridge on occasions great and small; and
Emerson and Hawthorne had come in from Concord; Harriet Beecher Stowe had breakfasted there, and the young
Henry James. James Fields had loved the theater from
boyhood, and at his table the New England writers had
met Edwin Booth and Joseph Jefferson, Charlotte Cush-
man and Christine Nilsson. Before and after his death
Mrs. Fields, it has been said, came nearer than any other
American to achieving a Parisian salon.

    In her house Willa Cather felt at once, and was to feel
increasingly, that the past continued alive. It seemed that
the step of a great actor or writer of another day might
again sound on the stairway that led to the long drawing-
room on the second story, "that pleasant Charles Street
parlor," as Whittier called it in his bucolic fashion. Here,
beside the windows that overlooked the Charles River,
Willa Cather was given her tea by a frail little woman who
was almost eighty, but had kept the clear blue eyes and
the bright lips of her youth, and who was not only, as her

guest had expected, kind, inquisitive, gracious, and deeply distinguished, but above everything else gay. Her years in the company of the great she had always borne with ease; and now she bore with ease her memories.

The house in Charles Street was full not only of memories but of mementos. Thomas Gray's copy of the 1673 edition of Milton's *Poems on Several Occasions* was here, surely an acquisition of the later poet's extreme youth, for his name was signed on the title page in a large boyish hand no fewer than nine times. Here too was Charles Lamb's copy of *The Rape of the Lock*, a defective copy in which the missing pages had been replaced in Elia's meticulous calligraphy; and Byron's working copy of *Don Juan*, III, IV, V, given to James Fields by his Edinburgh crony Dr. John Brown; and a book given him by Tennyson, the poet's own volume of Keats, "a battered little copy in green cloth, with the comfortable aspect of having been abroad with some loving companion in a summer shower." The Fieldses had a cult of Keats. There was a drawing of him executed at Fields's desire by Severn, who had tended the poet's deathbed; there were many books concerning him that had been acquired with Leigh Hunt's library; and there was also the bust by Amy Whitney, which after Mrs. Fields died was to rest in Willa Cather's living-room. Mrs. Fields had once led Dr. Holmes to talk about it; he talked more as a doctor than as a connoisseur, and ventured to criticize the hair, adding that he knew a great deal about the nature of hair, and doubted that this was like Keats's though, since he supposed nothing was now known of Keats's hair, it might as well be one way as another. Rash words to use in this house. "I told him on the contrary,"

said Mrs. Fields, "I owned some of it; whereat I got it out."
No wonder that in this house Willa Cather accused herself
of a "Bœotian ignorance" and undertook a campaign to
overcome it. If you wanted to know how Edwin Booth had
delivered a passage in *Hamlet*, or what were the gestures
of Turgenev's Pauline Viardot, in this house you could find
out; but, Willa Cather found, you must not "go at" Mrs.
Fields, you must involve your question in some general
talk about acting.

All her life Willa Cather had wished for the atmosphere
she found in Charles Street, an atmosphere where the arts
and manners of a past time lingered with none of the des-
iccation of the classroom but with the fragrant natural life
that can be maintained only by discriminating affection.
She had found a little of it in Lincoln, with the Westermanns, the Canfields, and Dr. Tyndale; more in Pittsburgh,
with the Andersons and George Seibel; but now she had
it in the finest form in which it could be found in America.
She had always liked old women, felt easy with them,
been kind to them, drawn them out; and now she was to
have a high reward. Mrs. Fields liked her at once, as Mc-
Clure had; and she was to return to this room many times
during the seven years her hostess had to live, and also to
stay with her more than once at Thunderbolt Hill, the cottage the family had owned at Manchester-on-the-Sea almost as long as they had owned the house in Charles
Street.

Much as she was to gain from knowing Mrs. Fields,
there was another person in that long green drawing-room
at the time of her first call from whom she would draw a
more precious benefit. This was the closest of Mrs. Fields's

friends in the long decades of her widowhood, Sarah Orne Jewett.

Miss Jewett was to die a little more than a year after this first meeting, and Willa Cather was the last person to whom she gave her friendship. Between these two women, separated by a quarter century in age, and by all kinds of superficial circumstance, there were deep affinities quickly recognized. Both had grown up in small towns, and had seen these towns, which they loved, decline through the play of economic factors nothing could check. At South Berwick shipping and shipbuilding had almost disappeared in the years after the Civil War; at Red Cloud there had been arrest, and then decline, in the drought and depression of the 1890's. Both women had entered eagerly into the life of their towns and had been imaginatively stirred by the interplay between the townsfolk and the farm people. They had both ridden tomboyishly about the countryside, loving every tree in it; and had been taken on long rides to lonely farmhouses by the country doctor. Both had cherished intimacies with an older generation and a way of life that was vanishing before their eyes and giving place to something they considered to be cheap and nasty. "I was brought up with grandfathers and granduncles and aunts for my best playmates. They were not the wine one can get for so much the dozen now." The words are Miss Jewett's; they might have been Miss Cather's except that she would have begun the enumeration with grandmothers. Both had turned early to an apprenticeship to writing and had taken for a master Flaubert. That sentence of his that Miss Jewett had pinned to her desk and kept there—*Ce n'est pas de faire rire ni de faire pleurer, ni de vous mettre à fureur, mais d'agir à la façon de la nature, c'est à dire de faire rêver*—might have been pinned to Miss Cather's. No epigraph would be more illuminating for *Death Comes for the Archbishop* or *Shadows on the Rock*. Their literary enthusiasms were in general alike: the pilgrimage Sarah Jewett had made with Mrs. Fields to Tennyson came from just the same kind of devotion that had led Willa Cather to make her pilgrimage with Dorothy Canfield and Isabelle McClung to A. E. Housman's lodgings. For each the chosen poet was the perfect verbal artist, the pure lyrist.

The most important of the affinities between them was in a conception of literature, or at least of prose fiction, assumed by Sarah Orne Jewett in the long letter of advice she wrote in December 1908, the most important letter, beyond a question, that Willa Cather ever received. It is an instance of something very rare in the arts, advice of a fundamental kind, arriving at the right time, and exercising a strong if not an immediate influence. "You must find a quiet place," Miss Jewett wrote from Charles Street. "You must find your own quiet center of life and write from that. . . . To write and work on this level we must live on it—we must at least recognize it and defer to it at every step." One of the main reasons for the letter was Miss Jewett's dissatisfaction with the stories Willa Cather had been writing since she had gone to *McClure's*. To Miss Jewett these stories revealed no deepening of the author's inward life, no ripening of her talent. The failure to deepen and ripen was alarming, for Willa Cather was now thirty-five, and it was Miss Jewett's feeling that if the early

years of an artist's activity were misdirected, some of the
highest effects would be forever unattainable.

What were these stories? Were they repetitions of those
in *The Troll Garden*? Or did they disclose some new qualities good or bad?

The first of them was "The Namesake," which appeared
in *McClure's* in March 1907. Willa Cather had used the
same title for a poem published in *Lippincott's* five years
before, and that poem was addressed to the memory of
her uncle William Lee Boak "of the Thirty-fifth Virginia,"
killed in the War between the States. The final feeling in
the poem is pride in relationship. That feeling reappears
in the story. The framework is simple, and introduces the
kind of persons who had dominated most of the stories collected in *The Troll Garden*. A group of young American
artists gather in the studio of Lyon Hartwell, in the boulevard Saint-Michel, the evening before one of them returns
for good to the United States. Their thoughts are fixed for
the time upon their country, and Hartwell, a great sculptor of the elder generation and a person of almost *farouche*
reserve, explains how he was able to accomplish what the
group considers his greatest statue, *The Color Sergeant*.
His explanation is the story; the rest is machinery.

Fifteen years earlier he had gone home to his grandfather's house a few miles from Pittsburgh, "on the high
banks of a river in Western Pennsylvania." Once the setting had been beautiful, but now it is ruined by the effects
of an industrial civilization—air polluted, dreams discol-
ored, vistas broken by coal shafts and oil derricks. What
he saw had no value for Hartwell, a *déraciné*, brought up

in Rome and Paris, obliged to stay amid the ugliness and
grime because a relative was ill and his heart was kind.
The only element that did achieve value was the group of
objects that reminded him of the uncle and namesake he
had never seen, killed, like Willa Cather's, in the War between the States. On one evening of concentrated appre-
hension the young artist broke through to a new level of
awareness:

> For the first time I felt the pull of race and blood and kin-
> dred, and felt beating within me things that had not begun with
> me. It was as if the earth under my feet had grasped and rooted
> me, and were pouring its essence into me. I sat there until the
> dawn of morning, and all night long my life seemed to be pour-
> ing out of me and running into the ground.

Willa Cather is not yet ready to draw strength from her
early environment, whether in Virginia or in Nebraska, to
let herself mix with it: she must write of Pennsylvania, and
the color sergeant must be a Union man and not a Confederate. She is developing an awareness of something, however, "that had not begun with me," of her family as a
source not only of happiness and comfort, but of spiritual
and artistic life. Her quest of that layer within herself from
which her great fiction was primarily to come has taken a
long step forward. But the story that records the step is
not a success, either spiritually or artistically. Compared
with the best of the stories in *The Troll Garden*, the rendering of the material in "The Namesake" is uneven and
has patches of crudity. The picture of an evening among
the American artists in Paris does not have the pressure of
experience that gave a steady force to the picture of Paul
in his luxurious room in the New York hotel or of the ill-

assorted pair listening to Wagner at the Boston Symphony, to say nothing of the Western scenes in "A Death in the Desert." The evening in Paris is done not as Henry James might have done it, or even Edith Wharton, but as it might be done by someone who had read their works and assimilated something of their manners. Yet since the picture of this evening is subordinate, it does not make or mar the story which hangs on the realization of the feelings that came to Hartwell in his grandfather's house. In the rendering of these feelings the patches of crudity appear, melodramatic or sentimental, as in Hartwell's magnification of the simple drawing his namesake had executed in his dog-eared school text of Virgil. It may have been of passages like this that Sarah Orne Jewett was thinking when she warned Willa Cather that her recent stories fell short because they did not proceed from a quiet center, "her own quiet center of life." Even in the writings of her own twenties in the sketches of *Deephaven*, Miss Jewett had written from that. Her insight told her that Willa Cather, though it would take her much longer to do so, might attain to it.

Another story of this time, "Eleanor's House," which appeared in *McClure's* later in 1907, was, Willa Cather knew, a Jamesian experiment, almost, one might claim, a pastiche. All the personages are Americans who live abroad, so detached from their country that when something drives one from the countryside near Paris he goes to Normandy or the Riviera, or, a great decision, to Surrey. America does not exist. One of the personages is a typical Jamesian outsider—the clumsy girl from ordinary folk, with a heart of gold. The four others—Eleanor, who is dead, her

husband, who has married the clumsy girl, and the West-
erfields, a pair of Eleanor's understanding friends—are lei-
sured, worried Jamesians, with nothing to interrupt their
questionings of themselves and of one another. They talk
with the Jamesian inflections and aposiopeses. The mellow
French settings are drawn with a good deal of the light-
ness and sensitiveness of stroke that James applied to landscape. The story is not, however, authentic James: the re-
nunciations are somewhat unreal, the conflicts a little
sullen. The pain that Eleanor's bereaved husband feels is
healed too easily, and his state after escape from his grief
is not an enlargement, but a reduction. The elaborate
Jamesian form has no real affinity with the simple sequence
of feeling. "Eleanor's House," like "The Namesake," does
not proceed from a quiet center: it is a sketch in another's
manner, not an organic development from the author's
own fiber.

There were other stories published in 1907 and 1908, in
McClure's and the *Century*, but none that had appeared
by the end of 1908 would escape Miss Jewett's criticism:
in a letter written at the end of November 1908 she expressed her dissatisfaction with the artifice in "On the
Gull's Road," which was in *McClure's* for that month.
"The lover is as well done as he could be," she wrote,
"when a woman writes in a man's character." But she felt
that there was some artifice in that, and she urged that it
was "safer" to avoid becoming involved in what was, in
her view, a "masquerade." She told Willa Cather she could
almost "have done it as yourself—a woman could love her
in the same protecting way—a woman could even care
enough to wish to take her away from such a life, by some

means or other. . . ." The problem raised by Miss Jewett
—which indeed all writers face in their delineation of the
opposite sex—was to be encountered again and to provide
great difficulties for Willa Cather when she assigned the
narrative of *My Ántonia* to Jim Burden. Miss Jewett felt
that "On the Gull's Road" just missed being good, while
offering the promise of the work Willa Cather could
achieve, given the right circumstances. In later years Willa
Cather disliked to be reminded of the short stories she had
written during her years at *McClure's*; she was glad that
she had the copyright and could prevent the republication
of any among them. She compared her attitude to that of
an apple-grower careful of his reputation: the fruit that
was below standard must be left forgotten on the ground;
only the sound apples should be collected. She was in the
habit of saying almost exactly what Miss Jewett had said
of them: she felt that these stories had the defects insep-
arable from creative work done in a hurry, when one was
tired, and seeking relief from exacting work of another
sort.

III

Soon after Willa Cather had finished her revision of the
Milmine manuscript she sailed for Europe, in April 1908,
taking the Mediterranean route, and enjoying a long and
carefree vacation with Isabelle McClung. Their time was
spent mostly in Italy and France. A few poems were written, but the journey was one of pleasure and absorption
rather than of direct literary effect. On her return to New
York she entered on her duties as managing editor of the
magazine. Her salary was liberal, but she was determined
to lay aside every dollar she could, withdraw at the first

safe moment from any kind of office work, and depend for a living on what she could write. Her first years in Pittsburgh had been so hard and precarious that she never got over some fright about money. With Edith Lewis she took in September 1908 a small and rather uncomfortable apartment in Washington Place, just off the square where she had lived when she first came to New York. From the time they shared this apartment they were separated only when one or the other of them was traveling or called home by illness in the family. Besides the salary there was another great compensation for the heavier anxieties of the managing editor's post. S. S. McClure believed in travel not only for himself but for his staff, especially those who were charged with bringing in manuscripts and determining policy. He was convinced that the last place from which a magazine could be well edited was the editor's chair. He pressed Willa Cather to make trips to England, and in the spring and summer of 1909 she spent several months in and near London meeting a variety of striking people.

One of her encounters is described in a preface she wrote for a serial that began to run in *McClure's* in December 1909, David Soskice's *The Secrets of the Schluesselburg: Chapters from the Secret History of Russia's Most Terrible Political Prison.* She was present when on the 23rd of June in that year the Russian colony in London gathered at South Place Institute, Finsbury, to welcome a political heroine, Vera Figner, who had spent twenty-two years, most of them in solitary confinement, in the Schlüsselburg prison, on a lonely island in the Neva. Prince Kropotkin and Soskice addressed the meeting in English, and

Vera Figner spoke in Russian. It was characteristic of Willa Cather that in this hotly political company her deepest impression was of Vera Figner's voice, "one of marvelous resonance and power, beautifully modulated in spite of the fact that it was mute for so many years." Besides arranging for a long series of articles by Soskice, she was responsible at least in part, for a series of reminiscential pieces by Xavier Paoli, who had spent a quarter of a century as officer in charge of the security of royal visitors to France.

During the London visit she had other experiences nearer her usual habit than the meeting in South Place. William Archer, who became her guide to London, and was for many years her principal friend in England, took her to the funeral of George Meredith in May, and to the first London performance by the Abbey Players, where she sat with Lady Gregory in Yeats's box. *The Rising of the Moon* was the curtain-raiser, followed by *The Playboy of the Western World*. Synge's play was a puzzle to that audience, as to so many since, and at first Willa Cather shared the general feeling. At supper afterward Archer inquired about her judgment of the *Playboy*; she said, somewhat tentatively, that she had found it interesting but lacking in the dramatic, to which he replied that he thought anything that was interesting had its dramatic quality and its place in the theater. It was a remark she never forgot, and it was to have its effect when she began to loosen the conventional structure in her fiction. It told as Sarah Orne Jewett's theory and practice told, on the side of freedom. Archer, Yeats, and Lady Gregory all contributed to *McClure's*; so did another writer with whom

Willa Cather formed a lasting friendship, Katherine Ty-
nan. Archer introduced her to a number of stage people,
and it was on memories of them that she drew in writing
the London chapters of *Alexander's Bridge*. She had a
strong sense of Anglo-American community; she was at
ease in England, and in the years before the First World
War she was reading at least as many English books as
American. But none among her English literary friends
ever had an influence on her work comparable to Sarah
Orne Jewett's, and the visit was saddened by the news of
Miss Jewett's death in June.

As managing editor Willa Cather continued to read a
great variety of manuscripts; indeed, she read more than
she had before. The impressions she formed were to have
a strong effect on her own later practice of fiction. More
than ninety per cent of what she read seemed to her incurably conventional: written according to formulas, written not for the sake of the subject but to display the cleverness of the author. The few manuscripts that were
unconventional were almost all from writers so unprac-
ticed that their crudities rendered what they wrote un-
publishable. It seemed to her that a true writer would submit to his subject, and by submitting to it arrive at a form
that was ideally suited to it, provided he had the command
of his instrument, which might be assured him by an honest apprenticeship. She was probably aware during her
years as managing editor that she had been an honest ap-
prentice long enough, and that it was time to discover
what she could achieve if she gave over experimenting and
submitted to a subject from her early experience. Miss
Jewett had said: "The thing that teases the mind over and

over for years, and at last gets itself put down rightly on paper—whether little or great, it belongs to Literature." This was strangely like the words of Stephen Crane.

Shortly before she went to England she wrote a short piece that belongs to Literature. This is "The Enchanted Bluff," which appeared in *Harper's Monthly* in April 1909. Perhaps she went elsewhere to have it published because she appreciated how unlike her other writings of this time it was, how remote from formulas. One hopes that Sarah Orne Jewett saw it—her fatal stroke occurred before it was printed—for it was the first evidence that Willa Cather was working in the vein she advised. "The Enchanted Bluff" evokes one of the sandbars in the Republican River where she had spent so many of the intense hours of her youth. On the sandbar, camping overnight, are six boys: the narrator, unnamed and unspecified, but by implication male; the two Hasslers, sons of the local tailor and mighty takers of catfish; Percy Pound, the dime-novel fanatic; Tip Smith, the grocer's son and jester to the group; Arthur Adams, son of the town gambler and a wanderer in the fields and marshes. By way of the stars and memories of Coronado's legend, the talk turns to a bluff in the Southwest, the Mesa Encantada. Tip's uncle had seen it, and reported its aspect as mysterious, its history as terrifying. Before they turn in, the boys agree that, of all places, this is the one to which they would like to go. The group gathers again in skating weather and, reaching the sandbar, reiterates the wish. There is a short epilogue, written, it is said, twenty years after the gatherings at the sandbar. The narrator returns to the Nebraska town. No one has seen the enchanted bluff; the Hassler boys have settled into being the town

tailors, though one did have a try at railroading and lost
a foot; Percy Pound is a stockbroker in Kansas City, who
will travel only where his car will take him; Arthur Adams
died in the garden of the town's saloon; Tip Smith, care-
worn and henpecked, still intends to go and has imparted
the story of the bluff to his son, who is as full of it as Tip
used to be.

That is all. "The Enchanted Bluff" is just the recalling
of persons and places and moments that have value,
poured out in a quiet sensitive prose, and ending in suggestive indeterminacy. The persons and places and moments call for exactly the rendering given them: perhaps
there is a brief obtrusion of the author in the epilogue,
where the grip of the town and the region on the personages is emphasized with a bitterness that seems excessive,
though it cannot be called irrelevant. Willa Cather had
not yet made terms of peace with Nebraska. "The Enchanted Bluff" was never republished; but before the appearance of the next collection of Willa Cather's stories
she had reworked this sketch into one of the most moving
chapters in *My Ántonia*.

Under her direction *McClure's* prospered. During the
first year of her responsibility the circulation increased by
sixty thousand, and in the next the outcome was even more
brilliant. In the issue for June 1910 McClure stated in the
bold type he reserved for special announcements that
within a twelvemonth three issues had gone out of print;
the current issue was the largest June edition in the history of the magazine; and advertisers were guaranteed a
continuation of the high circulation. The price of Willa
Cather's success was nervous exhaustion. A remark she

applied to Alexandra Bergson in *O Pioneers!* applied to
her own work in the years at *McClure's*: "It was because she had so much personality to put into her enter-
prises and succeeded in putting it into them so completely,
that her affairs prospered better than those of her neighbours." Willa Cather did not have Alexandra's stolid temperament. She could not meet a new person or one she did
not know well without feeling stimulated; whether she was
drawn to him or felt antipathetic, the encounter was intense. Elizabeth Shepley Sergeant, whose first meeting
with Willa Cather concerned an article offered to the
magazine, was astonished at the warmth of her reception;
before she left the office she felt, as was true, that she had
made a friend for life. Others felt Willa Cather's immediate hostility. After a morning of such encounters she would
often retire to her apartment for the afternoon to read
manuscripts and write letters in healing privacy. But such
an escape was not enough. McClure understood, as he understood almost everything about Willa Cather. He would
propose his grand nostrum of travel, and she was often
glad to accept it. Every year she spent some weeks at Red
Cloud; and sometimes she would visit her brother Roscoe,
or go on a camping trip with him. In her own generation
of the family Roscoe was now, as he always had been, the
one with whom she was most intimate. He cared for what
she wrote, and for the magazine; and she was eager to
know how he responded. She was often in Pittsburgh, staying with Isabelle McClung, or in Boston staying with Mrs.
Fields. Once she had the good fortune to find at the house
in Charles Street another guest whose poetry she admired.
Louise Imogen Guiney had written few poems in late

years; but Willa Cather's interest led her to write again, and a number of her pieces appeared in *McClure's*. The meeting was less fortunate when Willa Cather, accompanied by George E. Woodberry, called on another of Mrs. Fields's friends, Amy Lowell. Miss Lowell's rudeness to Woodberry was so insultingly discourteous that Willa Cather formed an immediate dislike of her that nothing could relieve.

In New York also there were literary friendships, though none of them was at all decisive. There was a brief meeting with Mark Twain, and a morning spent at his bedside listening to his vivid talk. Edwin Arlington Robinson was living in the house of Mrs. Clara Potter Davidge near Washington Square; meeting him there and occasionally in the houses of other friends, Willa Cather was delighted with his intelligence, and more than a little puzzled by his reserve and the abruptness of his commentary on life and letters. For his poetry she cared less than for the man; it seemed to her unnecessarily enigmatic and somewhat clumsy. She was much more at ease with George Arliss and his wife, who had taken an apartment in the neighborhood. She always remembered conversations she had in the months when Arliss was studying the role of Disraeli; and she found the reminiscences of the drama, the theater, and the stage that the Arlisses could be persuaded to offer a perfect enchantment. Her interest in all that touched on acting and actors was as lively now as when she waited at the station in Red Cloud to watch a traveling company get off the train. The Arlisses often invited her to after-theater supper parties; and these were among the chief pleasures of her early years in New York. But it was not from her associates in Greenwich Village or from the staff at the magazine that her ideas and feelings about her art took shape, and it would be idle to list the people she saw or the places to which she went.

IV

In the intervals of her work, she completed by the fall of 1911 a short novel that she called *Alexander's Bridge*. Under the title *Alexander's Masquerade* it appeared in *McClure's* in three parts, from February to April of 1912.[1] It is a study in the split personality of Bartley Alexander, taking him when he is forty-three, eleven years after his marriage, and carrying him to his death a year later. All the other characters—Winifred, his wife, Hilda Burgoyne, his mistress, Lucius Wilson, his old teacher, Mainhall, his London friend, and the few minor persons who crop up in an episode—are in the novel only to furnish him with stimuli or to comment on his nature. The economy is somewhat rigidly perfect; not a chapter, not a scene, could be spared; hardly a word is excessive or distracting. There are moments when a fuller rendering of a mood, a more emphatic presentation of an interchange, would probably have deepened, and would certainly have clarified, the effect. The weight of Bartley Alexander's personality would have borne a more massive presentation. If the book has fineness, it is also a little thin. One might say that Willa Cather was using some of the resources of Sarah Orne Jewett in approaching a subject that Miss Jewett would have thought beyond her bounds.

[1] The title *Alexander's Masquerade* was probably invented in the office of the magazine. As early as November 1911 the work is mentioned in the files of Houghton Mifflin Company as *Alexander's Bridge*. The English edition was titled *Alexander's Bridges*.

The stronger part of Alexander's personality, which is also the larger, is in keeping with his Western origins. If the state where he grew up is not named, he comes from Willa Cather's country. The Western touches are few but perhaps sufficient. Alexander grew up on a ranch, where he learned how to deal with "locoed" horses; as a boy he used to hunt jackrabbits; he liked to recall a campfire on a sandbar in the river that ran near his early home; he went to a Western university; and he had the bigness and hardness of physique that go with the pioneer hero. He was a "tamer of nature" as his forefathers had been; they subdued the land, he subdued the rivers of the continent with a dozen daring bridges. What Lucius Wilson has remembered is the force of the young Alexander, who had been "a powerfully equipped nature" and "simply the most tremendous response to stimuli" the professor had ever known.

In this strong nature Wilson had divined a flaw, which he could not find, much less name, but which might nevertheless bring complete ruin. In the first chapter, when he comes to stay with Alexander, he speaks of his misgivings, which had continued long after Alexander made a name. The greater the performance, and the greater the reputation, the more did Wilson expect that a big crack would appear "zigzagging from top to bottom" and leading to a crash of the whole man in dust and ruins. Wilson is free to mention his misgivings because they have at last been set to rest. He has observed Alexander in his Boston home overlooking the Charles River and (it would appear) around the corner from Mrs. Fields's house, and has found to his surprise that Alexander belongs in a setting of mellow traditional beauty. He has responded to the charm of Alexander's distinguished wife and felt her depth and strength, and has found that the relation between husband and wife is excellent. Either the flaw has worked out of the mature man or it was imaginary.

The mention of the vanished misgivings leads Alexander to a remark from which the action of the novel flows. He is unsatisfied with his life: it is not, he feels, a true expression of himself, but a building of himself into a social structure he does not care about, a swallowing of himself in a million details. "I sometimes wonder," he says gloomily, "what sort of chap I'd have been if I hadn't been this sort; I want to go and live out his potentialities, too." This is what he begins to do on a trip to London that follows close on Wilson's visit.

Hilda Burgoyne, an Irish actress whom he had not seen since he met Winifred, becomes his mistress; but what is significant is not his wish to make her this, but the wish it evolves from—to live out some of the potentialities that had gone unrealized in his marriage and his career. A long time elapses between the evening when he sees her act and the evening they are first alone together. The finest psychological probing in the novel is in the period between these two evenings. In long, introspective walks Alexander tries to pick his way from the cramping years of his middle life to his uncommitted childhood and youth. The process is extraordinarily like what Godfrey St. Peter was to undergo in *The Professor's House*. There was still, Alexander felt, "something unconquered in him, something besides the strong work-horse that his profession had made of him. . . . He remembered how, when he was a

little boy and his father called him in the morning, he used
to leap from his bed into the full consciousness of himself.
That consciousness was Life itself." It was this consciousness Alexander was bent on recovering. To make sure that
the reader will not for a moment suppose that what he
feels for Hilda is a great love, Willa Cather gives the most
emphatic signal in the novel. "He walked," she says,
"shoulder to shoulder with a shadowy companion—not little Hilda Burgoyne, by any means, but someone vastly
dearer to him than she had ever been—his own young
self. . . . It was not until long afterward that Alexander
learned that for him this youth was the most dangerous of
companions."

The emergence of this second self was for a while delightful to Alexander. "This new feeling was so fresh, so
unsatisfied and light of foot. It ran and was not wea-
ried. . . . At this moment, it was tingling through him,
exultant, and live as quicksilver." So it had been with
Dr. Jekyll, whose second self was also much younger than
his respectable nature, which might be described in the
words Willa Cather applied to Alexander's—"the strong
work-horse that his profession had made of him." When
Dr. Jekyll first assumed the personality of Edward Hyde,
what he felt was what Alexander would wholly have understood: "There was something strange in my sensations,
something indescribably new, and, from its very novelty, incredibly sweet. I felt younger, lighter, happier in
body. . . . I stretched out my hands, exulting in the freshness of these sensations." The outcome for Alexander is
what might be predicted in the light of our memory of
what befell Dr. Jekyll. Although Stevenson was one of the

authors Willa Cather most often reread, and his symbolic tale may have suggested, or clarified, the idea for *Alexander's Bridge*, between his work and hers there are immense differences. She keeps well within the round of realistic psychological portraiture, and the effect she seeks is far less violent and extreme than the horror of *Dr. Jekyll and Mr. Hyde*.

Yet the division in Alexander's nature ends in his destruction. The second self exerts a constantly increasing pressure on the first, twisting it out of shape and inhibiting its life. "Something had broken loose in him of which he knew nothing except that it was sullen and powerful, and that it wrung and tortured him." As it won control it would, Alexander knew, make him hateful even to Hilda, perhaps to Hilda above all. It is always—like Mr. Hyde—completely sterile: no new life can grow out of it; Alexander never so much as ponders a marriage with Hilda, or a new career apart from engineering. The growth of this new self began, he reflects just before his death, in "a mere folly, a masquerade"—the phrase from which the magazine title was taken—and quickly it escaped from his direction and reached over to ruin his severely patterned life. It threatens, but does not actually ruin, his marriage (if he had lived it would doubtless have ruined this), but it ruins his career.

The bridge he is building across the St. Lawrence during the year covered in the narrative is his first failure. In her account of the construction and collapse of this bridge Willa Cather follows closely the story of the Quebec bridge that was to span the river five miles from the city of Quebec. This bridge, though there was a subsidy from the government of Canada, was undertaken on a tight budget; the designing engineer knew he must use materials as sparingly as he could, just as Alexander yields to pressure from the contractors that he use less steel than he thought quite prudent. The principal designing engineer for the Quebec bridge, Theodore Cooper of New York, one of the great bridge engineers of his time, would not withdraw from the undertaking, just as Alexander would not, because the bridge offered the excitements of new problems in design to conquer and the promise of unrivaled fame. The most striking of the likenesses between Alexander and Theodore Cooper was that when signs of danger which they could have interpreted correctly began to appear, neither was on the scene. On August 27, 1907 the bending in some of the lower chords in an anchor arm of the bridge at Quebec, noticeable for some days, greatly increased. On August 28 ordinary workers began to be alarmed. The Royal Commission of three engineers appointed by the Canadian government to inquire into the disaster and assess blame gravely declared: "It was clear that on that day the greatest bridge in the world was being built without there being a single man within reach who by experience, knowledge and ability was competent to deal with the crisis." A warning sent by Alexander's assistant did not reach him in time, as he was at a tryst with Hilda. The series of warnings from Cooper's assistant had not clarified the situation for him, partly because the assistant was inadequately prepared for his responsibility, partly because Cooper, old and ailing, had never seen the bridge in all the years it was under construction. A final warning did stir Cooper into action; at one p.m. on August 29 he dispatched a telegram ordering the suspension of work; but in what seems to have been confusion of mind he sent it not to the office at the scene, but to the headquarters of the contracting company at Phoenixville, Pennsylvania, where it was decided that nothing should be done until the next day. At 5.37 p.m. the bridge collapsed, crushing or drowning almost a hundred workers. The Royal Commission declared that the blame for the collapse rested on Cooper, and the blame for the collapse of Alexander's bridge rests on him. Both men fail for the same essential reason: because they were no longer the men who had been commissioned to build a bridge, they are not what their employers, judging them by the past, assumed them to be. When Alexander at length receives the warning from his assistant, he hurries to the scene; but when he reaches the bridge, all he can do is make a vain attempt to draw the workmen off. He is carried to his death with them, one of them clutching him to the end, just as in *Lucy Gayheart* Sebastian drowned in the clutch of his accompanist, Mockford. The image Wilson had used to describe the flaw he divined in Alexander acquires a more literal truth than he had ever expected. From the moment Wilson has uttered it—spoken as it was of a builder of bridges—it broods over the novel. There are enough supporting references to ensure its being remembered by even a desultory reader.

In commending the manuscript to his associates at Houghton Mifflin, Ferris Greenslet wrote of its varied sorts of distinction, its "excellence of workmanship," its "perceptiveness," its "actuality"; but his heaviest stress fell on "the spiritual sense of life that informs it." Forty years afterward the phrase may seem a little vague, but it is a response to what is essential in the book. Only if it is read in the way Greenslet must have read it, as a study in the psychological processes of the protagonist, can it be understood. It has not often been read so. The objection that is taken to *Alexander's Bridge* is that its characters do not come to life, that they are not people as Ántonia Shimerda and Alexandra Bergson are people. Alexander is not a rounded person as these two women are; and certainly his wife and his mistress are not. There is no need why any of them should be. The subject is not Alexander, but the process through which he passes. That process is presented with a stern concentration and a cold accuracy that Willa Cather did not often use in rendering the central datum in a novel, although she was to use just these qualities again in *My Mortal Enemy*, and again to face deep critical misunderstanding. There also the subject was to be not a person but a destructive process within a person.

The severest critic of *Alexander's Bridge* was its own author in later years. She came to believe that it was not her sort of book, and in some degree it was not. She constantly disparaged it to her friends, and one who knew her very well and very long was surprised on rereading it after Willa Cather's death to find what power of psychological portraiture it has. In a preface that first appeared in the edition of 1922, and in an article of 1931, "My First Novels (There Were Two)," Willa Cather is forthright in her blame. She was right of course in saying that *Alexander's Bridge* was imitative, both in the choice of a milieu that was upper-class, sophisticated, cosmopolitan, and in the choice of a form that was bare and contrived. But the core of the novel is not touched by criticism of this kind. *Alexander's Bridge* gains nothing at all by the use of the superior milieu, and gains little by the contrived bare form; it would have gained something if the people in it were of the sort Willa Cather was profoundly at home with, people from the Western plains living on those plains, and if she had felt free to be discursive and lambent, as Sarah Orne Jewett had seen and as she was to be in the Nebraska novels. But the gains would not have been fundamental: the process in Alexander would have been the same if he had been a farmer on the Divide, with a hired girl for his wife and the daughter of a new settler for his mistress.

The reason for Willa Cather's aversion to her first published novel was a sudden turn in the direction of her life and writing that followed it. When she was writing it she was still uncertain of herself, and composition was a task, not the pleasure it was later to be. The usual way of describing what happened after it was written is to say that she left the editorial office of *McClure's*, went on a visit to the Southwest, a long one, gained a clear understanding of herself there, and wrote *O Pioneers!* So far as it goes the description is sound; substantially it is what Willa Cather has said in "My First Novels" and elsewhere. It is, however, a simplification. It ignores some things that are too important to be ignored. For instance it ignores "The Bohemian Girl." Before Willa Cather left the editorial office for good, she took a long leave and late in 1911 wrote this story, which appeared in *McClure's* in August 1912, only four months after *Alexander's Masquerade* had been concluded. Cameron Mackenzie, McClure's son-in-law, was managing the magazine at the time; he was so delighted with the story that he proposed to pay $750 for it; Willa Cather protested—would take only $500—but added, with a laugh, the next story might deserve $750.

In "The Bohemian Girl" Willa Cather for the first time wrote at length and appreciatively of life on the Divide. At length—the story runs over sixteen thousand words and is shorter than *My Mortal Enemy* only by four thousand— and appreciatively, with a smiling recognition of values not only different from those which had shaped her own life but inimical to these. Almost everything that is said of *O Pioneers!* in the article on her early novels is true of "The Bohemian Girl." This also is "a story about some Scandinavians and Bohemians" who had been neighbors of the Virginia colony in Webster County; it is in some degree a story "of the soil": it has the air of a "spontaneous" effusion; everything in it appears to have "taken its own place right or wrong." It is not quite so discursive as *O Pioneers!* nor does it give such an impression of the author's own pleasure in recalling her material.

Our guides to values in "The Bohemian Girl" are a man and a woman who were born on the Divide, but are conscious of not belonging and leave it for an entirely different form of life. Nils Ericson, the protagonist, is returning when the story opens, after an absence of twelve years, roughly the length of time Willa Cather had spent in Pittsburgh and on the east coast. In the introductory picture of Nils what is stressed is assurance to the point of insolence; and the same quality is diffused through his dialogue in the early chapters. His silences and ironies and brief laughs are those of a person who has become invulnerable to the people with whom he has to do, and enjoys

giving them the conviction that they have no hold upon
him. Once they had had a strong hold upon him: he had
been the atypical, disapproved, ridiculed child, the child
who instinctively disliked the standards his family lived
by, and was made to feel guilt for his deviation. What he
had not been able to endure was the Ericson denial of life.
This was embodied in his parents' house, "a grim square
house with a tin roof" and the accompanying windbreak
of mutilated poplars and straggle of small outbuildings, a
landmark on the road that led from Red Cloud to the
Cather farm. It was embodied also in the Ericson reduction of life to hard work done to get on in the world, and
to a domestic routine marked by "mess, full of babies and
washing and flies." As a child he had determined to get
away; and he was no more than a boy when he did run off
—as far as Bergen in Norway, where he made a new life
for himself.

Our other guide is the Bohemian girl, Clara Vavrika,
daughter of the tavern-keeper in a village to the north of
the Scandinavian settlement (unnamed in the story, and
very like Blue Hill), and bored wife of Nils's stolid and
joyless brother Olaf. Olaf had always been the brother
Nils cared for the least: "the one thing he had always felt
in Olaf was a heavy stubbornness, like the unyielding
stickiness of wet loam against the plow." No one could
have been a more exasperating mate for Clara, mercurial,
avid for pleasure, and finding it only in the desperate
forms of baiting the Ericsons and "being witty" for herself
alone. Nils persuades her in a series of carefully graduated talks that her one chance to live is to come back with
him to Bergen. Her sense of desolation in living on the Di-

vide has a parallel in a remark that Willa Cather made to her young friend Elizabeth Shepley Sergeant at about the time when she was writing "The Bohemian Girl," that her pleasure in revisiting Red Cloud was flawed by a feeling that a sudden death would overtake her somewhere on the prairie. That feeling would come on her obsessively and darken her life for days.

Clara's response to the Divide and its people is entirely hostile; only her father, whose fun-loving nature is irrepressible, escapes. Nils, however, makes discriminations interesting in themselves, and recurring in most of Willa Cather's later stories about the region. The most elaborate scene in the story is the supper at the raising of Olaf Ericson's barn, developed with the happy accumulation of detail that Flaubert allowed himself in the wedding chapter in *Madame Bovary*. All the neighborhood is there, and Nils cannot contain his appreciation of the grandmothers. He is amazed at how much they have done in their lives, and how much life they still have. Most of them have brown or blond hair still, and old Mrs. Oleson, a grandmother twelve times, has "yellow hair whose braids are as thick as her own wrists." Despite the mountains of food they have cooked, they delight in a feast; and even in the dancing they take a radiant vicarious pleasure. Even for his own mother, so dour, so unloving, so insensitive, he has a smiling appreciation: "a regular pile driver!" he says with enthusiasm. He does not have a particle of filial love for her; but for the "vigor and force" she has kept, his appreciation is unbounded. Clara is impatient at the praise of the grandmothers; they are her natural enemies; she detests them all. Nils's reply is an index to the author's feeling. "You won't," he says, "when you look back on them from Stockholm or Budapest. Freedom settles all that." One must know the world, Willa Cather had been warned by Miss Jewett, before one can draw one's own part of it, which is an artist's natural subject. In Nils's response is the first strong evidence that the years in Pittsburgh, Boston, and New York, the travels in Europe, the association with artists and cultivated persons, were qualifying Willa Cather for the profound æsthetic realizations of Nebraska which she was now on the eve of making.

The appreciation of the older generation, the true pioneers, has no parallel in Nils's attitude toward his brothers. Clara remarks that "the second generation are a tame lot," and it is as tame, dull individual people they figure in "The Bohemian Girl." The good ones in this generation, the ones with a spark, like Clara and Nils, must leave, and the farms of the pioneers be occupied, as a cheerful old failure remarks, by the commonplace ones who "run over this here country like bindweed." What is remarkable, if one recalls the bitter early Western stories such as "The Sculptor's Funeral," is not that the appreciation has limits, but that it exists at all.

The degree of appreciation has a bearing on the unexpected and unsatisfactory close of the story. Nils had a special feeling for the youngest of his brothers, Eric, who had deviated from the family type in early childhood and always exhibits a delightful gentleness. At the end of the story, established now with Clara at Bergen, he sends Eric money for his passage. Eric begins the journey, but in western Iowa he changes his mind and returns to the farm after only one night of absence. If his return were rendered as a final proof of his gentleness and that alone, it would be satisfactory, and by contrast the hardness in Nils would be established as one of the conditions for his successful escape. But the end also involves a sudden and striking shift in the character of the mother: this woman, who has always acted and spoken as a hard-bitten feelingless nature, responds to the softness in Eric, and the final tableau is warm with a sentiment that not only confuses one about the meaning the story bears but also embarrasses by its unprepared demand on one's feelings. Only on the supposition that as she read over the story Willa Cather found it too severe in its estimate of the Divide and the people who live there can I account for the unlikely close, and it may have been because she was later aware of its weakness that she never republished "The Bohemian Girl." It has had many admirers, among her intimate friends and among her own family. The next book in which it might have been included was *Obscure Destinies*, twenty years in the future; and "The Bohemian Girl," vigorous and shapely as it is, would have needed more than superficial revision to take its place among the finest expressions of Willa Cather's powers in short and intermediate narratives.

PART TWO

7

The Ancient People and
the Pioneers

1913–1918

O PIONEERS!

THE SONG OF THE LARK

MY ÁNTONIA

IN THE SPRING of 1912, after resigning from *McClure's*, Willa Cather went to Winslow, a town in northeastern Arizona where her brother Douglass worked for the Santa Fe. Douglass, who never married and who delighted in the out-of-doors, was living in the most primitive simplicity, with a little group of railroadmen. Willa Cather was exhilarated by the rough life and interested in the character and idiom of her brother's associates. One of them suggested many of the traits that went into the personality of Ray Kennedy, the freight conductor in the early chapters of *The Song of the Lark*, who knew the Southwest "like the blisters on his own hands"; another was the model for the Englishman in Tom Outland's narrative in *The Professor's House*. This was the frontier, and Willa Cather felt that once more she was among pioneers, men who might have founded Red Cloud or put the first plows into the earth of the Divide. It was not merely exciting, it was reassuring in the West to find in men of her own age or younger than she, not the "tame lot" who had formed the second generation in Webster County, but the "great-hearted adventurers" to whom only beginnings are stimulating. The vacation she had intended became a discovery —a discovery of the Southwest she had divined three years before in "The Enchanted Bluff." It was a discovery, and an enjoyment, of the land and the people.

She did not remain at Winslow. She took long pack-trips —riding was always a pleasure to her—and camped out for a week at a time. She crossed into New Mexico briefly. The colors and shapes of things were unlike anything she had seen before. How much she was affected by the joy the landscape of the Southwest gave her will appear in the record of later and even more important stays in the country. It was not only by the land that the Southwest charmed her; it was at least as much by the people, especially the Indians and the Mexicans, in whom she discovered survivals of Aztec beauty. The delight she had found in the company of some Latin Europeans in her trips abroad was renewed as she responded to the gaiety and vitality in some of these simple folk it was so easy to meet and, superficially at least, so easy to know. She felt in some of them a tragic and heroic quality, associated with the Aztec strain which gave to their other traits an intensity that was quite new to her. The picture of Johnny Tellamantez and his "Spanish" friends in *The Song of the Lark* caught a great deal of what she felt in her first encounter with Indians and Mexicans of the Southwest.

The most important of her discoveries was one that involved both persons and places, but the persons were dead. It came when she saw the ruins of the Cliff-Dwellers in Walnut Canyon, Arizona, the "Panther Canyon" of *The*

Song of the Lark. In Nebraska there was no past unless
one was geologically minded; everything that had not happened yesterday had happened the day before. In the villages of the Cliff-Dwellers Willa Cather found something
that was not only extremely simple and extremely beautiful, but extremely old. The discovery was a lengthening of
one's past as an American, especially if one were a Western American, an enlarging of one's frame of reference.
The woman who was to inspire *The Song of the Lark* had
never been in this canyon; but it is here that Willa Cather
set the crucial phase in Thea Kronborg's history as an artist, and this is a proof of how very personal a work *The
Song of the Lark* is. It is the one of her novels in which
she is not recalling or resurrecting, but working in the impressions of the present or the immediate past.

During the months she stayed in the Southwest Willa
Cather was unusually receptive. She had firmly closed the
door on one career, which had brought her to great success. In 1906 she had left Pittsburgh a high-school teacher;
within two years she had become managing editor of a
magazine that was successful to the point of the fabulous,
and during the next four she had exercised, with an inspired skill, a measure of power and earned a comfortable
living. It had required courage to close the door on so
much so quickly gained. She had the courage, and she was
determined to live for a while in the present, which poured
in on her more powerfully and with less resistance than,
perhaps, at any other time in her mature life. "I did no
writing down there," she has said, "but I recovered from
the conventional editorial point of view." What such a recovery meant she has told in her account of the growth in

Thea Kronborg, the central person in *The Song of the Lark*
—this also occurred on a first exposure to the Southwest.

All her life she [Thea] had been hurrying and sputtering, as
if she had been born behind time and had been trying to catch
up. Now, she reflected . . . it was as if she were waiting for
something to catch up with her. She had got to a place where
she was out of the stream of meaningless activity and undi-
rected effort.
Here she could lie for half a day undistracted, holding pleasant and incomplete conceptions in her mind—almost in her
hands. They were scarcely clear enough to be called ideas.
They had something to do with fragrance and colour and
sound. . . . She had always been a little drudge, hurrying
from one task to another—as if it mattered! And now her power
to think seemed converted into a power of sustained sensa-
tion. . . . What was any art but an effort to make a sheath, a
mould in which to imprison for a moment the shining, elusive
element which is life itself . . . ? Her mind was like a ragbag
into which she had been frantically thrusting whatever she
could grab. And here she must throw this lumber away. The
things that were really hers separated themselves from the rest.
Her ideas were simplified, became sharper and clearer. She felt
united and strong.

In a new state of mind, very like Thea Kronborg's, conscious of how she had grown as a person and eager to discover what the change might mean to her fiction, Willa
Cather returned to the East by way of Red Cloud and the
Divide, where she saw the wheat harvest and visited the
Bohemian settlement, and Pittsburgh, where she stayed
for some months with Isabelle McClung. At McClure's
urgent wish, she kept a thread of connection with the
magazine—she was to furnish two stories, and the business

office as well as the proprietor hoped they would resemble "The Bohemian Girl." These stories were not written: instead Willa Cather went back to an old manuscript that became *O Pioneers!*

How much of *O Pioneers!* had been written before the stay in the Southwest is not precisely known. The mark of that country is on the fourth section of the book, "The White Mulberry Tree," and to a less extent on the third, "Winter Memories," in the allusions to Emil Bergson's happiness in Mexico, his response to the happiness and expressiveness of a Latin people so unlike the heavy, dour Scandinavian atmosphere in which he grew up. "The White Mulberry Tree" is known to have been written or perhaps expanded from earlier material after Willa Cather's return from the Southwest, and so, presumably, was at least a part of "Winter Memories." It was originally intended to be a self-contained story of middle length. The first section of *O Pioneers!*, "The Wild Land," must have been expanded at a relatively late stage in the composition of the novel. No other hypothesis will, I believe, account for a repeated error in the time schedule most unusual in an author who was meticulous in arranging this element in her fiction. So much for late additions. About the first state of the work there is a little precise knowledge. Some time after joining *McClure's* but before her journey to the Southwest, Willa Cather wrote a story shorter than "The Bohemian Girl" and called "Alexandra" after its heroine, who became the Alexandra Bergson of *O Pioneers!* It is probable that the early story was a study in a single character, with the other members of the Bergson family and their neighbors drawn only as stimuli for

her and factors in her life. The shift in title from "Alexandra" to *O Pioneers!*—however much it may have been
prompted by its similarity to the title of her first novel—
pointed to a shift in interest: in the novel Alexandra remains the principal personage, but she is now presented as
part of a study in the history of a family characteristic of a
time and a place. All the additions that have been noticed
build up the roles of other characters. In "The White Mulberry Tree" Alexandra is less important than Emil: in this
section Willa Cather records his tragic love for Marie
Shabata, which goes unperceived by Alexandra. The emphasis on Emil's Mexican adventures in this section and in
"Winter Memories" adds to his importance. The changes
that must have been made in the first section, whatever
else they included, delayed the departure from the Divide
of Carl Linstrum, who is in love with Alexandra, and assured him of more importance when he returns. Emil and
Carl present a response to the Divide very unlike Alexandra's, but rendered with equal respect and almost equal
sympathy.

The originality of "The Bohemian Girl" was in its material; in structure it was a conventional work. Nils Ericson returns home; he persuades Clara Vavrika to run off;
they are happy in their new life. In *O Pioneers!* there is a
conventional story parallel to this: Emil returns home; he
wins Marie Shabata's love; they are killed by her husband.
The unconventional element has its center in the portrayal
of Alexandra. She too has her conventional story: Carl
Linstrum returns to the Divide; he wins her love; they
agree to go away for a while and then to live on the Berg-

son farm. But how small a part this story plays in the portrayal of Alexandra!

Her quality is impressed upon us by a very emphatic passage that closes an early chapter. With her brothers and Carl, she drives out to Crazy Ivar's, to ask this strange old seer how to protect her hogs from the cholera. Ivar, a delightful splotch of color in the grayness of the first section, bursts out: "I tell you, sister, the hogs of this country are put upon!" and bids her enclose a sorghum patch for hers and allow them plenty of clean water and clean feed. On the return of the party to the Bergson farm the boys go swimming after supper, and Alexandra sits on the kitchen doorstep. The chapter ends:

It was a still, deep-breathing summer night, full of the smell of the hayfields. Sounds of laughter and splashing came up from the pasture, and when the moon rose rapidly above the bare rim of the prairie, the pond glittered like polished metal, and she could see the flash of white bodies as the boys ran about the edge, or jumped into the water. Alexandra watched the shimmering pool dreamily, but eventually her eyes went back to the sorghum patch south of the barn, where she was planning to make her new pig corral.

Out of context the passage is comical, even farcical; but read in its place it has pathos, and a queer sort of austere heroism. Alexandra scarcely had a childhood; at twelve she was a help to her father's thinking about the land. She had no real youth, no religious elation, no romance, no personal life of any definable kind. "Her personal life, her own realization of herself, was almost a subconscious existence." When she has a falling out with her brothers Lou and Oscar late in the novel, Lou complains that Oscar offended their sister quite unnecessarily by blurting out that she was forty and beyond the age for falling in love. He comforts himself with the rationalization: "Of course, Alexandra ain't much like other women-folks. Maybe it won't make her sore. Maybe she'd as soon be forty as not!" To the misunderstanding of their sister is added this final failure in perception; Oscar is not capable of allowing her even those emotions which most persons, men and women, experience with the passage of their youth.

The pathetic quality in Alexandra requires to be stressed because, though it is essential to the emotional effect she has on a reader, it is overshadowed by her austere heroism. She was in her early twenties when her father died, and the responsibility for all decisions devolved on her: through a series of years harder than he had endured, she kept the land he had broken, imposing her will on her brothers, and forcing on their stupid routine-loving natures modes of farming suited to the soil. It was in the land that her impersonal nature expressed itself. The large house she had built for herself is a disappointment; but "you feel that, properly, Alexandra's house is the big out-of-doors." By the kind of feeling she has for the land she rises far out of the circle of strong, austere, vital Scandinavian women in "The Bohemian Girl." It is something to her that the land she lives on was first settled by her father; and something too that it was land she could work with and subdue; but at the heart of her feeling for the land is a poetic appreciation that no character that preceded her in Willa Cather's fiction had even adumbrated. Early in the book, when she returns to the Divide from a

few days spent on the farms in the valley, appreciation
fairly flows through her frame. "For the first time, perhaps,
since that land emerged from the waters of geologic ages,
a human face was set toward it with love and yearning. It
seemed beautiful to her, rich and strong and glorious. Her
eyes drank in the breadth of it, until her tears blinded her.
Then the Genius of the Divide, the great, free spirit which
breathes across it, must have bent lower than it ever bent
to a human will before." Much later, after she has subdued
the land, making it yield a succession of rich crops, its
power to enchant her is not so strong. "I even think," she
admits to Carl Linstrum, "I liked the old country better.
This is all very splendid in its way, but there was something about this country when it was a wild old beast that
has haunted me all these years. Now, when I come back to
all this milk and honey, I feel like the old German song,
'Wo bist du, wo bist du, mein geliebtest Land?' " The
austerity and strength of the woman are in unison with the
austerity and strength of the land—"the wild land" as it is
called in the title of the first section; and it is in the unison
that the poetic force of the novel has its center. Sometimes
one wonders why Alexandra was never driven, like old
Chapdelaine in Louis Hémon's novel, to give up the acres
she had tamed and begin again in a new frontier. Her regret for the passing of the first phase in the development of
Nebraska, the phase of hardship, heroism, and imagination, was to be echoed more and more deeply in the novels
to come.

Alexandra rises above the Scandinavian women in the
earlier fiction by her appreciation of forms of life and character unlike her own, and in some ways at odds with her

own. Clara Vavrika was right in feeling that the old women Nils admired were her natural enemies; and Nils admitted that in order to appreciate them he had to begin by assuring his freedom from any pressure they could exercise. Alexandra has none of the Scandinavian intolerance that is so strong in her brothers Lou and Oscar. Marie Shabata delights her; she is happy attending the services at the Catholic church in the French settlement; and, most striking, perhaps, of all, she draws from knowing how life goes on in other places a wider and more satisfying sense of its significance. "If the world were no wider than my cornfields, if there were not something besides this, I wouldn't feel that it was much worth while to work." She does not believe that Carl Linstrum made a mistake in leaving the Divide, in being an artisan in big Eastern cities, in wanting to seek his fortune and much else in the Klondike. She appreciates in him a sensitive nature, somewhat uncertain of its powers, and determined, above all, on freedom. The perfect test of her liberal judgment of the world outside, which she has never seen and does not wish to see, is in her attitude toward the one brother she really cares for, Emil, almost twenty years younger and rather her son than her brother. She is delighted that Emil wishes to live away from the Divide and beyond its values: "Out of her father's children there was one who was fit to cope with the world, who had not been tied to the plough, and who had a personality apart from the soil. And that, she reflected, was what she had worked for. She felt well satisfied with her life."

Alexandra is a large woman. No man on the Divide, we

are told, could have carried her gleaming white body very far. It is a case of a large frame, large nature. Never for an instant does she seem in the least unreal; yet when the novel ends she is a personality of more than life-size. Her last act is the final proof of the extraordinary largeness of her nature. Emil has been killed by Frank Shabata, and Frank has begun a ten-year prison term. Alexandra visits him to say she will not rest till he has been pardoned. Unalterable fact, once more: "Being what he was, she felt, Frank could not have acted otherwise"; and jail is bad for him, will destroy him.

The style and the structure in *O Pioneers!* are what they should be if the substance of the book is to have the fullest effect. There is nothing of the tightness of organization, the cold clearness of style, that were so right for the story of Bartley Alexander. The structure of *O Pioneers!* has a happy looseness and the style an easy strength that belong in a story where the great values are the land, the large nature of Alexandra, and the warm love of Emil. At last Willa Cather was writing as a person writes when he is doing what he came into the world to do.

II

Early in 1913, before Ferris Greenslet was telling the others at Houghton Mifflin that *O Pioneers!* "ought to . . . definitely establish the author as a novelist of the first rank," Willa Cather and Edith Lewis took an apartment at 5 Bank Street, in Greenwich Village. Here they lived from 1912 to 1927, when the house was torn down to give place to a more modern apartment building. These were

Willa Cather's best working years. The apartment, its furnishings, and its atmosphere are described by Miss Lewis
in this note:

5 Bank Street was a wide, brick, five-story house which had
been built by a rich brewer as a wedding-present to his son,
and had later been made, with very few changes, into an apartment house. A wide staircase ran up through the middle of the
house, dividing it into two apartments on each floor. The one
we rented was on the second floor above the street. It had
seven rather large rooms, with high ceilings, and all the rooms
had big windows, facing east, south, and west. The three front
rooms we used as one large living-room. It was heated (as was
the dining-room) by a coal grate, under a white marble mantel-
piece; there was no central heating-system in the house. We
bought little copper-lined gas stoves to heat the two bedrooms.
The house was lighted by gas, instead of electricity, and in cold
weather the gas sometimes froze.

We were delighted with the spaciousness and fine propor-
tions of this apartment, so different from the boxlike place we
had on Washington Place. We did not mind certain discom-
forts, such as having to make our own coal fires and carry coal
for them, and having the gas freeze occasionally. The house
was very solidly built, with thick walls which shut out the cold
in winter and the heat in summer. . . . We got very little
noise from our neighbours. Overhead, a German family lived.
Their place was thickly carpeted, and the only sound we heard
from them was the daughter's practising of the piano in the
mornings. She never practised but the one thing—Beethoven's
Appassionata; but after a while Willa Cather came to like this
practising—she said it was like a signal to work, and she associated it with her working hours. . . .

We had very little furniture when we moved into 5 Bank
Street, but at auction rooms on University Place we bought ma-

hogany chests and a round mahogany dining-room table for a
few dollars. Among our possessions were a number of large
oriental rugs; and we got some comfortable chairs. An Italian
carpenter built us low open book-shelves for our books. Willa
Cather found a large etching, by Couture, of George Sand, and
had it hung over the fireplace in the living-room—not because
she particularly admired George Sand, but because she liked
the etching. She had brought back a number of photographs
from Italy—copies of Tintorettos, Giorgione, Titians, etc.—and
these she now had framed and hung. She also discovered some
fine Piranesis at a little print shop which was selling out its
wares—she was very much pleased by this find, I remember,
and considered them a great treasure.

After we had made the apartment fairly comfortable, we
gave no more thought to acquiring new things, or getting better ones than those we had. What money we had we preferred
to spend on flowers, music, and entertaining our friends.

It is in the setting of the apartment in Bank Street that
most of Willa Cather's friends have cared to remember
her. The spaciousness of the living-rooms, the generous
coal-fire, the warm colors in the rugs, the large, comfortable chairs, all belonged to her way of life and her outlook
on it. There was nothing mannered or fancy or constrict-
ing about her home—or about her. During the early years
in Bank Street the apartment was often full of her friends.
She was not so pressed for time as she had been; and the
fatigue that often settled on her in later years was still a
rare visitation. For a while she was at home to her friends
on Friday afternoons: people from Nebraska and Pittsburgh, people she had met at *McClure's*, stage people, musicians, writers. The spirit of these highly informal at-
homes is captured in another note of Miss Lewis's:

These Friday afternoons became very popular—so popular, in fact, that eventually she had to give them up; instead of half-a-dozen or so of her friends dropping in for tea, more and more people came, sometimes bringing strangers with them; and it became at last too much of a responsibility. But those informal gatherings . . . were very pleasant while they lasted. Every one talked as if there were not nearly enough time for all they had to say. Often a small group of Willa Cather's more intimate friends would stay on after the others had drifted away, lingering until eight o'clock or later, and driving the cook, Josephine, to despair; and the talk was then always at its best.

During her first year in Bank Street Willa Cather did a final service for S. S. McClure. Writing came hard to him; yet he was determined to publish an autobiography. He would talk to her at length of the main episodes in his life; she would listen, taking no notes; then when he had gone she would set down the gist of what he had said, so far as possible in his own words and units of thought. He was, as Kipling said, "one of the few with whom three and a half words serve for a sentence." She allowed the special McClure words and ideas to recur much as they would have recurred in his own speech; but she supplied the connective tissue and the perspective that were beyond McClure's powers. Technically *My Autobiography*—which ran in *McClure's* from October 1913 to May 1914, and appeared as a book in the latter year—belongs to the canon of Willa Cather's writings, but she was right in her opinion that in every sense that matters it was McClure's. McClure was so pleased with the outcome of their collaboration that long afterward he would plead directly and indirectly for her help in getting his ideas about government on paper. She was sorry that she could not accede, but the years of indiscriminate writing were over; now she could write only what came to her as irresistible impulsion.

Her part in the autobiography is only one of many evidences of the friendly relations she kept with the magazine after she had resigned. For the issue of October 1913 she prepared an article: "Training for the Ballet—Making American Dancers," an account of the Metropolitan School of Ballet Dancing, founded by Dippel and Gatti-Casazza to furnish dancers for the Metropolitan Opera. Her sympathies were warmly with the classical ballet as it was understood in this school. A remark on Isadora Duncan is in the vein of the sharper critical writing she had done in the years at Lincoln and Pittsburgh: "This kind of interpretative dance is for those who like it. I agree with the New York reporter who in summing up Miss Duncan's dancing of *The Rubaiyat* said that on the whole he preferred Omar's lines to Miss Duncan's." In February 1914, in "New Types of Acting: the Character Actor Displaces the Star," she sets George Arliss at the head of recent actors in America; and in an estimate of Alexander Carr and Barney Bernard in *Potash and Perlmutter* she deviates to express her deep discontent with New York City. The life of the city is dominated by the desires of people intent on getting on in the world, and gorging on the material things that are the rewards for having got on. "This city roars and rumbles and hoots and jangles because Potash and Perlmutter are on their way to something." One has to wear the kinds of clothes that have been "designed to enhance the charms of their wives"; and most apartment

houses were garish jerrybuilt monsters because they were
built by Potash and Perlmutter to be lived in by Potash
and Perlmutter. The discontent with New York City was
to grow until it became a problem with Willa Cather
whether its pervasive horrors were outweighed by its special delights—ballet and theater, music and galleries.

Another article, which appeared in the issue of December 1913, led to a new friendship, which was to determine
the subject of Willa Cather's next novel, *The Song of the
Lark.* To write this article, "Three American Singers," she
was obliged to interview Louise Homer, Geraldine Farrar,
and Olive Fremstad, all of them familiar to her as singers
from her years of opera-going. Much as she admired Louise Homer's even competence as a woman and an artist,
and Geraldine Farrar's charm and vitality, it was only by
Olive Fremstad that her imagination was captured. Miss
Lewis has recorded the peculiar facts of the first meeting
with Fremstad:

Fremstad had given her a late afternoon appointment at her
apartment near Riverside Drive. Willa Cather was to interview
her there, pick up a hasty supper somewhere, and join Isabelle
McClung (who was visiting us) and me at the Metropolitan
Opera House, for we had tickets for *Tales of Hoffmann* that
evening. But when she arrived, just before the curtain went up,
she told us, to our great disappointment, that the interview
had not come off.

She had gone to Fremstad's apartment—waited—Fremstad
was away on a motor ride, and there was some delay about getting back. Finally she came in, very tired, and began at once
to apologize; but she could scarcely speak—her voice was just a
husky whisper. She was pale, drawn—"Why, she looked forty

years old!" Willa Cather told us. She begged Fremstad not to
try to talk—said she would come back for the interview another time, and left.

This was all she had time to tell us before the opera began.

The second act of *Tales of Hoffmann* is of course the Venetian scene. The intermission seemed very long, and the audience got very restless. Finally the manager came out before the
curtain. The soprano, he announced, had been taken ill, and
would be unable to appear; but Mme. Olive Fremstad had
kindly consented to sing in her place. Then the curtain went
up—and there, before our astonished eyes, was Fremstad—
whom Willa Cather had left only an hour before—now a vision
of dazzling youth and beauty. She sang that night in a voice
so opulent, so effortless, that it seemed as if she were dreaming
the music, not singing it.

"But it's impossible," Willa Cather kept saying. "It's impossible."

The experience of that evening was to give Willa Cather
one of the most dramatic chapters in the later part of *The
Song of the Lark*, with Thea Kronborg taking the role of
Sieglinde in *Die Walküre* at the beginning of the second
act.

The interview came soon afterward and led to many
other meetings. Fremstad was often at the apartment in
Bank Street for dinner, and Willa Cather at her apartment
for tea. In the summer of 1914 Willa Cather visited her at
Bridgeport in Maine.

In Fremstad Willa Cather found an artist of a kind that
had always given her deep pleasure, and a woman who
might have been Alexandra Bergson's sister. Fremstad was
born in Sweden and brought to America as a small child.
The family settled at St. Peter in Minnesota—it might as

well have been Red Cloud—where her father combined the practice of medicine with a stormy religious life and a passion for music. Fremstad's childhood was hard: she was driven hard and punished hard. "She grew up," as Willa Cather said, "in a new crude country where there was neither artistic stimulus nor discriminating taste. She was poor, and always had to earn her own living"—she had to give piano lessons, at her father's demand, when she was twelve—"and pay for her music lessons out of her earnings. She fought her own way towards the intellectual centers of the world." In her early twenties she was studying in Germany, and had just turned thirty when Willa Cather heard her soon after she began to sing at the Metropolitan Opera. "The most thrilling to us of all the new stars that came up over the horizon," Miss Lewis has said, "was Olive Fremstad. We heard her nearly every time she sang." Her singing, which was usually in Wagnerian roles, was so profound an experience for Willa Cather because so much brain work lay behind the voice, and the brain work had been carried on within a personality of austere strength and fierce originality. In her originality there was nothing of the petty sort; Fremstad was sparing in gesture, she disdained stage business, she never cared to enrich a commonplace conception of a part with superficial embellishments. She evolved her conception of a part from the depths of her nature, passed what her nature told her through her brain, and made her voice and all else serve the conception. "With Madame Fremstad," Willa Cather wrote, "one feels that the idea is always more living than the emotion; perhaps it would be nearer the truth to say that the idea is so intensely experienced that it becomes emotion." The qualities that Willa Cather found in Fremstad are qualities one might hope to find in a great artist who came from the frontier; in her singing were the force and originality of the pioneers, translated into the terms of disciplined art. In Fremstad she saw realized what she was soon to realize in her own art. In *The Song of the Lark* it was not difficult for her to combine what she felt about Fremstad with what she felt about herself: in Thea Kronborg both are projected.

Some others who knew Fremstad in her great years, and shortly afterward when her voice was ruined, found her to be unperceptive and overbearing. Undoubtedly she could be rough with those who crossed her even in trifles; and with triflers she was habitually merciless. Like S. S. McClure she knew how to raise a rumpus, and like him she did not always have just reasons for doing so. She was often, perhaps she was usually, withdrawn and cold. To Willa Cather none of this mattered. She believed, she always had believed, that the artist is not amenable to the standards by which other folk may rightly be judged. For mastery of an art, she thought, a fearful tax is levied on the entire personality of the artist. Artistic achievement means a constant bleeding of a person's strength. Imaginative understanding of the artistic process should bring, she thought, a deep compassion for what the personality of the artist undergoes, if not homage for his acceptance of his destiny. In *The Song of the Lark* Willa Cather brought together the imaginative understanding, the deep compassion, and the homage. It is no wonder that after reading the novel Fremstad flung her arms about Willa Cather, exclaiming that she could not tell where Thea left off and she began.

The writing of *The Song of the Lark* was begun in the winter of 1913–14. Willa Cather was able to work at it without much regard to where she happened to be. In the spring of 1914 she was in Pittsburgh staying with Isabelle McClung, and happy about the progress of the manuscript. She paid short visits to Maine, staying with Fremstad and with Mary Jewett, the surviving sister of Sarah Orne Jewett. In midsummer she was in Nebraska: the outbreak of war in Europe found her on a farm, and her memory of the way the news was received there and in Red Cloud gave her some of the most moving pages in *One of Ours*. After a stay with Roscoe Cather in Wyoming, she went again to the Southwest, but even in the Sangre de Cristo country the reports from France made her inattentive and restless. In the late fall she was again staying with Isabelle McClung, enjoying the company of her youngest brother, Jack, a student at the Carnegie Institute, and writing so successfully that she could not bear to leave until almost midwinter 1915. The interruptions to which she was subject in writing *The Song of the Lark*, and the stimulating, disturbing variety of experiences and associations among which composition went on, account in part for the special qualities, good and bad, in that novel.

She was happy writing it, and it came quickly. Although it is by a great deal the longest of her novels, extending almost to two hundred thousand words, it was finished in little more than a year. Among her books it has the most conventional structure, a typical massive *Entwicklungs-*

roman in the tradition of *Clayhanger* and the early Dreiser. In retrospect it seems curious that the novel in which
Willa Cather is most explicitly engaged with artists and
the artistic process is the least artistic of her works. In
later years she was deeply dissatisfied with the artistry of
The Song of the Lark. She had said of Fremstad that she
"rejects a hundred means of expression for every one she
uses"; and she was sorry that in her novel she had not
shown the same austerity. For the reissue of 1932 she revised *The Song of the Lark* as no other of her novels has
been revised. Nearly a tenth of the text was cut away, the
longer excisions coming in the later parts. The conversations Thea Kronborg's friends hold about her are so cut
down that one feels the author's impatience with her earlier impulse to drive an idea deep into presumably inattentive heads. Now and then Thea's own account of her processes, whether in dialogue or unspoken reflection, meets
the same fate. Sometimes what is removed is an expansive
comment by the author, which may shine like a jewel but
does not cast any light on the essential subjects of the
book. It was when I looked in vain through one of the
lately printed copies of the novel for an agreeable phrase
about Denver that I became aware of the excisions. What
inspired them is plain in a sentence from William Heinemann's letter rejecting the book which Willa Cather quotes
in "My First Novels—There Were Two." She had known
Heinemann when she was collecting material in London
for *McClure's*; and he had taken both *Alexander's Bridge*
and *O Pioneers!* About *The Song of the Lark* he wrote: "As
for myself, I always find the friendly confidential tone of
writing of this sort distressingly familiar, even when the

subject matter is very fine." Certainly in revision the novel
is less confidential, less familiar; it is also less explicit. But
even in the revised form Willa Cather was critical in
later years about *The Song of the Lark.*

In "The Bohemian Girl" and in *O Pioneers!* she had written of the Western countryside and farm people, not of
towns and townsfolk. At the beginning of "The Bohemian
Girl" Nils Ericson, on leaving the train, avoids the town
and sets off across country—at Red Cloud it would be easy
to do so, for the town is a mile from the station. Until he
and Clara go to the train on their way to Europe, everything happens on the Divide or at her father's saloon near
by. Townsfolk do not appear in that story; nor do they in
O Pioneers! That novel opens with a great winter scene
in town, but the cold has swept the townsfolk from the
streets and kept them from visiting the stores. Only the
farm people are about, and the storekeepers, who remain
unindividualized and even unnamed. To little Emil Bergson, whose kitten has been put out of doors and has
climbed a pole, "this village was a very strange and per-
plexing place where people had fine clothes and hard
hearts." His sense of the town as something marginal and
alien to his life remains with us through the book. But in
The Song of the Lark the town is everything until Thea
goes east. Farm people do not appear; and the countryside, which might as well be uninhabited, is only the few
miles around town.

There was an excellent reason for placing Thea in a
town rather than on the Divide, the same reason for making her a minister's daughter. She must have the maximum
of exposure to the Philistines; she must suffer "the fear of

the tongue, that terror of little towns." On a Western farm she would not have been exposed to anyone beyond her family; the disapproval of the neighbors would not have been something to reckon with. Willa Cather does set Thea in a disapproving family; her sister and all her brothers except the baby, Thor, have a natural enmity toward her. But this is not the enmity that counts for most, since during almost all the time she is in Moonstone the idea that anyone in her family might be hostile does not occur to her as even possible. Only in her last summer she "suddenly realized" that her sister "had always disliked her." In accounting for this dislike, and her brothers', she merges the family in the town. "She had done them the honour . . . to believe that though they had no particular endowments, *they were of her kind,* and not of the Moonstone kind. Now they had all grown up and become persons. They faced each other as individuals, and she saw that Anna and Gus and Charley were among the people whom she had always recognized as her natural enemies." That phrase "her natural enemies" occurs more than once in the novel: it is used of the principal of the high school who in addition to lethargy and stupidity has the deeper sin of diagramming poems in the manner of Professor Sherman. It is used of Mrs. "Livery" Johnson, who intrigued to give her protégée, "the angel child of the Baptists," a mean victory over Thea at a concert. None of her natural enemies, whether inside the Kronborg family or outside, is strongly individualized: there is no one in the novel like the Ivy Peters of *A Lost Lady* or the Wick Cutter of *My Ántonia*. It would have been easy to add to the portrait of Dr. Archie's mean and petty wife some jealousy of her

husband's romantic and innocent attachment to Thea.
Mrs. Archie does not care about it, she remains only mean
and petty, and so do the rest of Thea's natural enemies.
Among them there is a lukewarm malice that never comes
to a boil, and is never exhausted. By contrast, Thea's
friends are highly colored individuals: the heartbroken,
decaying music teacher Wunsch, Johnny Tellamantez,
Dr. Archie, the railwayman Ray Kennedy, Thea's queer
maiden aunt, and—the most complex of the portraits in
this group—her mother.

To anyone who has seen Red Cloud and taken his bear-
ings there, the topography of Moonstone will seem familiar. Moonstone has been set, however, in Colorado,
some distance to the west of Denver. It lies not among
farmlands but in the desert: it is a "frail, brightly painted
desert town . . . shaded by the light-reflecting, wind-
loving trees of the desert." The desert is constantly emphasized: the beauty in the countryside is a desert beauty.
Moonstone is also a town with a Mexican settlement—
something Red Cloud did not have—and toward the Mexicans, so graceful, with such a feeling for beautiful turns
of speech, so dependent on music and dancing, Thea is
strongly attracted. By the combination of a desert landscape and a Mexican colony we are prepared for Thea's
being immediately at home in Arizona.

The desert setting is important to another effect. Like
O Pioneers! this novel opens in January, but with what a
difference! *O Pioneers!* begins when a "mist of fine snowflakes was curling and eddying about the cluster of low
drab buildings huddled on the grey prairie, under a grey
sky." The sidewalks were "grey with trampled snow"; the

countryside with "its sombre wastes" had an "uninterrupted mournfulness." In *The Song of the Lark*, when
Dr. Archie steps out of his office into the January night,
"overhead the stars shone gloriously. It was impossible not
to notice them. The air was so clear that the white sand
hills to the east of Moonstone gleamed softly." Brilliance
of light pervades the novel. In the picture of Chicago the
stress comes on brightness: when Thea stepped out of the
Auditorium, after hearing the *New World* Symphony for
the first time, "the sun was setting in a clear, windy sky,
that flamed with red as if there were a great fire somewhere on the edge of the city"; and what is most vividly
represented in the street scenes is simply the brilliance of
the shop windows at Christmas. Thea's life in Arizona
"was simple and full of light, like the days themselves"—
"she had loved the sun, and the brilliant solitudes of sand
and sun" as "the earliest sources of gladness that she could
remember," and now the sun filled her being, for months
on end. Even in the seedy hotel in Union Square which is
her first lodging in New York her room is "flooded by thin,
clear sunshine." But it is the final part of the novel, the
rendering of Thea's triumph, that brings to its height
the effect of light to which we became accustomed in the
early desert scenes. This section opens in Denver, which,
"under a thrilling green-blue sky, is masked in snow and
glittering with sunlight." The blaze of the sun on the Capitol is so dazzling that the outlines of the building are lost
in light. On the peaks of the mountains "the fiery sunshine
is gathered up as by a burning-glass." When the scene
shifts to New York, the sun continues to shine, the snow is
bright in Central Park, and when dusk comes the lamps

banish any possibility of gloom. In the last scene, when, after singing Sieglinde, Thea left the Metropolitan, she stepped into the same kind of sunset that had met her years before when she left the Auditorium in Chicago. A more subdued brightness streams through the epilogue, in which Thea's queer old maiden aunt, the only Kronborg left in Moonstone, shows how happy she is in the reflected glory of a great name.

The white and gold colors of the sunlight playing on sand and snow are matched in the appearance of Thea herself. Her beauty has a much finer correspondence with the play of sunlight. It is not a constant thing, like the sensuous fairness of Lena Lingard in *My Ántonia*, or like the steady blond beauty of Alexandra Bergson. It comes and goes as her feelings shift. Just as the canyons in Arizona are like "a grey ghost, an empty, shivering uncertainty" when the sun does not shine, Thea's face is heavy and lifeless when she is balked or worn.

The use of light, repeated and varied with an artistry more resourceful than analysis can mirror, is never painfully obtrusive. Its principal value is not intellectual but emotional: without quite knowing why a sympathetic reader is suffused with warmth as he moves through the story, and long afterward when most of the events have been forgotten and most of the characters have grown dim, a mention of *The Song of the Lark*, a sight of the faded blue cover on the bookshelf of a friend, is enough to bring back a radiant feeling that no other writing by Willa Cather can evoke. The spirit of the book is too strong for the massive structure to crush.

III

In the summer of 1915, with the manuscript of the novel already at Houghton Mifflin, Willa Cather returned to the Southwest for a third long stay. For years she had wished to visit the Mesa Verde in Colorado. On this trip, accompanied by Edith Lewis, she traveled by rail to Mancos, twenty miles or so from the Mesa, and engaged there a team and driver to take them to it. Miss Lewis describes the visit to the Mesa Verde in this striking narrative:

Willa Cather had heard that one of the Wetherill family, a brother of the Dick Wetherill who first "discovered" the Mesa Verde, was still living in Mancos, and on the evening before we started for the Mesa she went to call on him; and from him she heard the whole story of how Dick Wetherill swam the Mancos river and rode into the Mesa after lost cattle, and how he came upon the cliff dwellings that had been hidden there for centuries.

We spent a week on the Mesa Verde. Very few people visited the place then—we were, I think, the only guests for the greater part of that week—and the forest ranger and guide, a young man named Jeep, who ran the government camp for tourists, was able to spend a great deal of his time taking us around to the different cliff dwellings. I recall that we spent a whole day in Cliff Palace, the cliff dwelling with a tower, described in the *Tom Outland* part of *The Professor's House*, cooking our lunch there and drinking from the spring behind the cliff houses.

The day before we were to go back to Mancos, Jeep had planned to take us to a cliff dwelling called the Tower House, which had not then been excavated. But just as we were about to start on this excursion, a large party of tourists arrived; and

Jeep announced that he would not be able to go with us. He said that, instead, he would send us with his brother-in-law, a young man named Richnor. We were disappointed, for Jeep was a splendid guide, familiar with every foot of the Mesa, and we knew nothing about Richnor. However, as Jeep made this announcement in Richnor's presence, we could hardly decline, and we started off with him.

To get to the Tower House, one had to walk through the woods to the rim of Soda Canyon, climb down to the bottom of this canyon, and follow along it for some distance. The Tower House was up the other wall of the canyon.

Richnor got us to the Tower House all right, but by a very rough trail—in climbing down to the bottom of Soda Canyon, we had in many places to hang from a tree or rock and then drop several feet to the next rock; we could not have returned by this trail without ropes. Richnor said he would take us back by another trail, further down the canyon. But by five or six o'clock that evening, after we had done a good many miles of walking, he was still unable to find this trail, and had to admit that he did not know how we were to get back. (The sides of the canyon were everywhere precipitous, and for several hundred feet beneath the rim the bare rock generally overhung.)

We had by then come to a place where another canyon, Cliff Canyon, opened at right angles from Soda Canyon. Richnor told us he thought, but was not sure, that about four miles up Cliff Canyon there was an archaeologist's camp (Dr. Fewkes' camp), and suggested that we try for it. But Willa Cather sensibly told him he had better go up Cliff Canyon and find out whether the camp was really there; we would wait, in the meantime, at the intersection of the two canyons.

The four or five hours that we spent waiting there were, I think, for Willa Cather the most rewarding of our whole trip to the Mesa Verde. There was a large flat rock at the mouth of Cliff Canyon, and we settled ourselves comfortably on this rock

—with the idea, I believe, that we should be able to see any rat-
tlesnakes if they came racing up. We were tired, but not worried, for we knew that we should eventually be found. We did
not talk, but watched the long summer twilight come on, and
the full moon rise up over the rim of the canyon. The place was
very beautiful.

We were sitting there in the moonlight, when we heard
shouts from up Cliff Canyon, and presently two men came in
sight. They were two of the diggers from Dr. Fewkes' camp,
whom Richnor had sent down to get us. He himself was so exhausted by the time he reached the camp that he was unable to
come back.

Soda Canyon has a wide, grassy bottom—one simply walks
along it—but Cliff Canyon is a very difficult canyon to climb—
just a mass of broken rocks all the way, some of them as big as
a house. We could never have got through without the help of
the two diggers, who were both splendid men—kind, chival-
rous, resourceful, and full of high spirits and encouragement. . . . Their names were Clint Scarf and Audrey Grey
Pearl. Each of them took one of us by the hand and steadied
us over the rocks. (At one place we had to lie down and be
pulled through a sort of tunnel in the rocks.) . . .

About four miles up the canyon one could reach the top of
the cliffs by mounting part way on the lopped-off branches of
a huge pine tree, which was laid along the side of the cliff like
a ladder. We got to Fewkes' camp at about two in the morning. Our two diggers then went out into the pasture, caught
a couple of horses, hitched them to a wagon, and drove us
back to our own camp. At eight o'clock that same morning our
team and driver arrived to take us back to Mancos.

Much of what befell Willa Cather on that day and night,
and something of the spirit in which she took it, were to
go into "Tom Outland's Story." After the visit of 1915

Willa Cather never saw the Mesa Verde; but her feeling toward the Cliff-Dwellers, her sense of the contrast between their way of building and living and the modern American way, were to shape *The Professor's House.* These were to be long delayed effects; never again did she convert the present or the immediate past into fiction as she had done in *The Song of the Lark.*

From Mancos Willa Cather and Edith Lewis traveled southward to Taos, at that time a very isolated place, approached only by team over a long distance of rough road. There was no American hotel, only an adobe hotel, run by a Mexican woman, which Willa Cather found comfortable if primitive. She stayed at Taos for a month or so, exploring the country either on horseback or behind a team she drove herself. She was always glad she had seen the Southwest before the invasion of automobiles, when one still had to be on the alert for every landmark and had time to note all the contours of the land and all the detail.

In the summer of 1916, accompanied again by Edith Lewis, Willa Cather returned to Taos, for a longer stay. She also spent some time at Santa Fe, explored Frijoles Canyon and the Espanola Valley, and at Santa Cruz talked with a Belgian priest, Father Haltermann, who knew the history of the French and Spanish missionaries in the Southwest. The impressions were now accumulating for the greatest of her novels, but many years were to pass before they fell into place and she could write the first word of *Death Comes for the Archbishop.*

On the way back to New York after each of these two summers Willa Cather stayed for some weeks in Red

Cloud. One day in 1916 she drove out to a farm on the
Divide and saw, surrounded by many children, Anna Pa-
velka, a Bohemian woman whom she had known well, very
well, when they were girls. It seemed to her that this woman's story ran very close to the central stream of life in Red
Cloud and on the Divide, that she stood for the triumph of
what was vigorous, sound, and beautiful in a region where
these qualities so often seemed to suffer repression or defeat. Before she returned to New York, Willa Cather had
begun to write this story in *My Ántonia*.

She always showed impatience at the complaint that
My Ántonia is not precisely a novel. Why should it be?
She had never said it was. In this book she was gathering
her memories of some persons and places very dear to her,
and as she was a writer of stories, the memories had taken
a narrative form. Besides, in the very curious preface she
had given notice of what the book would be like. This introduction, like so many of her writings, opens on a scene
in a train to the west of Chicago. She is talking, she says,
with Jim Burden, whom she had known when she was a
girl, and who is now the legal counsel for a Western railway. They both live in New York, but she rarely sees him,
for she dislikes his wife. Mrs. Burden, who is not aboard
the train, is given a full page: she is a superficial, spoiled,
restless woman, who has her own money and lives her own
life. The failure of Jim Burden's marriage has not injured
his character: he remains what he always was, romantic
in disposition, in love with the Western country, as impres-
sionable as a boy. They talk of the early days in Nebraska,
and find they "kept returning to a central figure, a Bohemian girl, whom we had known long ago and whom both

of us admired. More than any other person we remembered, this girl seemed to mean to us the country, the conditions, the whole adventure of our childhood." Willa
Cather says she had the feeling that Jim Burden could tell
the story of Ántonia better than she could: "he had had
opportunities that I, as a little girl who watched her come
and go, had not." It was agreed that both would record
their memories of Ántonia; but when in the course of the
next winter Jim Burden called at her apartment with his
manuscript complete, she had not gone beyond a few
straggling notes. Jim was taken aback at the mention of
notes for what was to be not a created fiction but a record
of fact and impression. "I didn't arrange or rearrange," he
says, "I simply wrote down what of herself and myself and
other people Ántonia's name recalls to me. I suppose it
hasn't any form. It hasn't any title either." Then across the
cover of the manuscript he wrote "Ántonia," prefixing in
a moment "another word, making it 'My Ántonia.' " When
she read his memoir she was so pleased, Willa Cather says,
that she did not write hers, and it is his she presents.

This is the substance of the preface in the early editions. Willa Cather was never happy about it; she had
found it, unlike the rest of the book, a labor to write. For
the reissue of 1926 she revised it in important ways. The
agreement that both she and Jim would record their memories of Ántonia is removed; and instead of Jim's undertaking to write because of his talk with her, he has been at
work on his manuscript long before the meeting in the
train. By these changes the effect is, I believe, improved.
Jim's concern with Ántonia seems more profound when
the decision to record his memories stems not from a

meeting with a professional writer but from his own inward impulse. The agreement had, besides, the defect
of starting in the reader's mind a question that could do
the book no good—whether in fact it would not have been
better told by another woman, the query Miss Jewett had
raised about "On the Gull's Road." Most of the satirical
account of Mrs. Burden was removed, though enough was
left to establish the failure of Jim's marriage. The excision
at this point is also a gain: for the earlier text left one wondering whether Jim was not ignominiously weak in continuing to lend himself to the purposes of such a creature.
Unless Jim can satisfy the reader that his impressions and
judgments about women are sound, his value as an appreciative recorder of Ántonia is threatened. What was important in the original preface remains: that the book is to be
taken as the work of an unprofessional writer; of a man
who had left the Divide, Red Cloud, the West, but kept
his attachment to all three; of a man whose personal life
in later years has been frustrated and who has judged the
phase to which Ántonia belonged to have been the high
water-mark of the whole.

It could do the book no good, I suggest, for the reader
to ponder whether it might not have been better told by
a woman. The new preface does not raise the question; but
readers are likely to raise it for themselves before the book
ends. A young man who feels that a young woman is the
most important thing in his life might be expected to fall
in love with her. Jim is curious about Ántonia, interested
in her, charmed by her, but he does not fall in love with
her; nor when in later years he visits her at her farm (as
Willa Cather visited the original of the character), does

202 Willa Cather: A Critical Biography

he have any feeling that he ought to have married her, though he does say that when he was a young boy he had been unconsciously in love with her. At the very center of his relation with Ántonia there is an emptiness where the strongest emotion might have been expected to gather. A comment on *My Ántonia* that Willa Cather made in an interview she gave in Lincoln a few years after the book came out shows that in her use of Jim as narrator she had been trying to achieve two effects that were not really compatible: Jim was to be fascinated by Ántonia as only a man could be, and yet he was to remain a detached observer, appreciative but inactive, rather than take a part in her life.

Jim's failure to take a part in Ántonia's life is made conspicuous by one of the main social themes in the book. In *O Pioneers!* as in "The Bohemian Girl," people of old American stock had no roles; apart from the Scandinavians and Bohemians the only other racial group to appear (in "The White Mulberry Tree" section of *O Pioneers!*) was the French. In *The Song of the Lark* individuals of old American stock had important roles even in the early Western chapters, but they appeared as individuals; there was no study of a family of old American stock, nothing to approach the account, so tenderly discerning, of the old German couple with whom Wunsch, the music teacher, lived. In *My Ántonia* Willa Cather is deeply concerned with the relations between the families of old American stock and the families of the immigrants from Europe. The reader is constantly required to make comparisons, and to perceive superiorities in the immigrants. At no point are the comparisons more pointed, the superiorities more conspicu-

ous, than when the Scandinavian girls like Lena Lingard
and the Bohemians like Ántonia are set beside the girls of
old American stock who have grown up not on the Divide
but within the rigid code of the leading families in town.
For the young man in one of those families who has marriage in his mind, the choice is between life and death.
Sylvester Lovett, the son of a local bank president, appears in the book for a moment to make his choice. He
has danced with Lena Lingard, taken her driving, and
shown the world that he is infatuated; but marry her he
will not, he chooses a well-to-do widow much older than
himself. Jim Burden had hoped that Lovett would marry
Lena; if he had done so, Jim thinks the "foreign girls"
would all have taken higher places in the town's scale of
values. When Lovett did not, Jim burned to find some way
of manifesting his contempt for the white-handed high-
collared young man.

Jim too had his chance to marry Lena and did not take
it. Lena is the most beautiful, the most innocently sensuous of all the women in Willa Cather's works. The portrait
of Lena has a merciful softness as if the novelist's critical
power were deliberately withheld except for an occasional
touch of humorous realism. Lena is never a rival for the
central place in the book—she has not Ántonia's force or
her insight, she is never so much alive. At times she is a
foil: her fairness against Ántonia's sparkling nervous dark
beauty, her slowness and quietness against Ántonia's vi-
vacity. It is easy to understand how in her rosy semi-naked
beauty she became so constant a figure in Jim's adolescent
dreams. Despite her richness in what a younger generation than Willa Cather's calls "sex appeal," her hold on

Jim never becomes firm. She and Jim were attracted to
each other early in the book; but it is only after he has
gone to Lincoln as an undergraduate and Lena as a dressmaker that he singles her out. In his own town he did not
have the daring. Just as Sylvester Lovett had found her a
girl who could really dance, Jim finds her a girl who can
really respond to the theater. Their relation is one of the
most beautiful elements in the book, with the charm of
an idyll (it is intertwined with his study of the *Georgics*),
of a sharing of youth rather than a relation between two
personalities. Jim is no better than the Sylvester Lovett he
had so despised. When his favorite instructor warns him
he should part from his "beautiful Norwegian," who is
"quite irresponsible," he does so without even an appearance of struggle. I seem to hear the creaking of the novelist's machinery as the idyll ends and Jim retreats so easily
into the status of a detached observer. What is excellent in
My Ántonia does not depend on a masculine narrator. It
inheres in the material itself and in the appreciation of it,
which might have been just as sensitive, just as various, if
Willa Cather had presented this story omnisciently—as
Miss Jewett counseled earlier—as she had presented Alexandra Bergson's, or if she had made herself a part of the
structure.

The beauty of the book was at once apprehended by
W. C. Brownell in a letter (still unpublished) to one of
Willa Cather's associates at *McClure's*, Viola Roseboro'.

I feel somehow [he wrote] as if the proper epithets to charac-
terize the book were something "up," almost physically floating
above the material, as it were. I don't mind being incoherent,
if I convey my notion in the least by my flounderings. Arnold,

on Homer, talks about Homer not (like a Dutch painter) "sinking with his subject." This has that air. But would it be too much to say it *lifts* the subject somehow—not, of course, by treating it idealistically, since it is one of the most notable instances I know of the contrary—but by a sort of continuous and sustained respect for the material: a sort of "what God hath made call thou not common" implication, putting Nature for God, of course. . . . At first I thought it was casual and episodical (though *so* well written, so simple, so obviously saying all it felt and with such ease) and though large minded and as unmeretricious as salt itself, still rather a desultory document of Western civilization. But ere long it differentiated itself imperceptibly and subtly into a picture crowded with real people, made somehow real, given souls, by—well, by what? I don't know. I don't remember any art more essentially elusive.

Where so penetrating a critic as Brownell was aware of floundering, and pronounced an author's art "essentially elusive," one hesitates to offer clarifications. I believe that something can be said of the means that have given this book its effect of "almost physically floating above the material." The elements that weigh a book down scarcely exist here. In *My Ántonia* there is no massive central trunk such as the development of Thea Kronborg, phase by phase, provided for *The Song of the Lark*. In *My Ántonia*, instead, there is a gallery of pictures. For a while, as happened to Brownell, the pictures seem to be hung in a casual and episodical fashion; before long they affect one as illuminating one another and contributing to a general tone. They have been painted and arranged so that one may apprehend the values in that old Nebraska world, gone forever before the book was written.

The epigraph and the comment upon it taken together are a sufficient clue to the method of the book. The epigraph, from the third *Georgic*, runs: *"Optima dies . . . prima fugit."* Jim was preparing this part of the poem and translating this passage as "the best days are the first to flee," when Lena Lingard made her first visit to him at Lincoln. When she had gone, "it came over me, as it had never done before, the relation between girls like those [Lena, Ántonia, and their friends] and the poetry of Virgil. If there were no girls like them in the world, there would be no poetry." His old dream of Lena returned to him awake, and "it floated before me on the page like a picture, and underneath it stood the mournful line: 'Optima dies . . . prima fugit.' "

Everything in the book is there to convey a feeling, not to tell a story, not to establish a social philosophy, not even to animate a group of characters. The feeling attaches to persons, places, moments: if one were to pin it in a phrase it might be called a mournful appreciation of "the precious, the incommunicable past"—those are the last words in the book. Earlier Jim Burden has voiced the feeling in the remark: "Some memories are realities, and are better than anything that can ever happen to one again."

This feeling attaches itself above all to Ántonia. She is the person whose inner strength enables her to live the enviable life. At the foot of Willa Cather's scale, as usual, are people who live in the town or on the Divide and make nothing of the opportunity. These are the narrow money-minded people like Wick Cutter and Ántonia's brother Ambrosch. Then come the people who must go away to achieve a life. They are much more important to the book;

Jim Burden and Lena Lingard are among them. Their lives will not bear comparison with Ántonia's. Jim has become wealthy and "important"; but he is childless and has no attachments to any person or any place except what he preserves of the Nebraska past. Lena has been successful —and her friend Tiny Soderball, another girl from the Divide, has had almost unbelievable success; but their lives in San Francisco are solitary and rootless. Ántonia has remained on the Divide; she had found a good husband, who has fragrant memories of Prague and Vienna, of music and song; she has a dozen children, all of them delightful; the farm is big and fertile; and Ántonia has given it some of the amenities that would have pleased her fastidious father—orchards and hedges and a grape arbor. She had worked herself and worn herself to accomplish her life, but if she was "battered" she was not "diminished." In middle life, when she makes her last appearance, her hair is grizzled and most of her teeth have gone; but she "was still there in the full vigour of her personality." Looking at her, one feels that is how one should have lived—if one could.

My Ántonia marks a new phase in the long process of Willa Cather's reconciliation with Nebraska. In this book she values not only the land and the pioneers, but aspects in the life of the town which have taken on an affecting charm in the long retrospect. The simplest experiences become charming by the play of a strong retrospective emotion: the casual warmhearted fun in the Harlings' kitchen, the dances in the park on summer Saturday evenings, the lonely walks at night under the cottonwoods to the edge of town. What was harsh, narrow, and malignant in the town, so strong an undertone in *The Song of the Lark*, has lost its menace; the face of Wick Cutter's wife is the "very colour and shape of anger," but she can do no real harm.

In the reconciliation with Nebraska the Southwest continued to have a role. The last summer before he went to the university Jim spent a long day by the river with Ántonia, Lena, and two other Scandinavian girls; in this episode Willa Cather reworks "The Enchanted Bluff" with deeper meanings and happier implications. In "The Enchanted Bluff" the wish of all the boys is to go away, and the failure of their lives is in not going away, or not going far enough. Now in *My Ántonia* the story of Coronado is told again. On a sword dug up by a farmer breaking sod near by, the parish priest found the name of a Spanish maker and an abbreviation that stood for the city of Cordova. Jim and the girls wonder about the motives for the long northward journey and how the country looked when the Spaniards first saw it. "Why had Coronado never gone back to Spain, to his riches and his castles and his king? I couldn't tell them. I only knew the school-books said he 'died in the wilderness, of a broken heart.' " As they wondered, the sun was setting; the "edge of the red disk rested on the high fields against the horizon," and "a great black figure suddenly appeared on the face of the sun." This was a plow left standing on an upland farm. "Magnified across the distance by the horizontal light, it stood out against the sun, was exactly contained within the circle of the disk; the handles, the tongue, the share—black against the molten red. There it was, heroic in size, a picture writing on the sun." The mention of Coronado, the feeling of a Spanish past in which inexplicable adventure had ended in heart-break and disaster, has woven an enchantment about the region. It is no longer a place to leave, it is a place to live in—if one has, like Ántonia, the stuff of which the heroic Spaniards were made.

8

The World Broke in Two

1919–1923

THE THREE NOVELS about the West, published within six years, had pre-empted most of Willa Cather's imaginative activity; but writing them had not dulled her awareness of what was interesting in the lives of the people she knew or heard about in New York. Most of these were artists or devotees of the arts; and among them, from the time of her getting to know Olive Fremstad, the opera singers had most to say to her imagination. She did not care to write about them at length, but when she was free for a while from the weight of a novel, she found herself writing short stories about them. There was "The Diamond Mine," which came out in *McClure's* in October 1916, when she was beginning *My Ántonia*; "A Gold Slipper," which came out in *Harper's* in the following January; and "Scandal," another episode in the life of the same singer, which came out in the *Century* in August 1919.

In these stories the center of interest is not where it had been in most of the earlier treatments of artists—in the greatness, growth, or decline of a talent or in the destructive force of Philistinism. Such grave matters usually do come in, but they receive only a secondary emphasis.

What now has most interest for Willa Cather is the kind of relationships artists have with those who are not artists but are brought into contact with them. At the core of "Scandal" is a shabby trick played on the singer Kitty Ayrshire by a garment-manufacturer whose hobby is pretending to intimate relations with women who are highly successful in the arts. The trick hurts her personal reputation, but it does not hurt her; and in retrospect she can afford to smile at it. In "A Gold Slipper" the core is even slighter: Kitty has a forthright talk in the course of the one meeting she will ever have with a pillar of the coal industry and the First Presbyterian Church in Pittsburgh; his scorn for artists cannot make her even momentarily uncomfortable, and there is nothing he could do to jeopardize either her talent or her personal life. The effect in "The Diamond Mine" is a little graver. The theme of an artist's suffering exploitation by her family, sounded briefly in "A Gold Slipper," runs through this story; it is disheartening to think that there are people like Cressida Garnet's sisters and brother, as it is disheartening to think that there are people like the coal-man and the garment-maker; but the artists are too strong to be injured. In Pittsburgh, before she had an intimate knowledge of serious artists, Willa Cather had felt that the failure of an artist's family and friends to understand him was a horrible disaster, disabling to the artist's personal life, if not fatal to his talent. She had said so in "The Sculptor's Funeral." She had misread the artistic nature: now that she knew Olive Fremstad and George Arliss and had observed for some years at first hand many artists practicing their craft on many levels and in varied fields, she was aware of the toughness of

fiber in an artist. She knew that his talent could not be
ruined or his life embittered just because clever scoun-
drels exploited him, or stupid people wrote him down for
a fool.

In another story of these years, "Coming, Aphrodite!"
Willa Cather pits one kind of artist against another—an
original painter against a conventional opera singer whom
he loves. His disappointment with her, her failure to perceive his distinction do not really matter. His painting is
not lamed by his experience, nor does it seem to change
the independent curve of his life.

Early in 1920 Willa Cather decided to bring out a second collection of short stories. It was fifteen years since
The Troll Garden was published, and it had long been out
of print. For the new book she would keep four of its seven
tales, submit some of them to much revision, and add the
four recent tales about artists. From this decision came
Youth and the Bright Medusa, the first of her books to be
published by Alfred A. Knopf. She had been happy when
Alexander's Bridge was accepted by the Houghton Mifflin Company; she knew that this house was one of the few
in the country with a history and standards; and she had
found in Ferris Greenslet a sympathetic counselor as well
as a firm friend. His report on *My Ántonia,* the last of her
books to appear with a Houghton Mifflin imprint, was
everything an author could wish. "Of all the remarkable
portraits of women that Miss Cather has done," he wrote
to his colleagues, "no other is so poetic and appealing. . . .
This is undoubtedly Miss Cather's best book so far. It is a
very distinguished piece of work and with a human quality
that will, I think, make it a permanent success." He had

been entirely right at every point; the portrait of Ántonia
was the most poetic and the most appealing in her writings; the book was her "best . . . so far" (and when she
wrote a better, Ferris Greenslet was prompt to say so); it
did have permanent success both popular and critical. But
if Ferris Greenslet's attitude toward her work was generous as well as perceptive, he had not been able, Willa
Cather believed, to persuade the rest of the directorate to
accept it. The company did not get behind her books, she
thought, did not give them sufficient play. She was especially displeased with what she thought a torpid interest
in making *My Ántonia* known and getting it into the bookstores. Besides, she was not happy about the format of her
novels. A company that had been giving soberly beautiful
covers and pages to Irving Babbitt (to name but one other
author) had given a crowded page to *The Song of the Lark*
and an awkward drab cover to *My Ántonia*. The parting
came without acrimony, and Ferris Greenslet was a close
friend as long as Willa Cather lived.

In *Alfred A. Knopf, Quarter Century*, Willa Cather has
related her first conversations with the man who was to
publish all her books in the last twenty-seven years of her
life. She went to see him because she had liked his lists and
the format of his books. During her first call she picked up
some samples of blue paper from his desk; he had gone to
the Metropolitan Museum of Art "to find exactly the right
shade among the Chinese blues" for a volume of translations from Chinese poetry. She liked the way he talked
about the works he had published and wished to publish.
She liked his independence, and the blend of "a fiery temperament" with "a rather severe taste." In their second talk

she formally asked him to become her publisher, and entered on a relationship that was as happy as the world
knows it to have been successful. Miss Lewis notes:

Next to writing her novels, Willa Cather's choice of Alfred
Knopf as a publisher influenced her career, I think, more than
any action she ever took. It was not so much that with him she
was able in a few years to achieve financial security . . . as
that he gave her great encouragement and absolute liberty to
write exactly as she chose—protected her in every way he could
from outside pressures and interruptions—and made evident,
not only to her but to the world in general, his great admiration and belief in her. Life was simply no longer a battle—she
no longer had to feel apologetic or on the defensive. She was
always very modest about her work, but she was a person of
great pride. Her pride was no longer threatened.

II

When she first talked with Alfred A. Knopf in the spring
of 1920, Willa Cather mentioned the novel she was writing—*One of Ours*, then tentatively named *Claude*. That
book had its inception when she learned, in May 1918, of
the death in battle at Cantigny of a young cousin who had
grown up in Webster County and about whom she had
cared a great deal. G. P. Cather, Jr., who had served in the
navy and in the national guard before the war, had shown
unusual skill with big guns, and became a lieutenant almost as soon as he enlisted. He was extremely happy in the
armed services and was believed to have great promise by
his superior officers, one of whom was Theodore Roosevelt,
Jr. But it did not require a personal loss to make Willa
Cather feel the impact of the war. For a year before her

cousin was killed, soldiers from Red Cloud and Lincoln and Pittsburgh, friends, students, friends of friends, had come in groups to see her, often when they were on the last leave before embarkation. One of her students in the Pittsburgh years, Albert Donovan, had an army post in New York which drew him into touch with great numbers of soldiers, and he was always encouraged to bring to call on her those he thought would care to come.

After her cousin the soldier who interested her most was a young violinist, whom she saw only four times, David Hochstein. She met him first in the winter of 1916 when he played in a quintet at an informal musical party in a New York hotel. In his playing and in the man himself she found poetic insight and a mixture of reticence and sincerity that delighted her. Hochstein was a relative of the anarchist Emma Goldman, and an admirer of the civilization of Germany, where he had received much of his training in music. She did not meet him again until after the United States had declared war, and he was in much doubt about its issues and outcome, and about the course he should himself pursue. He entered the army, and when Willa Cather saw him next he was in the depression that the first months of military training so often bring. Some months later she saw him for the last time, and marveled at the change in him: he was now delighted with the kind of men he had to do with and the special terms on which they lived. In the autumn of 1918 he was killed in the Argonne. Willa Cather was allowed to see some of his letters to his mother, as she also saw some of her cousin's letters home, and was moved by the intellectual and emotional maturity in both. How had a Nebraska farm-boy, with lit-

tle education and slight experience of life, and how had a
New York musician of solitary and pessimistic temper,
changed so much and so quickly? How could war and the
army and France produce such effects? These were the
questions that led to the writing of *One of Ours*. Willa
Cather was mystified when Sinclair Lewis, in a review, remarked: "The whole introduction of the great war is
doubtful; it is a matter to be debated." One might question the authenticity of the war scenes, and argue about
the conception of war and the army, but there is no doubt
whatever that the war was an intrinsic part of her original
conception.

One of Ours was written slowly. In August 1918 Willa
Cather visited Red Cloud, and in the early fall she stayed
with her brother Roscoe in Wyoming. The novel was in
her mind before she went west, and as soon as she returned to New York she started to write. She was at work
on it during the whole of 1919. In the autumn of that year
she made a long stay at Jaffrey, New Hampshire, which
she had found a good place for work when she was reading the proofs of *My Ántonia*. She came down with in-
fluenza and was treated by a local doctor who had served
as medical officer of a troopship when a severe epidemic of
the disease broke out. From his diary she drew much of the
material for the fourth part of the novel, "The Voyage of
the *Anchises*." By the spring of 1920 two thirds of the novel
existed. To write the remainder, which is laid in France,
Willa Cather felt that she must live in that country for a
time. In June, accompanied by Edith Lewis, she went to
Paris by way of Cherbourg, and for almost two months
lived at the Hôtel du Quai Voltaire, with windows opening

on the Seine. She used no introductions, seldom crossed over to the Right Bank except to hear opera, and acquired impressions of the older Paris that went into *Shadows on the Rock* as well as into the pages she was preparing to write. There are no Paris scenes in *One of Ours*, but from her absorption in the past of the city she drew what she felt she had needed: a feeling of the meaning of French civilization and culture as a whole. She visited the battle-fields with Isabelle McClung and Jan Hambourg, moving for two weeks through a countryside still pitted and scarred by war, and visiting the grave of her cousin. Almost as soon as she had returned from this trip she was eager to go home—she was ready to write the rest of the novel. It did not come quickly, and the proofs did not begin to arrive until the summer of 1921. She read a part of them during her first stay at Grand Manan, an island in the Bay of Fundy, where before long she was to find her summer home. *One of Ours* appeared in the autumn of 1922, four years after she had begun writing it.

Of her earlier novels only *The Song of the Lark* has any resemblance to *One of Ours*. Each is a novel of development, with a large number of carefully detailed phases, beginning on the Western plains, ending far away when the development has been completed, with an epilogue to show what the development meant to someone who remained in the original setting. In the Western part of each novel the developing character lives in a crisscross of alliances and enmities. Thea Kronborg's youth, roughly contemporary with Willa Cather's, came in the pioneer phase of her society; in Claude Wheeler's the next phase has succeeded, prosperous, mechanized, prosaic. In the second decade of the century the pioneers are still living on their farms and in the town; but except for Claude's own family they do not often appear, and when they do, as when old Troilus Oberlies is charged with disloyalty, they have a force and a color somewhat out of scale with the rest of the cast. One reason why the dramatis personæ seem dull in comparison with those of the earlier novels is that the immigrants have no important parts, nor do their children. There are no Scandinavians, and there is only one Bohemian, a pleasant thoughtful boy, of no force or imagination. The world in which Claude grew up needed to be a dull world; what Willa Cather wished to show was how a boy who had an exceptional nature, but no exceptional gift or strength of will, was undergoing a slow strangulation of intellect and feeling until the war provided an escape from Nebraska. The dullness was necessary, but even when one rereads the early parts of *One of Ours*, aware of what the theme requires, interest often flags.

The forces that are hostile to Claude's nature are best rendered in his brother Bayliss Wheeler, a new type in Willa Cather's fiction, and a preliminary sketch for Ivy Peters in her next novel, *A Lost Lady*. Because Bayliss was undersized, his father had been ready to see him leave the farm and set up a business in town. His interests were to make money, having made it to save it, and to make life disagreeable for anyone who had other interests. He suspected all forms of pleasure that did not relate to money-getting and was prone to suspect all other forms of activity. When he hears that one of Claude's friends in Lincoln plans to become a professor, he asks dryly: "What's the matter with him? Does he have poor health?" There is no active cruelty in Bayliss, no vicious scheming; he remains dull and petty, on the scale of the cast; it is Willa Cather's triumph that he nevertheless seems formidable. It does not seem silly that on his last leave, as he is turning over in his mind what his experience in the army and in France has taught him, Claude should say: "No battlefield or shattered country he had seen was as ugly as this world would be if men like his brother Bayliss controlled it altogether. . . . He knew the future of the world was safe; the careful planners would never be able to put it into a strait-jacket—cunning and prudence would never have it to themselves."

About Claude's younger brother Ralph there is nothing sinister; but he represents another trait in the generation that followed the pioneers which alarmed Willa Cather, the cult of machinery. In "Coming Aphrodite!" at the end of the preliminary picture of the beauty of Washington Square in the years before the First World War, she wrote: "Looking up the Avenue through the Arch, one could see the young poplars with their bright, sticky leaves, and the Brevoort glistening in its spring coat of paint, and shining horses and carriages—occasionally an automobile, misshapen and sullen, like an ugly threat in a stream of things that were bright and beautiful and alive." Ralph Wheeler yearned after every machine he saw or read of; no sooner had his mother and old Mahailey, her general helper, found out how to operate a washing machine or a churn than he produced another, more complicated and more vexatious. The cellar was full of machines that had been superseded or had never been useful. Claude reflects that Ralph spent more money on unnecessary machinery than his friend in Lincoln, Julius Erlich, would use for his graduate study in Germany. The Erlichs, he reflected, might be poor, but they knew how to live, spending "their money on themselves, instead of on machines to do the work and machines to entertain people. Machines . . . could not make pleasure, whatever else they could do. They could not make agreeable people, either."

The machine is a recurrent symbol of disaster in the Nebraska part of the novel. One day when Claude is at work with a mule team, a gasoline motor-truck frightens them, and Claude's face is driven against a barbed-wire fence. Erysipelas follows, and, what is much worse, during his recovery the visits of Enid Royce lead him to marry her. His marriage to this loveless bigoted girl is the worst of his misfortunes. Its failure is symbolized in her creeping about the countryside for hundreds of miles in her black electric spreading leaflets for the cause of prohibition while Claude picks up a lonely meal and broods through a lonely evening.

In the last part of the novel machinery loses its evil sense. One of Claude's friends, Sergeant Hicks, who had intended after he got home to open a garage with his pal Able, plans to have his sign read "Hicks and Able" though Able has been killed. Machinery serving a humane man, with vistas of experience and some imagination, is a very different force from machinery at the Wheelers' or the Royces'. For Ralph Wheeler and Enid Royce, it is part of a way of living. How deeply mistaken Willa Cather felt this way of living to be was made plain in her essay "Nebraska," written a few years after *One of Ours*. "The generation now in the driver's seat," she said, "hates to make anything, wants to live and die in an automobile, scudding past those acres where the old men used to follow the long corn-rows up and down. They want to buy everything ready-made: clothes, food, education, music, pleasure." An old lady who grew up in Red Cloud with Willa Cather remarked to me that boys and girls no longer went walking or on horseback to swim in the Republican and loll on its sandbars; they drove forty or fifty miles to an artificial pool. The generation after Ralph's and Enid's, as Willa Cather was to notice, prolonged their attitudes.

It was those attitudes, the glorification of money-getting and the cult of the machine, that Willa Cather wished to produce for the reader of *One of Ours*, not elaborate individual characterizations of people such as Ralph and Bayliss and Enid. The characters ruled by money and machinery must merge into the gray world, and do. None of them actively harms Claude, or has any wish to harm him. Seeing around him so many people sure of these miserable values, and scarcely anyone to deny them, is what does the harm. Claude asks himself the most dangerous question that can arise in a person of exceptional nature who is without an exceptional gift or exceptional strength of will: Am I mistaken, weak, queer?

In the choice and rendering of Claude's sympathizers Willa Cather again needed to avoid creating persons of great comprehension or vitality, who would have vigorous roles in Claude's story. There could be no Wunsch, no Dr. Archie. If there were, Claude would not be so full of self-distrust as he needs to be, and the world would not be gray enough. The rendering of Enid's father, Jason Royce, is an instance of Willa Cather's skill. Jason is a pioneer, the first miller of the county, a strong, heavy man, with a gentle heart. He had seen something exceptional in Claude long before the novel opens, and envied his unperceptive father; when the water-power in the mill was replaced by an engine he had felt that little Claude Wheeler was the only person who would regret the change. But Jason has been broken by his wife and daughters; he does not have the strength to say the right things, much as he wants to, in his one great scene—when he tries to avert the disaster of Claude's marriage. Gladys Farmer is rendered with equal skill. If her full strength had been let loose on the novel, there would have been an end to grayness. She is an exceptional nature—as much so as Claude— and she discerns and admires his way of being exceptional. They could easily have fallen in love, and were indeed on the way to doing so before the novel opens; then the lines of communication between them were cut. She appeared to encourage Bayliss as a suitor, and Claude was so outraged that he avoided her and the thought of her as "a sore spot in his mind." Not until he is in uniform and back on his last home leave is there a clearing up of the difficulty that has kept him apart from Gladys Farmer.

Within his own family Claude has sympathizers, much more active in the story than Jason Royce and Gladys Farmer. His mother is a portrait of great pathos. A sensitive, affectionate, and somewhat cultivated woman, she has been dominated so roughly by her husband that her frail spirit and her wandering step are the index to her inability to do for Claude anything at all like what Mrs. Kronborg did for Thea. She understands much of what makes life hard for her son, but cannot be a confidante because she is so rooted in a narrow religious code that she translates anything he says into terms with no reality for him. Mahailey, her servant, is the one character in the novel who might have stepped from the pages of *My Ántonia* or *O Pioneers!* The affections and instincts that have faded in all the other characters who have much to do or say in the novel have kept their full strength in Mahailey. But she is simple-minded like the Margie Anderson in the household of Willa Cather's parents from whom she was drawn; and if she has a queer wisdom of her own, much like Crazy Ivar's in *O Pioneers!* which lets her glimpse what is wrong in Claude's circumstances, her efforts to bring them right are as ineffective as his mother's.

The early parts of *One of Ours* are the product of Willa Cather's close observation of Red Cloud and the Divide during the long visits she paid nearly every year. It had become plain to her that the day of Ántonia was over: now one had to go away to grow, there was no other choice. The world she had known in the eighties and nineties was ceasing to exist; everything in it that had encouraged her own growth was dead or dying, and what had opposed her growth was now victorious. In *One of Ours* she turned from the pleasure of recalling memories that were full of life and charm to the comparatively dreary task of rendering a world as humdrum as that of *Madame Bovary.*

But with that humdrum world she proposed to contrast the belated growth of Claude Wheeler once he came into circumstances that would give him his great unforeseen second chance. These were, in ascending importance, the army, the war, and France.

Of the three, as a woman, Willa Cather has least to say about the army. Nothing in her earlier stories since the historical romance about Lord Fairfax's castle was so remote from her experience as the representation of Claude's life in the army. Much as she learned from the young soldiers who came to see her, she left Claude's sense of what he drew from associations within the army a suggestion rather than a realized picture. It was an opportunity for forming friendships, as with the violinist Gerhardt, that would in peace have been impossible. It was a coming together for reasons more satisfying than making money, or getting the upper hand. The effect of war on a soldier is also suggested rather than worked out. Taking part in it was responding to an idea or a feeling, and was therefore outside the range of the life Claude had known in Nebraska. "History had condescended to such as he . . . the feeling of purpose, of fateful purpose, was strong in his breast."

With the impact of France on Claude, Willa Cather could work more freely. One understands her need to return to that country and immerse herself in its life and its history before she wrote the last part of the novel: here was a factor she could master. What Claude takes from France comes to him from places and persons. He is like Niel Herbert in *A Lost Lady*, who "had no curiosity about what men had thought; but about what they had felt and lived he had a great deal." For Claude, France is the Church of Saint-Ouen at Rouen, with its arches, windows, and chimes; the glades in the forests, green beyond a Nebraskan's imagination; the devotion of the people to their flowers and their cooking; the language that "couldn't be mumbled, that had to be spoken with energy and fire or not at all"; the bright sympathetic understanding of French women; above all, the interweaving with the lives of individuals of something lasting and strong that sustains them. "Life," he reflected, "was so short that it meant nothing at all unless it were continually reinforced by something that endured; unless the shadows of individual existence came and went against a background that held together." Otherwise it was what he had known in Nebraska: "buying and selling, building and pulling down," it was Bayliss Wheeler, who put the proceeds of his buying and selling into the one place near by that had tradition and beauty, and proposed to "tear down that old trap and put up something modern."

The army, the war, and France combined to give Claude the youth he had never had. When he has had it, he may die. Indeed, Willa Cather insists it was best he should. When he was killed in the fall of 1918, it was "believing his own country better than it is, and France better than any country can ever be." The beliefs would have perished had he seen the postwar world. In the last pages of the novel, speaking briefly in her own person, Willa Cather says:

"One by one the heroes of that war, the men of dazzling soldiership, leave prematurely the world they have come back to. Airmen whose deeds were tales of wonder, officers whose names made the blood of youth beat faster, survivors of incredible dangers—one by one they quietly die by their own hand. Some do it in obscure lodging-houses, some in their offices, where they seemed to be carrying on their business like other men. Some slip over a vessel's side and disappear into the sea."

This passage needs to be set beside her remark in the prefatory note to *Not under Forty*: "the world broke in two in 1922 or thereabout." By the time she had finished *One of Ours* she was beginning to feel that estrangement from modern American life that was to grow more acute as she got older.

In a lecture at Omaha, in October 1921, she pointed to tendencies in Nebraska that were contrary to life itself and would surely suffocate art. Democracy was more and more applied as a regime of sameness, in which the Bohemian housewife must be encouraged to give up her ancestral recipes for roast goose and draw food from an array of tins, and her children were to be denied instruction in their rich and beautiful tongue so that they might speak English like all the rest of Nebraska, and nothing else. The new god was the short cut, dependent on the machine. "We have music by machines, we travel by machines—the American people are so submerged in them that sometimes I think they can only be made to laugh and cry by machinery." In art there were no short cuts and, besides, a dead level of sameness would be the end of art. To an interviewer in New York not long afterward she was more explicit about how the failure in American life would lead to a deterioration in American art.

"The Frenchman," she said,

doesn't talk nonsense about art, about self-expression; he is too greatly occupied with building the things that make his home. His house, his garden, his vineyards, these are the things that fill his mind. He creates something beautiful, something lasting. And what happens? When a French painter wants to paint a picture, he makes a copy of a garden, a home, a village. The art in them inspires his brush. And twenty, thirty, forty years later you'll come to see the original of that picture, and you'll find it changed only by the mellowness of time.

Restlessness such as ours, success such as ours, do not make for beauty. Other things must come first; good cookery, cottages that are homes, not playthings; gardens, repose. These are first rate things, and out of first rate stuff art is made. It is possible that machinery has finished us as far as this is concerned. Nobody stays at home any more; nobody makes anything beautiful any more.

That art depended on the artist's being able to find beauty and individuality in the world about him was not a conclusion to which she had come by reasoning: her own art was characteristically a flow of memories. The theme of a novel or a shorter story was hers as the outcome of much living and feeling. For the rest she depended on what she had observed and divined. If there had been no people within her experience in whom personal life flowed richly, she felt that as an artist she might as well have lived in an igloo. Sometimes, as she looked about her in the years after the First World War, she wondered if there would be much lost if she did elect the igloo.

Her friends noticed the pessimism that was so strangely unlike the exuberance of her youth and her first years in New York. In conversation she avoided self-analysis—she detested it in others as well as forbidding it to herself. The seriousness with which she was examining the world and herself in 1922 appears more sharply in an act than in anything she said. On December 27, in the company of her parents, she was confirmed in the Episcopal Church

by the Bishop of Western Nebraska, her old friend Dr.
Beecher. She had set her foot on the way that led to
Death Comes for the Archbishop and *Shadows on the
Rock*; and in the books that intervened she touched more
and more closely on religious issues.

III

One of Ours brought to Willa Cather a Pulitzer prize and
her first great popular success, happy omens both for her
association with her new publisher. When the prize was
announced she had finished the next of her novels, *A Lost
Lady*. That book, so apparently effortless, so deceptively
simple, had cost her more labor and involved her in more
frustration than anything she had attempted before. Miss
Lewis describes the chief problem it presented and the
various approaches Willa Cather tried:

Although *A Lost Lady* has been regarded by many critics as
the most perfect in form of all her novels, Willa Cather had, at
the start, more trouble with it than with any of the others. As
a rule she was unhesitating in her attack on a new piece of
work. She did not try first one way and then another, but took
at once, with sureness and great momentum, the road she
wished to follow. Her difficulty in the case of *A Lost Lady*
arose largely, I think, from the fact that *Mrs. Forrester* was
more a direct portrait than any of her other characters except
Ántonia; and although Mrs. Garber, from whom *Mrs. Forrester*
was drawn, and her husband, Governor Garber, were both
dead, some of their relatives were alive and might be (and,
indeed, were) offended. Probably because of this, she at first
set the scene of her story in Colorado, and wrote it at some
length in this setting. But she found it would not work. Her

memories of Mrs. Garber, and of the Garber place were among
the strongest, most enduring impressions of her childhood; a
whole ambiance of thought and feeling surrounded them, and
she could not transfer them to an artificial climate. So she
started the story anew, writing of things just as she remembered them.

But she still was not wholly satisfied with the construction of
the story. As nearly as I can recall, her dissatisfaction arose
from the difficulty of maintaining what she felt to be the right
balance in the presentation, which is sometimes direct, but
more often done through the boy *Niel*. When she had written
perhaps one-third of the story, she decided to change and
write it all in the first person, and she recommenced it a second time, and wrote several chapters in this manner.

That June [of 1922] she had accepted an invitation to give
two or three talks before the English classes at Breadloaf, Ver-
mont. . . . She took the two versions of *A Lost Lady*, so far as
she had written them, along with her, and in the week or so
that she spent at Breadloaf she went over them; and came then
to the conclusion that her first method was right. She discarded
the chapters she had written in the first person, and from that
time on wrote the story without any break or hesitation.

Even without the personal reason, one can see why to
maintain a balance in presenting the lost lady Mrs. Forrester was a problem, why Willa Cather needed the intelligent, appreciative young Niel Herbert (who is simply
Jim Burden from *My Ántonia* renamed, even to being
from the South), and why she could not trust the whole
story to Niel. He could not know how fully Mrs. Forrester was lost, living in the little Nebraska town of Sweet
Water, and he could not know how fully she was a lady

according to the code of the society in which she was a
figure. For that society is not in Sweet Water; no one else
in Sweet Water belongs to it, though Niel's bachelor uncle, Judge Pomeroy, hangs precariously on its edge. It is
the society of the "railroad aristocracy," about which
Willa Cather begins to speak in the first sentence of the
novel when she qualifies the Forresters' house as "well
known from Omaha to Denver for its hospitality and for
a certain charm of atmosphere." Later we are told that
railroad presidents leave their private cars on the siding
and scramble up the hill in their eagerness to be with the
Forresters; and that among the guests at one party was
Marshall Field—he is not reported as saying anything, but
the fabulous name is enough. For the effect Willa Cather
wants, the reader must believe from the beginning of the
novel that in this society Mrs. Forrester is accepted,
missed, sought out. Willa Cather takes this society with
completely serious respect; it was always her view that
the men who put through the railroads and organized the
settlement of the land were pioneers just as truly as any
farmer on the Divide; in both kinds of pioneers she found
the imagination and daring and warmth of life that she
constantly looked for. When a former president of the
Missouri Pacific praised *The Song of the Lark*, she felt a
contentment more instinctive and complete than any
purely literary critic could give her. We are to feel that
Mrs. Forrester is receiving an award of merit in the respect, interest, and gallantry of the railway pioneers.

   Her story lies in her decline from being a member of
their world to being a member of the village world of
Sweet Water. It can be apprehended best by someone

who has a place in that village world and from it at first
looks up to Mrs. Forrester as to a visitor from another
planet. This is the position of Niel Herbert, and when the
author appears more directly, she often takes this same
position, which was her own as a girl contemplating the
life of Governor Garber and his wife. The stages in Mrs.
Forrester's decline are few and strongly marked: Captain Forrester, who is twenty-five years older than his
wife, has a stroke; she takes a lover in the society of the
railroad aristocracy; the captain loses most of his money
in the panic of the nineties; illness and poverty mean that
the Forresters must stay at Sweet Water the year round;
the captain has another stroke; Mrs. Forrester loses her
lover; she drinks more and more heavily; the captain dies
leaving her little more than the house; she falls into the
hands of Ivy Peters. To pass from the society of the railway aristocracy to that of village roughs was quite within
Mrs. Forrester's range, provided that she was never without the desire and devotion of some strong male.

   She is the central variable in the novel; and the strongest reason why *A Lost Lady* has the very texture of life is
the number of variables in it, and the force with which
they act upon one another. The changes in the woman are
matched, or almost, by the changes in the village. Sweet
Water also has disappointed expectations; some of the best
villagers leave; others are elbowed aside; and in the new
order Ivy Peters is the type figure—a Bayliss Wheeler
with an addition of malignant cruelty and sensuality. Mrs.
Forrester had kept aloof from the village in its earlier and
better days; she comes to terms with the new order. Ivy
Peters is her lawyer, her confidential man, and, it is

strongly implied, her lover. The shift in Mrs. Forrester and the shift in the village come to us mainly through another variable, Niel Herbert, to whom a few years, a little experience, and some travel gradually bring new shades of comprehension and reservation. His disillusionment with Mrs. Forrester and with the village—in which the author shares—adds to the force of the downward movement in the novel.

That downward movement, becoming stronger and stronger, distinguished *A Lost Lady* from the other Western novels. The best days may have been the first to flee in *O Pioneers!* as well as in *My Ántonia*, but the downward movement in those works did not affect the central person. Ántonia's own days were of the best up to her last appearance, and it is implied that only death could injure them; the phase that is about to begin for Alexandra Bergson as *O Pioneers!* ends will be in keeping with her early appreciations and victories and will have a gentler poetry of its own. In *One of Ours* the glory had departed before the story opens, and the novel has an eddying movement until, with the great chance for escape and expression that the war provides, the movement turns sharply upward. *A Lost Lady*, written for the most part in that very year, 1922, in which Willa Cather fixed the breakup of the world, records the passing of a woman and a village from the regime of a Captain Forrester to that of an Ivy Peters. As Niel got ready in the last chapter to leave Sweet Water he "felt that he was going away for ever and was making the final break with everything that had been dear to him in his boyhood. The people, the very country itself, were changing so fast that there would be nothing to come back to." Niel did not trouble to say good-by to Mrs. Forrester; even more quickly than the village she had ceased to be as he had known her in the first days, which were the best. Carl Linstrum could come back to Alexandra Bergson after twelve years of wandering and find her essentially unaltered; after twenty years Jim Burden could come back to Ántonia and find her essentially unaltered; such as it was, the world in which Claude Wheeler grew up survived his death and could have been revisited by his spirit; but the woman and the village that Niel Herbert admired were as if they had never been. In the first three novels of the West Willa Cather had evoked the great decades; in *One of Ours* she had recorded the tame decades that followed; in *A Lost Lady* she had shown how the great decades gave place to the tame ones. Her record of Nebraska in fiction stood complete. If she were to write again of Nebraska, it would be only after she had learned from life to look deeper into the meanings of her memories. For the present the subject was exhausted.

The lifelike texture of *A Lost Lady* depends also on the avoidance of what is rigid and massive in structure or in style. Helen McAfee recalls that some time after the appearance of *The Song of the Lark* Willa Cather declared she would never write a novel of that detailed sort again, that she would aim at a more concentrated effect. In *One of Ours* she did write the detailed sort of novel, for the last time; it was in *A Lost Lady*, even more than in *My Ántonia*, that she showed what she could achieve by concentration. Ántonia, Jim Burden reflected toward the end of her story,

had always been one to leave images in the mind that did not fade—that grew stronger with time. In my memory there was a succession of such pictures, fixed there like the old woodcuts of one's first primer: Ántonia kicking her bare legs against the sides of my pony when we came home in triumph with our snake; Ántonia in her black shawl and fur cap, as she stood by her father's grave in the snowstorm; Ántonia coming in with her work-team along the evening sky-line. She lent herself to immemorial human attitudes which we recognize by instinct as universal and true.

Mrs. Forrester also left images that did not fade, and grew stronger with time; and in *A Lost Lady* these images stand out more boldly than the sequence of images concerning Ántonia. The images that give us Mrs. Forrester are more highly colored, and sometimes more richly phrased; but what is best about them is the amount of vitality they have, the movement, the intensity. When Willa Cather needs to tell us just what it was that Mrs. Forrester drew from her affair with that early lover who moved in the railroad aristocracy, she concentrates her meaning in an image, to which a half chapter leads. With her lover Mrs. Forrester goes out driving one winter afternoon on the pretext of getting some cedar boughs. The pair leave the cutter and carry their buffalo robes deep into the wood; after hours have passed, a village boy sees them return to the cutter. The lover goes back into the wood to get the forgotten boughs, and little Adolph Blum, lying behind a log, so near to Mrs. Forrester he could almost have touched her, finds that "when the strokes of the hatchet rang out from the ravine, he could see her eyelids flutter . . . soft shivers went through her body."

Intensity and economy of this kind were to mark the highly experimental books to which Willa Cather turned next, *My Mortal Enemy* and *The Professor's House*.

9

Religion
and the Artist

1924–1927

THE PROFESSOR'S HOUSE
MY MORTAL ENEMY
DEATH COMES FOR THE ARCHBISHOP

IN THE SUMMER of 1923, *A Lost Lady* completed, Willa Cather left for a long stay in France. She went almost at once to Ville-d'Avray, where Jan and Isabelle Hambourg had arranged a study for her in the house they had bought since her previous visit to France, when she was absorbing impressions for *One of Ours*. Miss Lewis writes: "The Hambourgs had hoped that she would make Ville-d'Avray her permanent home. But although the little study was charming, and all the surroundings were attractive, and the Hambourgs themselves devoted and solicitous, she found herself unable to work at Ville-d'Avray. She felt indeed that she would never be able to work there."

One outcome of this summer was the portrait by Léon Bakst, which hangs in the Public Library at Omaha. When funds had been subscribed, the first striking recognition Willa Cather had from people in her own state, she was asked to choose a painter. On the advice of friends she chose Bakst, though such a portrait was far from the usual round of his work. It was an unfortunate choice, though Willa Cather was immediately delighted with the man and enjoyed the talks she had with him and his friends during the twenty sittings. At one of these Nijinsky appeared. After he had been introduced and had kissed her hand, he withdrew to a corner and stood with his face to the wall. He believed himself to be a horse. It was plain to Willa Cather that Bakst, who was supporting a number of White Russians, was in great need of money, and she could not bring herself to cancel the commission. At each sitting she felt the portrait become more mistaken—stiff, dark, dead, lifeless—and she could tell from Bakst's desperation that he knew better than she how bad it was. She felt that she was behaving unworthily to the kind admirers in Omaha, but she could not say the word that would have extricated her from the false position. No expression of complaint, reproach, or even regret ever came from Omaha, and she was deeply touched by the magnanimous silence. After the sittings were over she escaped to Aix-les-Bains, where she stayed for several weeks of the early fall. It was here that the idea of *The Professor's House* began to take shape, and on her return to the apartment in Bank Street in November, she began at once to write that novel.

The Professor's House, at which she worked steadily through 1924, in Bank Street and, during the summer, at Grand Manan, is among the most revealing of her novels. Toward the end of the book Professor St. Peter reflects on what Tom Outland was spared in escaping by an early death "the trap of worldly success." "What change," the professor wonders, "would have come in his blue eye, in

his fine long hand with the back-springing thumb, which
had never handled things that were not the symbols of
ideas? A hand like that, had he lived, must have been
put to other uses. His fellow-scientists, his wife, the town
and State, would have required many duties of it. It
would have had to write thousands of useless letters,
frame thousands of false excuses. It would have had to
'manage' a great deal of money." No writer of her time
was more successful than Willa Cather in keeping freedom and anonymity. She never became an official personage, and the crucial decisions were taken in the years
of her first popular success, from 1923 to 1927. She declined to join societies, no matter who asked her, no matter what their aim; she declined to recommend books,
and wrote a review so rarely that she could decently avoid
pressures to be nice and helpful. Instead of working for
charities she gave as if from a bottomless purse to old
friends fallen on hard times, or institutions in Webster
County. If a letter appeared useless, she did not write it;
and instead of a false excuse she preferred a frank explanation, which usually saved her from repetition of a re-
quest she could not grant or an invitation she could not
accept. Her royalties mounted substantially with the popular success of *One of Ours* and she handled all money
matters herself; anything, she felt, was better than living
like the singer in "Coming, Aphrodite!" who used to drive
down to Wall Street and review her holdings in the light
of the latest oscillations of the market. Miss Lewis writes:

The struggle to preserve the integrity of her life as an artist,
its necessary detachment and freedom, cost her something—cost
a considerable expenditure of nervous energy, for it meant a

steady exertion of her will against the will of the public. But it was not disdain for the tributes people wished to pay her, or a feeling of superiority or indifference, that caused her to withdraw more and more from the world. It was self-preservation.

Into Professor St. Peter Willa Cather poured her grief at the decline of so many of the values she cherished. The postwar students at the small Midwestern college where he has taught since before the end of the last century are now, he thinks, a common lot. The young professors are utilitarian, political, self-interested. The programs have suffered by the pressure of the will of the state legislature and the community, for whom the ideal in higher education is a trade school passing under the name of college. The war which had taken the life of Tom Outland had, "in one great catastrophe, swept away all youth and all palms, and almost Time itself." [1]

The novel is a revelation of an attitude in Willa Cather more desolate by far than any fear of the price that worldly success tries to impose, or a disapproval of new forces in American life. There is a startling comment on its meaning in Alexander Porterfield's essay on Willa Cather, perhaps the most considered English estimate of her fiction. Mr. Porterfield says: "Briefly, it is the story of a scholarly professor at a Middle Western University passing through that critical, uneasy period between middle and old age—at least, it should be taken as a study of such, otherwise its meaning is difficult to perceive exactly." *The Professor's House* is a study of the passing, prematurely, from middle to old age, and St. Peter, at fifty-two, is exactly at the age the author reached in the year of the

---

[1] This sentence was deleted from the collected edition.

novel's appearance. But it is disquieting to find a critic shutting the door on his perception that there is in a book more than he can comprehend, and deciding that his comprehension is the measure of its meaning.

It is by a scrutiny of the approach to houses that the deepest meaning in the novel will disclose itself, and by the same token clarify the beautiful relation among the three parts in which it is arranged. At the outset Willa Cather presents St. Peter living between two houses. There is the expensive conventional house that he has built because his wife wanted it and into which he has moved with reluctance, with indeed a positive distaste that greatly surprises him; and there is the old rented frame house, ugly, inconvenient, run down, in which he has lived for thirty years—for the whole of his adult life, the whole of his career, the whole of his marriage. He finds that he can write, and think, only in its attic study, encumbered with the forms on which a dressmaker has fitted clothes for his wife and daughters ever since he was a young husband. It is oil-lit and stove-heated; it has almost every disadvantage a room can have; but it has been the home of his mind and spirit. It is very easy to mark the two houses as symbols of no apparent depth, nor do they acquire in the first part of the novel any depth beyond the practice of a Sinclair Lewis or a James T. Farrell.

The obviously surprising element in the structure of *The Professor's House* is its second part, a long story inserted after the fashion of Cervantes or Smollett, and giving, as Willa Cather has said, an effect similar to those Dutch pictures of an interior where a square window offers a contrasting vista of a gray sea or the masts of ships.

The length, vitality, and power of the intercalated tale are surprising, and not only at a first reading. The substance in this middle part of the novel is the crucial episode in the life of Tom Outland. Once and once only in the thirty years of his teaching St. Peter encountered a mind and personality of the first order, a student from whom he learned, and whose impress is strong upon the many-volumed history of Spanish exploration in America which brought St. Peter his fame, gave him his full mental and personal growth, and as a by-product provided the new house, built with literary prize money. When the novel opens, Tom is dead.

That crucial episode in Tom's life was the discovery of a Cliff-Dweller village in a New Mexican canyon. The discovery gave a new dimension to American life for Tom Outland. "I had read of filial piety in the Latin poets," he says, "and I knew that was what I felt for this place." Here was beauty, the beauty of pure and noble design, unspoiled by clutter or ornament, undistracted by cosiness, uncontradicted by the ugliness of machinery or industry. An expert to whom Tom showed some of the pottery was struck by its likeness to the decorative art of early Crete. The effect Willa Cather produces in her account of the Cliff-Dwellers, so much more vivid, so much more austere, than in the parallel passages in *The Song of the Lark*, is very near the evocation of the Greek town in the "Ode on a Grecian Urn." "It was as still as sculpture—and something like that. . . . The tower was the fine thing that held all the jumble of houses together and made them mean something. . . . That village sat looking down into the cañon with the calmness of eternity.

The falling snowflakes, sprinkling the piñons, gave it a special kind of solemnity . . . preserved in the dry air and almost perpetual sunlight like a fly in amber, guarded by the cliffs and the river and the desert." The houses of the Cliff-Dwellers are never overtly contrasted with those in the Middle Western college town where the first and third parts of the novel are laid; and in the modern town the emphasis falls on individual buildings, in the ancient village, significantly, on the architectural as well as the social unity of the whole.

A light but telling touch will show how firmly the novel has been stitched together. Between his discovery of the village in the canyon and his death a few years later, Tom made physics his principal study. He devised and patented a bulkheaded vacuum, which after his death became the nucleus of a great improvement in aircraft. He had willed everything to his fiancée, one of the professor's daughters, but with not a particle of the professor in her make-up. With some of the immense fortune the invention brought, she and her entrepreneur husband, a born front-office man, built a country house and called it Outland. The professor's new house is a wrong house, but wrong only by its acceptance of prevailing convention. Outland is much more deeply a wrong house. Although it stood on a high site, it held no reminiscence of the village in the canyon—it was a Norwegian manor-house set down in the sultry Middle West, without a vestige of American feeling. We are spared a sight of its interior, but are told what is to furnish it—the loot of the antique shops of Europe imported by way of a Spanish-American port in a dodge to avoid customs duties. This is the worst of all the houses in the novel, but there are a number of wrong modern houses—for instance, that in which the head of the physics department lived, "in the most depressing and unnecessary ugliness"—and none has any affinity with the village of the Cliff-Dwellers. With the kind of past it stands for, the ugly insensitive present seems to have no conceivable bond.

But in the third and final part of the novel the bond is suddenly revealed. The first and second parts, which have seemed so boldly unrelated, are brought into a profound unity. In the first part it was plain that the professor did not wish to live in his new house, and did not wish to enter into the sere phase of his life correlative with it. At the beginning of the third part it becomes plain that he cannot indefinitely continue to make the old attic study the theater of his life, that he cannot go on prolonging or attempting to prolong his prime, the phase of his life correlative with that. The personality of his prime—the personality that had expressed itself powerfully and in the main happily in his teaching, his scholarship, his love for his wife, his domesticity—is now quickly receding, and nothing new is flowing in. What begins to dominate St. Peter is something akin to the Cliff-Dwellers, something primitive that had ruled him long ago when he was a boy on a pioneer farm in the rough Solomon Valley in western Kansas. To this primitive being not many things are real. What counts above all is nature, seen as a web of life and finally of death.

The binding passage is in terms of houses:

[The Professor] . . . really didn't see what he was going to do about the matter of domicile. He couldn't make himself be-

lieve that he was ever going to live in the new house again. He
didn't belong there. He remembered some lines of a translation from the Norse he used to read long ago in one of his
mother's few books, a little two-volume Ticknor and Fields edition of Longfellow, in blue and gold, that used to lie on the
parlour table:

> *For thee a house was built*
> *Ere thou wast born;*
> *For thee a mould was made*
> *Ere thou of woman camest.*[2]

Lying on his old couch, he could almost believe himself in
that house already. The sagging springs were like the sham up-
holstery that is put in coffins. Just the equivocal American way
of dealing with serious facts, he reflected. Why pretend that it
is possible to soften that last hard bed?

He could remember a time when the loneliness of death had
terrified him, when the idea of it was insupportable. He used
to feel that if his wife could but lie in the same coffin with him,
his body would not be so insensible that the nearness of hers
would not give it comfort. But now he thought of eternal solitude with gratefulness; as a release from every obligation, from
every form of effort. It was the Truth.

All that had seemed a hanging back from the future—
the clinging to the old attic study, the absorption in Tom
Outland's quality and the civilization of the Cliff-Dwellers, the ways of the missionary fathers, the revival of in-

[2] Miss Cather was quoting from memory the opening of Longfellow's
translation of the Anglo-Saxon "Grave":

> *For thee was a house built*
> *Ere thou wast born,*
> *For thee was a mould meant*
> *Ere thou of mother camest.*

terest in the occupations of childhood and its pleasures—
was something very unlike what it had seemed. It was
profound, unconscious preparation for death, for the last
house of the professor.

Willa Cather had begun on. the surface with a record
of mediocrities, of the airless prosaic world of a small college town—how airless, how prosaic, only those who have
lived in one know; and with the disenchantment a distinguished spirit felt in the narrowing utilitarianism of
the postwar years. The mediocrities and the utilitarians
do not have everything their own way. For all his short-
comings on the surface, the head of the physics department is as sound in essence as one of Willa Cather's pioneers. Even through the first part of the novel the aura
about Tom Outland's name is an assurance of other values,
not as yet defined. St. Peter himself cannot be hemmed in
by what is here and now: the descendant of a Napoleonic
soldier, he has the look and many of the tastes of a Latin,
and on him is the mark of his preoccupation with the
Mediterranean culture and the Spanish explorers. Yet he
and those who belong with him do not dominate this first
part of the novel; they belong to a minority not only weak
numerically but edging to extinction. In the second part
the balance is reversed: the mediocrities and utilitarians—
in the main civil servants, remembered with contempt
and pity from Willa Cather's stays in Washington a quarter century earlier—are few and feeble; and against them
is set something that is quite overwhelming—the life the
Cliff-Dwellers lived, and the understanding of that life by
the sensitive and civilized Belgian priest Father Duchene,
to whom Tom turned for interpretation; and, in the fore-

ground throughout, Tom's own ever growing understanding of the Cliff-Dwellers and everything else.

The profound surprise for the reader is in the strange, short third part. Between the life of the Middle Western college town and the life of the Cliff-Dwellers' village the common quality is simply that both end in death. Guided by the feeling that they both end in death, we know how to measure them. What aspect of beauty, of dignity, even of interest would the ruins of the college town hold for Macaulay's New Zealander if he were to pause on this continent on his way to sketch the ruins of St. Paul's?

Not by any answers it proposes, but by the problems it elaborates, and by the atmosphere in which they are enveloped, *The Professor's House* is a religious novel. The parallels in Willa Cather's earlier fiction for the depth of self-scrutiny and the anxiety about alternatives in St. Peter all have to do with the rendering of artists, with the development of Thea Kronborg's talent or that of the sculptor from Kansas in *The Troll Garden*. In the one specimen of St. Peter's lecture we are permitted to overhear, the link between art and religion is forged in our presence:

As long as every man and woman who crowded into the cathedrals on Easter Sunday was a principal in a gorgeous drama with God, glittering angels on one side and the shadows of evil coming and going on the other, life was a rich thing. The king and the beggar had the same chance at miracles and great temptations and revelations. And that's what makes men happy, believing in the mystery and importance of their own little individual lives. It makes us happy to surround our creature needs and bodily instincts with as much pomp and circumstance as possible. Art and religion (they are the same thing, in the end, of course) have given man the only happiness he has ever had.

The shift is not a weakening in Willa Cather's belief in the primacy of art, but a bracketing of religion with art. The same bracketing occurs when Father Duchene sums up the distinction between the Cliff-Dwellers and other tribes of the region. On their mesa he feels, with reverence, humanity "lifted itself out of mere brutality," and the agencies by which it did so were art (as expressed in the ancient people's "distinct feeling for design," whether in the shaping of a water-pot or the grouping of the village) and religion (as expressed in their "manifold ceremonies and observances"). Less explicitly, Tom Outland makes the same response: for him the mesa, which was at first a stimulus to "adventure," assumed a beauty like that of sculpture, and finally aroused "a religious emotion." So it is with the novel as a whole; one passes from a record of happenings to the achievement of startling and satisfying form, and then to the suggestion of essential feeling about final issues.

II

The Professor's House was published in September 1925. Willa Cather had spent the early months of that year in Bank Street, writing *My Mortal Enemy*, the first part of which is mainly laid near by, in an apartment overlooking Madison Square and in hotels and restaurants in the lower Fifth Avenue district. The New York of this story is the city of the early 1900's, the New York of "Paul's Case," with a sensuous richness and metropolitan glamour it had

held for Willa Cather in the years when she came on from
Pittsburgh for brief visits packed with going to the opera
and the theater and dining out. Myra Driscoll Henshawe,
the protagonist, is a study of a woman, older by a full generation, whom Willa Cather had known well through con-
nections in Lincoln, and who had died before the First
World War, but whose life and nature could be understood only by one whose religious sense had become acute.
Although the story was awkwardly short for a book, Willa
Cather believed that it should appear by itself, that it was
in fact a book. She had misgivings about the judgment
Alfred A. Knopf would pass. Twenty years later she still
spoke with enthusiasm of his quick response to *My Mortal
Enemy.* He made no difficulty about publishing it as it
was, and his opinion was speedily ratified by the sales,
which required five printings before the end of 1926, and
by the closeness with which the critics discussed a psychological portrait that was felt to be sharp and original,
if at points a little mystifying.

All that Willa Cather cared to do with Myra, all that
she needed to do, could be done quickly, by showing her
at two points—as a mature worldly woman and ten years
later face to face with death. Her childhood and youth
could be sketched in sparing strokes in a retrospect. The
first picture abounds in the poetry of worldliness. It is
drawn for us by a young provincial girl, agog at the re-
finements of Myra's dress, the distinction of her speech,
her imperial manner, the devotion of her husband, the
charm of her apartment, the interest of her friends, among
them an actor, a young poetess, and Madame Modjeska
herself, whom Willa Cather had once met and who is an

enriching thread through the story. But the worldliness is not a complete armor. At moments when there is not enough money—she had given up a fortune to marry as she wished—or when her husband's devotion, extreme as it is, comes short of what she requires, Myra becomes another being, malevolent and rough. In the first picture there is just enough of this other being to render the future ominous.

The second picture is drawn by the same person, but in the interval of ten years she has ceased to be provincial; she has as much insight and sympathy as are compatible with being twenty-five; but she is as much puzzled by Myra's new phase as when in her middle teens she had come under the spell of her worldliness. The distance between the subject and the portrayer has, if anything, increased. Myra has lost almost all that had given to her life the appearance and atmosphere of enviable achievement. Not only is she incurably ill (she is shown in the last four months of her life); she has drifted out of the orbit of her friends—Modjeska is dead; the money is gone; the New York apartment has given place to a miserable room in a jerrybuilt hotel on the west coast. What remains to her is simply her husband's devotion; and the growth of her other self has turned her against this and against him. He has become, she says, her mortal enemy, the idol that drew her away from the course of life that was natural to her.

Myra's feeling about her husband is bound up with the revival in her of a self that, like St. Peter's early self, found no expression in the values of her prime. It was a rough self that had nothing to do with artistic friends or

charming apartments or gentle husbands; it was the product of her Irish forebears, and of the fierce willful uncle
who brought her up. But within the roughness was an intense religious feeling. As death approaches, Myra feels
that her marriage to "a German freethinker" has separated her from religion, and she returns "ardently to the
faith of her childhood." Her thoughts run on profound religious values. The young priest who attends her exclaims,
to our amazement, "I wonder whether some of the saints
of the early Church weren't a good deal like her." His
remark amazes because Myra has none of the kindness,
charity, or humility that we conventionally associate with
a religious spirit; but it also illuminates—for it becomes
plain to us that this worldly woman has passed out of
worldliness into preoccupation with primary realities. Her
final mood is much like St. Peter's: she cares for light and
silence and solitude, the sweep of the wind, the sight and
smell of broad waters. It is her triumph that when she
comes to die she has all these circumstances—and unlike
St. Peter she has a crucifix.

My Mortal Enemy is a pure instance of what in an article for the *New Republic,* written in 1922, Willa Cather
had called "the novel *démeublé,*" the novel stripped of its
superfluous furnishings. It is the boldest experiment she
had made in leaving out, in the subordination of secondary characters, the abbreviation of incidents, the reduction of settings to where "they seemed to exist, not so
much in the author's mind, as in the emotional penumbra
of the characters themselves." Nothing distracts from the
rendering of Myra, least of all the style, fluid and transparent beyond anything Willa Cather had accomplished.

Economy and concentration do not lead to slightness: Bartley Alexander had been drawn rather as a theater in which two selves conflicted, but Myra Henshawe is a full personality, subject to development as well as to conflict, and she is as completely realized as Mrs. Forrester herself. Of all Willa Cather's writings this is the one on which Sarah Orne Jewett's judgment would have been most rewarding.

III

In the summer of 1925, accompanied by Edith Lewis, Willa Cather stayed for months in New Mexico, making Santa Fe her center. The essential story of the Southwest, she had come to believe, was neither that of its ancient Indian civilizations nor that of the Spanish explorers and martyrs: it was that of the French missionaries in the nineteenth century. About these remarkable men she had heard from Father Haltermann in her first visit to the region. He was now an invalid, after his service in the war; she had seen him but once and she was unable to see him again; but he had produced an impression. From old traders and Mexicans she had met during her many visits she had heard so much of the first Archbishop, Lamy, that she "never passed the life-size bronze of him which stands under a locust tree before the Cathedral in Santa Fé without wishing that I could learn more about a pioneer churchman" whose career had been so extraordinary, and whose countenance expressed, in every reproduction, "something fearless and fine and very, very well-bred— something that spoke of race."

While she was in Santa Fe in 1925 she came on an ob-

scure book, printed at Pueblo, Colorado, seventeen years
before, Father W. J. Howlett's *Life of the Right Reverend
Joseph P. Machebeuf, Pioneer Priest of Ohio, Pioneer
Priest of New Mexico, Pioneer Priest of Colorado, Vicar
Apostolic of Colorado and Utah, and First Bishop of Denver*. When Willa Cather opened the biography of Bishop
Machebeuf her interest was already fixed in the personality and experience of his friend Jean Lamy. How much
she may have known about Machebeuf before she read
Father Howlett's book cannot be said for sure—probably
it was very little. The record of his life, and especially the
long intimate letters to his sister and brother in Auvergne,
made a strong appeal to her feelings, for he was the ideal
of a missionary bishop, the very man to spread a faith and
found its institutions on the frontier. All the interest and
respect Bishop Beecher had aroused in her went to
strengthen and brighten her response to Bishop Machebeuf. He would have been in his element breasting the
winds on the Divide, raising a church for the Bohemians
near Blue Hill, trading secrets of cookery with Ántonia,
begging a horse from Captain Forrester. He was a man of
the people—his father was a baker—impulsive, cordial,
violent, enduring. He is drawn in the figure of Father
Vaillant, very much in the manner of the secondary characters in the Nebraska novels, with emphatic lights and
shades, massively, with no suggestion of mystery or hagiography.

   A character with such vitality, when given the second
place throughout an extended narrative, is likely to seize
the first just as Mercutio threatened to overshadow Ro-
meo. Nothing in *Death Comes for the Archbishop* is more

masterly than the novelist's instinct of how fully and
warmly Father Vaillant could be rendered without jeop-
ardy to the primary position of the Archbishop. In the
prologue there is no mention of Father Vaillant, and in
the first two chapters of the first part the Archbishop
comes to grips with the Southwest alone. The record of
the journey to Santa Fe in Father Howlett's book gave the
two priests equal prominence; but in the novel it is only
in the later chapters of the first part, after they are in-
stalled at Santa Fe, that the two friends appear together.
How much could be safely risked is best shown in the
first chapter of the second book, where Father Vaillant
appears by himself, in the vigorous episodes at Manuel
Lujon's ranch, where the priest marries, baptizes, cooks
his lamb *saignant,* begs the two beautiful white mules,
and by all he says as well as does fixes his nature for us
forever. Throughout the third and fourth books Willa
Cather again refuses him a role, and by the beginning of
the fifth, when he returns to the scene, the Archbishop's
less definite, less expansive character has by subtle and
gradual means made itself the center of the narrative. It
was not necessary, though it was a gain for the climax and
the symmetry of the book, that Willa Cather shift the
chronology of her materials and have the Archbishop out-
live his friend and go to his funeral.

The vitality of Father Vaillant is not the only hazard to
the effect the Archbishop is to produce. The obvious opportunity for a dramatic conflict between the Archbishop
and his circumstances is refused: the sensitive, aristocratic, scholarly man at once accepts and finally loves the
wild country of his diocese, the rough people, the alien

traditions. His troubles with the native clergy—all the
Spaniards had been required to leave in 1821, thirty years
before the Archbishop came, and all who remained were
natives of the region or of Mexico—do not disturb his inner peace, and his victory over those who oppose him appears easy and inevitable—much easier than Lamy's victory was in historical fact. No conflict of exciting force
enters the Archbishop's life. Most of the recorded events
occur in the late afternoon, usually toward sunset, and as
one succeeds another the record seems as serene and gen-
tly melancholy as the cadences in which it is conveyed.

The appeal the Archbishop made to Willa Cather hung
on the absence of such inner conflict as Professor St. Peter sustained. The Archbishop is the great example in her
fiction of a personality extraordinarily fine and cultivated
finding on the Western plains the ideal circumstances for
his life. Torn herself, during so many decades, between
the appeal of the Divide and her home in Red Cloud and
the appeal of the cities of the east coast, with their opera,
concerts, and galleries, she experienced an intense if
somewhat sad pleasure in contemplating a life that was
not torn but was a seamless unity.

The narrative is in essence, however, something much
more than a presentation of the two French priests and
of the traditions and qualities they embody. They would
not wholly suit Willa Cather's purpose—their story would
not be the story of the Southwest—if in any way they came
short in appreciation of the region—its aspect, its people, its
past. Here Indian villages, the exploits of the Spanish adventurers as well as of the missionaries, the coming of a
new layer of high civilization with the French priests, and

the small but true contribution of the best of the great-hearted Anglo-Saxon adventurers—men like Kit Carson—are set before us as on a frieze. The composition of this frieze, in the grouping of its figures and their portrayal against a living background, is the most beautiful achievement of Willa Cather's imagination. In it at last her craftsmanship and her vision were in relation, and that relation was complete. The length of her unconscious preparation to write it had served her well indeed.

Willa Cather had always understood that a person's relation to a place might be as valuable to him, and as decisive in his growth or retardation, as any relation he might have with other persons. What happens in one place could not happen in just the same way in any other. Thea Kronborg could not have taken from Moonstone or from Chicago what the villages of the Cliff-Dwellers gave her. But in the earlier novels the landscape did not impinge upon the reader with the vitality that distinguishes it in *Death Comes for the Archbishop.*

The Archbishop, from the first of his appearances, is "sensitive to the shapes of things." We see him as he rides alone through a waste area of New Mexico, a mass of uniform conical red sandhills on which conical junipers are symmetrically spotted; the "geometrical nightmare" oppresses his spirits and he shuts his eyes; when he opens them, the first thing he sees is a unique juniper—"living vegetation could not present more faithfully the form of the Cross." The sight of that juniper is a turning-point for him. Color matters to the Archbishop as much as shape. One day years after his arrival in the Southwest, following by accident an unfamiliar road on his way to Santa

Fe, he found among many green hills one that was yellow
—"a strong golden ochre much like the gold of the sunlight." This, he knew at once, was his cathedral. Better
no other church than the simple little adobe he found
when he came to Santa Fe—better than a red brick horror
such as he had known in his days in the diocese of Cin-
cinnati. The vicar was quite unmoved when he was shown
the yellow stone; he had always assumed that when there
was a cathedral at Santa Fe, it would be a large pile of
red brick, and he did not see that it mattered.

Much to his own surprise, Archbishop Latour decides
against returning to his native Auvergne to pass the years
of his retirement and preparation for death. The ties of his
family, the promise of fine architecture on every side, and
of the scholarly associations of which through his long
years in Santa Fe he had been deprived, were less powerful than the atmosphere of New Mexico. When he wakens
in the early morning at Santa Fe, the Southwestern air
communicates to him a conviction of eternal youth, of energy, of ever possible spiritual growth. A response of this
kind might have been a part of *My Ántonia* or of *The Song
of the Lark*, but at the time when she wrote those novels
Willa Cather could not have found such language as she
uses in conveying the quality of the atmosphere at Santa
Fe. "His first consciousness was a sense of the light dry
wind blowing in through the windows, with the fragrance
of hot sun and sagebrush and sweet clover; a wind that
made one's body feel light and one's heart cry, 'To-day,
to-day,' like a child's. . . . Something soft and wild and
free, something that whispered to the ear on the pillow,
lightened the heart, softly, softly picked the lock, slid

the bolts, and released the prisoned spirit of man into the
wind, into the blue and gold, into the morning, into the
morning!" Her craftsmanship in language, her sense of a
true economy, her command of rhythms individual without being eccentric, had never before reached such a delicate sureness. It is the language that makes the impressions of the New Mexican landscape superior to any
presentation of setting in the earlier books. She had borne
the memories of this landscape in her mind for a long
time; at last she had the words to convey them in simple,
perfect strength.

The same sure delicacy marks her manipulation of character and incident, a richer material than she had ever before worked in, more varied, more intense, and at times
more heroic. The deliberate and often pondered movement in the earlier narratives is now replaced by a
movement wonderfully quick and light, beautifully appropriate to the atmosphere. It is always through the Archbishop's eyes that we catch the splendor of Southwestern
sunsets, the spirit shining through the faces of Mexican,
Indian, and American types, the somber beauty of the
old Spanish churches, but it is the vicar who is our guide
to the appreciation of human qualities. The Archbishop
knew that he had difficulty in responding to people, that
he was impeded by a reserve and an inadaptability only
rarely to be overcome. He admired, and in a pious sense
he envied, the warmth in his friend, to whom every encounter with a person, even with a convicted murderer,
was an opportunity. No matter what parish the vicar was
given, no matter whom he met on his travels, he delighted
in the humanity of everyone, and everyone delighted in

his—"he added a glow to whatever human society he was dropped into." The Indians and Mexicans he met in the new diocese seemed to him the purest Christians he had known, souls like those in the primitive age of the Church. Guiding them was, he felt, "work for the heart, for a particular sympathy, and none of the new priests" from his own Auvergne understood "those poor natures" as he did. To the Archbishop he bursts out: "I am *their man.*" He responds to them both as groups and as individuals, always prizing in each not what is unlike others but the binding quality of humanity.

The Archbishop's appreciation was reserved for rare individuals such as Kit Carson. He had long wished to meet the scout, and when he did, he "felt a quick glow of pleasure in looking at the man. As he stood there in his buckskin clothes one felt in him standards, loyalties, a code which is not easily put into words, but which is instantly felt when two men who live by it come together by chance." The Archbishop had the same sense of immediate and instinctive unity with the Navajo chief Eusabio, who had the face of a Roman general in the time of the Republic, the authority of a natural force and fineness; it was through his intimacy with Eusabio that the Archbishop had so strong a compassion for the Navajos, long hunted for the bounty the Mexican government had set, under American rule driven from the region of their gods beyond the boundaries their gods had forbidden them to cross. The vicar would have loved them for themselves. A rare extremity of misfortune borne with courage by a very simple person would move the Archbishop as much as Kit Carson's splendid integrity and daring or Eusabio's austere intensity. In the chapter called "December Night" —Willa Cather liked it so much she allowed it to be republished as a Christmas book in 1933—the Archbishop responded to the devotion of an old Mexican woman living as a slave among people who despised her, a woman who could not read and could scarcely think, as the deepest experience of religion he had ever beheld. What led the Archbishop to feel with such strength was not the individuality of old Sada but the height to which religion rose in her. The complementary natures of the two clerics allow a record of all that called for appreciation in the people of the Southwest: at the center is the Archbishop's response to whatever is distinguished and exalted, surrounding it is the vicar's quick infectious pleasure in all that is human.

In the structure of the book what might have become solid masses, comparable with long reaches in the earlier novels, is broken up by brief tales inset with an apparent casualness that recalls the ingenious narrative manner of Cervantes or Smollett. Willa Cather had done this many times before; one has only to recall the story of the Russian wedding and the chase of the wolf pack interpolated early in *My Ántonia*; but in the earlier novels this material seemed sometimes to intrude and delay the march of the story; it was not a part of its organic structure. Willa Cather could not resist piling anecdote on story, and fable on anecdote; her largest experiment of this kind is the perfect placing of the *nouvelle* of Tom Outland into the novel of *The Professor's House*. By the time she wrote *Death Comes for the Archbishop* she had mastered the art of the inset. It is the manner appropriate to the older and better kind of hagiography, simple, concrete, unemphatic, concentrated. The material lends itself at every turn to the narrative within the narrative—tales of miracles and old Church happenings, miniature stories, such as the anecdote of the Mexican youth devoted to the rooster he had bred for cockfighting or the touching miracle of the neophyte to whom the Mother of God appears, clad in blue and gold, and leaves a painted picture of herself on his *tilma,* the mantle worn only by the very poor. The tale of the bold and evil friar who ruled on the crag at Ácoma is among the perfect short narratives, suggestive, swimming in the atmosphere of the time and the place, without a touch of false exaggeration or falser complexity. At every turn in the story the setting is alive, almost overpoweringly sensible: the friar and his clerical guests at dinner and the servant whom he kills say next to nothing, but we catch them in their characterizing attitudes and know them as human beings. The height in Willa Cather's success is in the pages that follow the death and evoke a silence and immobility as thick and ominous as Conrad with his more lavish methods could suggest. With the simplest of means, which are also the most difficult, she has accomplished a triumph.

In its simplest terms, *Death Comes for the Archbishop* is a chronicle of two missionaries and of the Southwest in which they carry out their appointed tasks; their response to the new land and their memories of the old; their relations to people and things each in his own way as well as to the past, and this interspersed by relevant anecdote and recollection, an accretion of story and tale which is the making of folklore, history, literature. In the pages in

which landscape and character merge in vivid pictorial
narrative there is much more than the *tableau vivant*, the
effect of a Puvis de Chavannes mural, for the muralist
painted with a purposeful thinness and an exaggerated
two-dimensionalism whereas Miss Cather is able to use
color in its richest and fullest tones and depth and perspective. There is a quality of feeling conveyed by material and language which, as Rebecca West discerned when
the book was first published, translates the work into the
realm of the senses so that on every page there are for the
reader not only the tones but the overtones: the mesas
and the cloud-mesas, the contrasts between the Southwest
and Auvergne, the constant balancing of pioneer life and
of civilization beyond the seas and the ever present sense
of a beneficent and also ominous nature—the crash of
thunder in the canyons, the sinister deep hum, like the
buzzing of bees, of an underground river heard through a
fissure in the rock. And there is food: the savory smell of
the *potage,* the rich swimming gravy which brings into
play the drama at Ácoma, the *gigot d'agneau saignant*
carved by Father Vaillant, "a delicate stream of pink
juice" following the knife. All the senses seem to have
been in Willa Cather's pen as she wrote the book.

There is another side to the book which Willa Cather
herself described—"a conjunction of the general and the
particular." She did not address herself at any point to
the larger problem of the paternal Church courting dominion and prosperity in the New World as well as carrying out the propagation of the faith; what Willa Cather
was trying to tell was the story of man's capacity to establish dominion over the immutable, as the farmers had

done in Nebraska. The Rock was here "the utmost expression of human need." Man too could learn to be as
hard and as steadfast as rock. In the rock, however, was
rigidity, while in man there was suppleness of spirit and
the endless realm of feeling. In no portion of *Death Comes
for the Archbishop* is this conjunction of general and particular better exemplified than in the chapter in which
the austere Bishop is confronted with the sensual, carnal
priest: Bishop Latour represents the triumph of discipline
and religion and the mind over things temporal; Padre
Martínez accepts the appetites and lust as a reality with
which he will not argue, yet he is exemplary and passionate in his religious devotions. The dramatic power of the
book is never higher than in the description of Latour's
visit to Taos and the home of the insurgent Mexican padre; the place is in disorder; the signs of worldliness and
of carnality are everywhere; "the place seemed overrun
by serving-women, young and old—and by large yellow
cats with full soft fur, of a special breed, apparently."
During their meal the talk gravitates to celibacy, and Martínez, who has defiantly introduced Latour to his son, at-
tacks it: it may be well for the French clergy, he argues,
but not for the Mexican. Had not St. Augustine himself
written it was better not to go against nature? "Celibate
priests lose their perceptions," Martínez says. "No priest
can experience repentance and forgiveness of sin unless
he himself falls into sin." A priest must not make of religion mere "dead logic." When Latour sharply demurs and
warns Martínez that he intends to have the priests in his
diocese keep their vows, Martínez responds: "We have a
living Church here, not a dead arm of the European

Church. Our religion grew out of the soil, and has its own roots."

Bishop Latour goes to bed troubled. He does not "like the air of this house . . . the clatter of dish-washing and the giggling of women across the *patio*" keep him awake, and on the floor he thinks he sees a mouse, only to discover it is a little "bunch of woman's hair that had been indolently tossed into a corner when some slovenly female toilet was made in this room."

Yet the same Padre Martínez, so rebellious, disorderly, and carnal, presides the next morning in a beautifully ordered church, clean and in good repair, and the Bishop "had never heard the Mass more impressively sung than by Father Martínez." His baritone emerges "from some deep well of emotional power" and "nothing in the service was slighted, every phrase and gesture had its full value." He discovers too that Martínez knows his country and finds him deeply versed not only in the Church Fathers but in the Latin and Spanish classics. Willa Cather traces the contrasting sides of this worldly scoundrel and libertine, yet devout and religiously inspired priest with such skill that Latour's decision not to change "the curious situation" comes as no surprise. "It is not expedient to interfere," he explains to Father Vaillant. "The church is strong, the people are devout. No matter what the conduct of the priest has been, he has built up a strong organization, and his people are devotedly loyal to him. . . . For the present I shall be blind to what I do not like there."

When Father Vaillant protests that Martínez's life is an open scandal, the Bishop replies: "I do not wish to lose the parish of Taos in order to punish its priest." What

Bishop Latour has seen in his wisdom is that the passion
Martínez gives to living is also given to the Church; and
that the Church must recognize realities and mold them
patiently to ultimate ends. Latour knows the Church's
time will come. "Padre Martínez is getting too old to play
the part of Don Juan much longer," he observes. And he
knows also that if ultimately Martínez is to be replaced, it
will have to be by a Spanish, not a French priest.

To the writing of this chapter, with its heightened
drama—the confrontation of two churchmen, the sensuous with the austere, the ebullient priest of the New
World with the disciplined priest of the Old—Willa
Cather brought not a heavy load of scholarship and reading, as Rebecca West seemed to think, but broad sympathies with men and an understanding of the problems
civilized persons encounter in the wilderness; one who
had made the jump from Virginia to Nebraska in childhood, and from Nebraska eastward as a young woman,
could understand the contrast between Auvergne and
New Mexico. Willa Cather suggested that writing the
book was "like a happy vacation from life, a return to
childhood, to early memories." This sense of the past per-
meates the work from beginning to end.

In their appreciation of the past, Latour responds to the
historical record, Vaillant to the interwoven strand of legend and miracle. Early in the narrative the contrast in interest is amusingly underlined. The Archbishop, who has
returned from a long journey, is awakened on the first
morning by a bell that the vicar has had hung. He dis-
misses the experience as a dream, a reminder of the mornings when he had awakened to the Angelus sounding at

St. John Lateran, but with a suggestion also, that puzzles him, of something Oriental. The vicar tells him that the bell is Spanish, with the date 1356 inscribed; that after its shipment to the New World it was brought by cart—the largest bell in North America!—the thousands of difficult miles from Mexico City, that it hung for over a hundred years in the Church of San Miguel at Santa Fe, and then lay for another hundred in a cellar. For the Archbishop the history of Spain in America is in that bell: a century of eclipse and ruin after an age of hardy achievement guided by a religious feeling that overrode all practical obstacles and expressed for the New World that affinity of religion with art and beauty which had grown up in the Old. The Archbishop broods, to the vicar's discomfort, on the Oriental suggestion in the bell's tone—it must come of Moorish workmanship or a Moorish formula, the infidels from Africa having taught the Spaniards to work finely in metals, as the Spaniards taught the Navajos. The vicar, for whom such musing is too thin-spun, too disengaged from faith, responds with a plea that the Archbishop receive a simple native priest who has just come back, edified, from the shrine of Our Lady of Guadalupe, burning to tell of the miracles wrought there since Mary's first appearance in the New World, in 1531. "Doctrine is well enough for the wise," he adds, "but the miracle is something we can hold in our hands and love."

10

The Rock

1928–1931

THE ORIGIN OF *Shadows on the Rock* was very unlike that of *Death Comes for the Archbishop*. The narrative of the Southwest was undertaken thirteen years after Willa Cather's first strong response to the country and the people; it drew on one of the most lasting enthusiasms of her life. For the narrative of French Canada there was no such background of slowly accumulating knowledge and feeling.

What associations with Canada she had had before she resolved to write *Shadows on the Rock* were unrelated to the French elements in its life and history. In the early years of their marriage Isabelle and Jan Hambourg lived in Toronto, and Willa Cather was often with them for short visits; but Toronto is as alien from French Canada as Pittsburgh itself. To Isabelle Hambourg, indeed, it seemed another Pittsburgh, another city ruled by the values of business and the social conventions of an incurious and intolerant upper middle class, where the only friends worth making were musicians and artists and an occasional exile from a more cultivated world.

In the summer of 1922 Willa Cather took an old cottage on the island of Grand Manan in the Bay of Fundy, off the coast of New Brunswick. The bright warm days and

cool nights, the natural beauty of the place, the great remove from all harassments, were ideal accompaniments
to writing. After another stay on the island she had a cottage built in the autumn of 1925. It still stands, unoccu-
pied since her death, on a sloping hillside about fifty
yards from the edge of the cliffs, in the middle of an open
meadow, and with a semicircle of spruce and birch woods
not far off. In the large undivided attic, with a vista of
cliffs and sea, she did her writing, and much of *Shadows
on the Rock* was written on Grand Manan. The pleasure
this place gave Willa Cather has been described by Miss
Lewis:

The outdoor surroundings were unsurpassably lovely. The
weather had a perpetual enchantment; it was always changing,
and all the changes were interesting and beautiful. There was
a kind of gentleness and innocence in the natural character of
the Island; wild flowers grew everywhere in the clean grass, the
streams that rushed in waterfalls over the cliffs were pure and
uncontaminated, the wild creatures that lived in the woods
never harmed anybody; even the slender, emerald-green snakes
one occasionally met on the paths seemed friendly and sociable
—did not glide away as one approached. The wild snow-shoe
hares that came close to the cottage to nibble at the clover
would creep under the very chair one was sitting in. Birds often built their nests four or five feet from the ground in the
little spruce trees. Sometimes, at dawn or dusk one encountered a deer or fawn.

There was solitude without loneliness. One could walk for
miles along the cliffs without meeting anyone or seeing any
mark of human life; but there was always activity on the water. Small craft of all kinds went to and fro, setting out lines,
visiting the herring weirs, carrying lumber. Indians from the

reservation at Point Pleasant sometimes paddled over to the Island in their canoes—looking down from the cliffs one would see a string of them rounding a point.

The "solitude without loneliness" of which Miss Lewis speaks was exemplified in the sense Willa Cather had of being securely hemmed in from the world, embraced in the soft damp intensity of isolation by the great all-engulfing fogs that settled around this pinpoint on the North Atlantic, sometimes for days. And on some days there was no sound but that of the beating rain, the roaring waters, and the British buoy whose bell melodiously seemed to call from a great distance.

The aspect of the island, and of its life, had much the same kind of charm that Sarah Orne Jewett had felt along the Maine coast, not many miles to the south. The people on the island, apart from the summer visitors, who came chiefly from the United States and the English cities of Canada, were maritime Canadians, akin to the people Miss Jewett knew in the Maine villages.

Willa Cather had been in Canada much more than most American writers before she wrote *Shadows on the Rock*, but there had been nothing in her Canadian associations to give her an awareness, let alone a feeling, of what was remarkable in the French region of that divided country.

Far more important as preparation was her long and admiring preoccupation with the literature, arts, and history of France. At the University of Nebraska she had found August Hjalmar Edgren a teacher of romance languages and a philologian of international reputation, and it was in part by the insight he communicated that even as a girl she could pierce beyond the techniques of the nine-

teenth-century novelists she read so constantly to some
sense of the European life and feeling that enabled men
to achieve techniques so subtle and so fine. Dorothy Canfield, who had passed much of her childhood in Paris, and
her mother, who felt Paris to be a second home, gave her
a yet more intimate sense of what it meant to be French.
In 1902, when she had visited France for the first time,
Willa Cather's enthusiasm was stirred not only at Rouen,
sacred to her because of Flaubert and Maupassant, or
Barbizon, but most of all in the south, especially at Avignon, where she came under the spell of a France that was
older than any of her literary or artistic cults, the France
from which the *ancien régime* in Canada derived. The
story she was writing in the last years of her life was to
express what Avignon, the Avignon of the popes, had
meant to her over a period of forty years. In the summer
of 1920 on the left bank of the Seine and on the Île Saint-
Louis she was exploring streets and churches not very different in aspect from the time when the footsteps of
Count Frontenac or Monseigneur Laval might have re-
sounded in them.

Memories and feelings from her experiences in France
and with French things stirred suddenly when in the summer of 1928, going to Grand Manan by a roundabout way,
she first saw the city of Quebec. As she was soon to write,
"These heavy grey buildings, monasteries and churches,
steep-pitched and dormered, with spires and slated roofs,
were roughly Norman Gothic in effect. They were made
by people from the north of France who knew no other
way of building. The settlement looked like something
cut off from one of the ruder towns of Normandy or Brit-

tany, and brought over." Willa Cather had an extraordinary power of obliterating from a historic scene its modern encrustations. She had done so at Avignon, and at
Paris, more recently at Santa Fe; she did so again at Quebec. Edith Lewis, who accompanied her, fell ill the evening of their arrival at the Château Frontenac Hotel and
was ordered to bed for ten days. Willa Cather walked
about the city and its environs; Miss Lewis remembers
the excitement with which she described her successive
discoveries—the convent of the Ursulines, the great Laval
seminary, the Church of Notre Dame in the lower town,
the old marketplace. In the evenings they read histories
from the hotel library, especially the chronicles of Parkman.

For Willa Cather, Parkman had always been the best of
American historians, and it was through his eyes that she
began to see the life of Quebec in the seventeenth century. The fifth part of his history opens:

The events in this book group themselves in the main about
a single figure, that of Count Frontenac, the most remarkable
man who ever represented the crown of France in the New
World. From strangely unpromising beginnings, he grew with
every emergency, and rose equal to every crisis. His whole career was one of conflict, sometimes petty and personal, sometimes of momentous consequence, involving the question of national ascendency on this continent.

Willa Cather adopted Parkman's conception of Frontenac,
the man from the heart of the Old World—aristocrat, intimate of princes, professional soldier—who, arriving in the
New when he was past fifty, acted with the vigor and
resilient adaptation to circumstance of a young Alexander

and proved precisely the leader the New World required. She followed Parkman, with some softening of the colors, in his picture of Frontenac's irascibility and contentiousness, his fiery, dominating nature, his harsh humor, his power to transmit his confidence in his invincibility; she also followed Parkman—perhaps went somewhat beyond him—in an almost tender sympathy with Frontenac's old age, his solitariness upon the rock of Quebec, his disillusionment with his associates and with his King, the frustration of his wish to die in France. It was in the last year of Frontenac's life that she set her story, and with his death it ended. Parkman's rationalism and anticlericalism had no effect upon her; of Frontenac's disputes with the Jesuits, and his determination to confine the Canadian church within the limits of an authority that was purely spiritual, despite Parkman's approving emphasis, she has little to say. She could enjoy, and repeat with a few changes for dramatic effect, his passage on Mother Catherine de Saint-Augustin's grinding a bit of Brébeuf's bone into the gruel prepared for a heretic she was attending and thus winning him for the Catholic faith. The skeptical apothecary Auclair is indignant at the entrance of such poisonous matter into a digestive tract; but though she sympathizes with his response, this passage is not characteristic of *Shadows on the Rock*.

Willa Cather's general attitude toward friars, nuns, and Jesuits, miracles and ceremonies, is in agreement with what she found in the second of her principal sources, the *Jesuit Relations*. She rejected entirely Parkman's conception of Bishop Laval, whom he disliked even more warmly than he admired the Bishop's great adversary, Frontenac.

Admitting what no one could deny, the energy of Laval's nature, the genuineness of his austerity, and the perfect consistency of his life and policy with his faith, Parkman's judgment is extremely severe:

He thought himself above human law. In vindicating the rights of the church, he invaded the rights of others and used means from which a healthy conscience would have shrunk. . . . He was penetrated by the poisonous casuistry of the Jesuits based on the assumption that all means are permitted when the end is the service of God; and as Laval, in his own opinion, was always doing the service of God while his opponents were always doing that of the devil, he enjoyed, in the use of means, a latitude of which we have seen him avail himself.

In her rejection of Parkman's view of Laval, instinctive and complete, Willa Cather was strengthened by conversations she had with Abbé Henri Arthur Scott, the elderly vicar of Ste. Foy, a village near Quebec. She was introduced to him by a bookseller in the city, and from the first day when she saw him in his library, "sensitive and kindly, reserved and discreet," as the late chief archivist of Canada described him, surrounded by old editions of the classics and a multitude of the best studies on modern thought and art, she felt that she could trust his judgment in his special subject. This was the ecclesiastical history of French Canada. His studies had brought him a fellowship in the Royal Society of Canada; and the respect in which he was held in English Canada had been shown when he had been asked to contribute the section on the history of the Catholic Church in the eastern parts of the country to *Canada and Its Provinces,* and the life of Laval to the revised edition of the *Makers of Canada.* His book on Laval had come out in 1926 and he was still afire with enthusiasm for his subject. Her conception of Laval's ideas and policies is substantially the conception that had appeared in the Abbé Scott's biography, though the effect she gives is far more moving, for she adds an artist's insight into the human temperament of the old Bishop. She continued to consult the Abbé Scott almost to the time of his sudden death, in January 1931, when her novel stood complete though it was not published until the following autumn; and to him she owed a sight of many rare and fugitive materials on which she drew for her account of the aspect and internal politics of Quebec at the end of the seventeenth century.

Willa Cather's Laval is in many ways an ecclesiastical analogue for her Frontenac. He is, to the shape of his foot, an aristocrat, a product (as a recent historian of Canada has said) of the exalted religious revival of seventeenth-century France, emerging from years in the mystical practices of Bernières's group at the Hermitage of Caen to organize and energize the Canadian church; and like Frontenac he is presented as precisely the leader the New World required. Laval was right, she thought, in insisting that the parish clergy remain a part of the great community of his seminary; right, too, in making sure that the ceremonies of the Church were accompanied by the same splendors on the rock of Quebec as he had known in the cities of France; right incontestably when he intervened in civil matters in defense of moral and spiritual values. Like Frontenac he is shown in his old age, a man approaching seventy-five when the story opens, long retired from his episcopal office, shouldered aside by his theatrical successor Saint-Vallier, painfully afflicted, miserably poor, formidably kind. The worst she will concede is that "he was a stubborn, high-handed, tyrannical, quarrelsome old man," only to add: "no one could deny that he shepherded his sheep"—and that was the crux. At the close of the novel, immediately after Frontenac's death, we are invited to make a common judgment on the two men when Auclair says to his daughter: "The Count and the old Bishop were both men of my own period, the kind we looked up to in my youth. Saint-Vallier and Monsieur de Champigny [the intendant] are of a different sort." The judgment is very like the one Willa Cather had rendered on the lapse from the generation of the pioneers in Nebraska to the generation of their children. It was because she looked at Laval and Frontenac with the same spirit in which she had looked at Governor Garber when she wrote *A Lost Lady* that she was able to be more philosophic and more profound than the historian who was betrayed by his harsh rationalism into taking a minor difference for a major distinction.

Into the shaping of her novel there entered the deep and painful emotions that followed on the first death in Willa Cather's immediate family. She had spent the Christmas of 1927 at Red Cloud, and during her visit her father had a first attack of angina. In March of the next year, shortly after her return to New York, he died. "There had always been the kindest and fondest relationship between her and her father," Miss Lewis writes, "and his gentle, modest pride in her achievements, and the high esteem they had won, were one of the chief satisfactions she got from what is known as success." Willa Cather went to Red Cloud for the funeral, and supported her brother Douglass's plea that her mother, who was worn out with strain, should go with him to California for a long stay. Mrs. Cather had depended on the hidden strength of her husband more than anyone had realized; it seemed impossible for her to make a life for herself. The death of Charles Cather was not only the loss of a father; it meant the breakup of what Willa Cather had always continued to think of as her home, the household in Red Cloud. Her mind was full of her father when she discovered Quebec; she was then reviving memories of her relation to him when she was a child in Virginia and a girl on the Divide and in Red Cloud. As she thought over the story that was beginning to take shape in her mind during the months she spent on Grand Manan, the relation between father and daughter, between Euclide Auclair and Cécile, demanded the foreground.

During the early months of 1928, when her feelings were so deeply engaged by her father's illness and death, she wrote a Nebraska story, "Neighbour Rosicky," the first of the three tales collected in 1932 as *Obscure Destinies*. It should be read along with the final part of *My Ántonia*, where Jim Burden, visiting Ántonia, whom he has not seen since her marriage twenty years before, is delighted by his first meeting with Cuzak, her husband, and by the quality of life in their household. "Neighbour Rosicky" is a study of the same man and the same household taken twenty years or so afterward, in the last few months of Rosicky's life. Like Charles Cather, Rosicky is an angina victim and learns of his ailment at the beginning of winter, to die of it the next spring. His last months are full of memories of the evil things he has escaped by fleeing from the harshness, ugliness, and deadness of big cities, and of experiences of the good things he has had in packed measure by living on the land, in a household full of warm-hearted, vigorous, and impulsive people, with Ántonia, who is here called Mary, as its perfect center. There is nothing simpler in Willa Cather's fiction than "Neighbour Rosicky"; the tone is quietness itself, and perfectly sustained; the emotion has a flawless purity. The choice of a friend's husband rather than of her own father as the main subject for a story into which she poured so much of what she felt about Charles Cather's life and death is a clue to the more elaborate work that she began later in the year.

When she returned to New York from Grand Manan in the autumn of 1928, Willa Cather began to write *Shadows on the Rock*. She felt almost at once that she needed to see Quebec again, and returned there alone in November for a stay of two weeks, in which she absorbed that strong feeling for the aspect of the city in autumn which was to be rendered so powerfully in the early and late sections of the novel. On this visit she ransacked bookstores and libraries, talked with historians, antiquaries, and other men learned in the past of French Canada, and returned to New York full of her subject and her eyes complaining of strain.

An ordeal even more severe than her father's death now came on her. In December she had the news that her mother, who was still in California with Douglass, had had a paralytic stroke. Willa Cather went to her at once.

The long illness of Mrs. Cather—it lasted two and a half years—had a profound effect on Willa Cather [Miss Lewis writes], and I think on her work as well. She had come to understand her mother better and better through the years—her strong-willed, imperious nature, full of quick, eager impulses— quick to resent, quick to sympathize, headstrong, passionate, and yet capable of great kindness and understanding. She realized with complete imagination what it meant for a proud woman like her mother to lie month after month quite helpless, unable to speak articulately, although her mind was perfectly clear. In Willa Cather's long stays in Pasadena, where her mother was cared for in a sanatorium, she had to watch her continually growing weaker, more ailing, yet unable to die. It was one of those experiences that make a lasting change in the climate of one's mind.

So great was Willa Cather's involvement in what her mother was undergoing that she could scarcely continue the writing of *Shadows on the Rock*. The death of her father had turned her mind on the life of the family when she was a child; and soon after her mother went to California she resolved to open the house in Red Cloud and refurbish it for Mrs. Cather's return. It was not the shabby, crowded house in which she had grown up, but a large, well-designed one in a better part of town which Charles Cather had bought after she went to Pittsburgh. She found a surprising pleasure in choosing new paper and new drapes, carefully avoiding any change in the parlor, to which she knew her mother's attachment. In one of her stays at Pasadena, where she had a cottage in the grounds of the sanatorium, she began the short story "Two Friends," finished in 1931, a study in a relationship between two intimates of her parents whom she had ad-

mired in the first years at Red Cloud. In Pasadena she began also the longer story "Old Mrs. Harris," another study
of those years, the most nearly direct representation of
life in the Cather household in the town's setting she ever
attempted. This also remained unfinished until 1931. If
she could write little of *Shadows on the Rock*, she could
take pleasure in reading about the world the novel was
to evoke. The difficulty in composing was perhaps the
main reason why she read so extensively in the *Jesuit Relations*, La Hontan's *Voyages*, Juchereau's history of the
Hôtel Dieu at Quebec, the letters of Mother Marie de
l'Incarnation, from which she drew the epigraph for the
novel, and a host of secondary works, among them the
Makers of Canada, which she bought.

During the winter of 1929–30, after another visit to
Quebec, which she now saw for the first time under deep
snow, she worked more steadily at the manuscript. She
spent the spring with her mother, and in May sailed for
France. In the course of the two months she stayed in
Paris she became as familiar with Frontenac's old quarter
as she was with the country about Santa Fe. With Jan and
Isabelle Hambourg she made her first visit to Saint-Malo,
evoked so delicately in the later part of the novel, where
Pondaven, the Breton captain appears. The news from
Pasadena was not disquieting, and Willa Cather decided
to visit again the Provençal country, which always made
her light of heart. After Avignon and Marseille she went
to Aix-les-Bains, and, staying at the Grand Hotel, had the
extraordinary encounter from which she drew the most
perfect of her essays, "A Chance Meeting."

In the dining-room she observed with an always grow-

ing interest an old French lady, lame and somewhat shape-
less, but with a head so fine that it reminded her of the
portrait busts of Roman ladies. This was Madame Franklin Grout, whose translation of *Faust* had been corrected
by Turgenev, and who had edited the *Bouvard et Pécu-
chet* of her uncle, Flaubert. In meeting the niece of Flaubert, the "Caro" of his letters, and finding her a person
whose talk of his writings joined subtlety and justice to
enthusiasm, Willa Cather felt that she had been "brought
up against a mountain of memories," and that the world
which survived in Madame Franklin Grout held most of
"her mental past." Their talks cast a special glory over
the summer of 1930, and when she heard of her friend's
death the next winter, Willa Cather's sense of loss went
deep.

   Late in September, after some days spent with Isabelle
Hambourg, who had become gravely ill, she returned to
America by the St. Lawrence route. I traveled by the same
ship and recall as if it were yesterday her warmth of expression and vigor of movement as she looked from the
promenade deck at the aspect of Quebec on a sunny October morning. Miss Lewis writes:

The whole voyage became a sort of home-coming to *Shadows*,
and the slow progress up the St. Lawrence, between woods on
fire with October, was its climax—a dream of joy. It had been
Willa Cather's intention to go straight on to Boston and Jaffrey;
but although her luggage had gone on ahead, she instantly decided to buy warm clothes and stay at the Frontenac for a
while. (During this stay she for the first time visited the Hôpi-
tal Général, and saw Bishop de Saint-Vallier's two small, poor
rooms where he humbly ended his life.) Everything she experi-

enced brought her closer and closer to her story, and when she
did finally start for Jaffrey, she could hardly wait to be at her
writing-table again. She wrote the last part of *Shadows* very
rapidly, part of it at Jaffrey, part at the Grosvenor, finishing it
December 27th.

II

It was inevitable that *Shadows on the Rock* should reflect
Willa Cather's longing for what in *My Ántonia* she had
called "the precious, the incommunicable past"—her personal past, the life in the Cather household when she was
a child and a girl, and the life in the pioneer society to
which it was related. In population the town of Quebec
in the year of her story, 1697–8, was a little short of two
thousand, as was Red Cloud in the years when she was
growing up. To the rock had come people who like the
Cathers and so many others coming to Nebraska from Virginia or New England, Norway or Bohemia, carried their
gods with them. A key to much in the material and the
scale in *Shadows on the Rock* is given in this passage on
which a chapter ends:

Inferretque deos Latio. When an adventurer carries his gods
with him into a remote and savage country, the colony he
founds will, from the beginning, have graces, traditions, riches
of the mind and spirit. Its history will shine with bright incidents, slight, perhaps, but precious, as in life itself, where the
great matters are often as worthless as astronomical distances,
and the trifles dear as the heart's blood.

The trifles at Quebec are like the trifles in the Nebraska
novels—old Vavrika's Tokay and Ántonia's grape arbor,
the garden of the old German couple with whom Wunsch,
the musician, lived, Mrs. Forrester's laugh, Mrs. Cather's

strange power, in "Old Mrs. Harris," to make a beautiful
occasion out of almost nothing, and Charles Cather's courtesy, in the same story, the courtesy of his grandfather on
the family farm at Flint Ridge.

Beyond the rock of Quebec, as beyond Red Cloud, lay
lonely farms where life was often rough and gross, and dividing them was the wild land. A lively episode in *Shadows on the Rock*, with much characterizing force, is Cécile
Auclair's unhappy visit to the Harnois farm on the Île
d'Orléans, where the people and the beds were dirty, the
rooms smelly and stuffy, the food heavy with lard. Cécile
returned home with a new appreciation of what cleansing
and polishing and cooking in the best French manner
meant in life, that they were a part of life without which
it would not mean much to her. What Cécile felt at the
Harnois' was what Jim Burden felt when in the middle of
winter he went with his grandmother to the sodhouse of
the Shimerdas, where the air was stifling and the food frozen or rotting, and Ántonia slept on a pile of straw in a
hole in the black earth. The Burdens—who are projections
of William A. Cather and his wife—accused themselves for
having allowed neighbors to live so, but on their return to
their own neat frame house they had a new appreciation
of its "atmosphere of comfort and security." The land in
O Pioneers! was the "great fact . . . which seemed to
overwhelm the little beginnings of human society that
struggled in its sombre wastes," a land that "wanted to be
let alone, to preserve its own fierce strength, its peculiar,
savage kind of beauty, its uninterrupted mournfulness."
The forests about Quebec are an equivalent for these Nebraska prairies: in their "dead, sealed world . . . an un-

charted continent choked with interlocking trees . . .
European man was quickly swallowed up in silence, distance, mould, black mud." It was because Quebec, as she
imagined it in the seventeenth century, had so much of
what she had responded to with such force in her years
on the Divide and in Red Cloud, in the Cather household
and in the society of her friends, that Willa Cather moved
with such sensitive ease in calling up its aspect and its
spirit.

To the qualities it shared with early Nebraska, Quebec
added the precious element Willa Cather had set at the
center of *Death Comes for the Archbishop*. Miss Lewis
writes:

I have sometimes thought that Willa Cather's great pleasure in
this Quebec visit came from finding here a sort of continuation,
in a different key, of the Catholic theme which had absorbed
her for two years, and which still lingered in her thoughts, after
the completion of the *Archbishop*, like a tune that goes on in
one's mind after the song is ended. Dickens, in his preface to
David Copperfield, tells "how sorrowfully the pen is laid down
at the close of a two years' imaginative task." I think Willa
Cather never got so much happiness from the writing of any
book as from the *Archbishop*; and although *Shadows on the
Rock* is of course altogether different in conception, in treatment, and in artistic purpose, it may have been in part a reluctance to leave that world of Catholic feeling and tradition
in which she had lived so happily for so long that led her to
embark on this new novel.

As in *Death Comes for the Archbishop*, Willa Cather
chose a later rather than an early period for the novel of
the French regime in Canada, and inserted a variety of

narrative reminders of what life had been when the colony was more primitive. These reminders are predominantly religious: a story about the first superior of the Hôtel Dieu, Mother Catherine de Saint-Augustin, related by her successor, Mother Juschereau de Saint-Ignace; a story about the Jesuit martyr Noël Chabanel told by another Jesuit, Hector Saint-Cyr; a story of the youth and vocation of the holy recluse at Montreal, Jeanne Le Ber, told by her former love, Pierre Charron. In the earlier time religious feeling had been more intense and exalted; the intensity and exaltation have survived in the aged and retired Laval, often called in the novel (as Willa Cather may have learned from the startling hagiography of the prelate in the first edition of the *Makers of Canada*) "Monseigneur l'Ancien." With the younger personages religious feeling has become quite different: in Mother Juschereau the "vigils, mortifications, visions, raptures" of Catherine de Saint-Augustin have given place to the "sunny outrightness" of "a religious of the practical type . . . a *Canadienne*, and the woman for Canada"; Hector Saint-Cyr, an imaginary personage modeled in his personal traits and his principal adventure on the soldier priest of the Sulpitians, Dollier de Casson, is heroic and devout, but with no overtone of Chabanel's passionate spirituality; though Jeanne Le Ber is still alive when the action occurs, she has receded into a long spiritual drought.

Much more potent in setting the tone for religious feeling at the end of the seventeenth century than contrasts with the age of the martyrs and mystics that had gone before is the amosphere in the households of the Auclairs and their bourgeois friends the Pigeons and the Pommiers.

In Cécile Auclair, for all her piety, her devotion to the Ursulines who had taught her, her pleasure in miracles, there was never a trace of a vocation for the religious life; like Madame Pommier's, her religion seemed to find its center and its preferred symbol not in a virgin or a martyr, but in the Holy Family. It was because of Madame Pommier's devotion that the cobbler shop had been opened on Holy Family Hill, and nothing delighted that old lady more than when Monseigneur Laval told her "that there is no other place in the world where the people are so devoted to the Holy Family as here in our own Canada. It is something very special to us." It was something very special to Willa Cather, writing when she felt her own losses. On its superior level this devotion is parallel to the practices in cooking, cleaning, and polishing by which the house and shop of the Auclairs became such a magnet for so many diverse persons. Religion also penetrated life and made it shine with grace and poetry.

As in the Nebraska novels, but to a greater degree, the pattern of *Shadows on the Rock* depends on responses to new circumstances and a new society. Throughout the novel there is a steady movement—of which the succession of the Canadian-born farm-girl Mother Juschereau to the place of Catherine de Saint-Augustin is an early instance—from what is French to what is Canadian. The importance of this element in the narrative is confirmed by its last incident, the arrival at the Auclairs' on the day after Count Frontenac's death of the *coureur de bois* Pierre Charron, Canadian-born and critical to the point of suspicion toward all who have about them the odor of Paris or Versailles. Cécile, born on the Quai des Célestins in Paris, but brought to Canada at four, reflects: "He had not a throne behind him, like the Count . . . not the authority of a parchment and seal. But he had authority, and a power which came from knowledge of the country and its people; from knowledge, and from a kind of passion. His daring and his pride seemed to her even more splendid than Count Frontenac's."

Although there were well-to-do Charrons, traders in Montreal and associates of Jacques Le Ber, the father of the recluse (and it was doubtless because she had come across their track that Willa Cather gave Pierre their name), he is an imaginary personage. To Auclair and his wife, Pierre "had seemed the type they had come so far to find; more than anyone else he realized the romantic picture of the free Frenchman of the great forests which they had formed at home on the bank of the Seine." In terms of the Nebraska novels Pierre is that rarest of all admirable kinds, the pioneer of the second generation who had to the full the finest qualities of the first; in his case we may say those that Willa Cather found in Robert Cavelier de La Salle. Pierre is another Ántonia; the wild land is for him an ideal setting and an opportunity. His marriage to Cécile Auclair, reported in the epilogue, is something like Ántonia's: it assures us that the future, evolving in the ways of a new society will also preserve the graces and traditions of Europe.

The main exception to the movement from what is French to what is Canadian is Cécile's father, another imaginary personage, many of whose traits are taken from the first of Canadian natural scientists, Michel Sarrazin, whose collection of botanical specimens was kept at the

Jardin des Plantes in Paris and who in 1699 was named a
corresponding member of the Académie des Sciences. On
the rock Euclide Auclair is out of his element. Left to himself, like Ántonia's father, he would have remained in a
European city; both men deferred to wills that were
stronger than their own. The shift from working in tap-
estry and playing the violin in Prague to a sodhouse and
the unbroken prairie was too much for old Shimerda—he
shot himself. I am not sure that Euclide Auclair would
not have done the same in similarly harsh conditions; but
he had Frontenac's protection, an apothecary shop in the
center of the town of Quebec, and a wife and then a
daughter to make the family's way of life in New France
so close to what it had been on the Quai des Célestins
that one had to step outside to notice the difference. There
were times when the desire to return to France grew very
strong, and it is significant that the final reason for Euclide's staying at Quebec was a feeling that when the
great King died, France would become a terrifyingly new
world. But in Quebec nothing would change. Charles
Cather, who spoke with a Virginia accent and kept Southern manners to the end of his life, who was not intended
for a farmer and came into town from the Divide as soon
as he could, also had his longings for the gracious society
he had left, and his compensations in the way of life in his
own household.

The novel in which Willa Cather traveled farthest from
Red Cloud drew most of its emotional power from her
memories of her life there as they flooded her mind during the years when that life had finally to take its place
in the irrecoverable past.

11

Winter Memories

1932–1940

OBSCURE DESTINIES

LUCY GAYHEART

THE OLD BEAUTY

SAPPHIRA AND THE SLAVE GIRL

THE DEATH OF her parents and the sale of the family house removed Red Cloud from its place in the rhythm of Willa Cather's year. Unless she was making a long stay in Europe she had "gone home," as she always spoke of her trips to Red Cloud, for a month or two every summer or early fall; often she made a second, shorter visit in the Christmas season. In the years after the Cather home was sold she was constantly asked by early friends who were still living in the village to stay with them. She never did, however; from the time when she began to be a novelist she was averse to staying with anyone who was not a member of her family, even though the hotels in Red Cloud were primitively uncomfortable. Without the visit or visits to Nebraska the entire year seemed emptier: nothing else could take their place. Roscoe and Douglass Cather were living in the Far West; and Willa Cather, who never traveled by plane, was almost dangerously exhausted by long transcontinental train journeys.

The Hambourgs were living in France; they had less money than in the early years of their marriage and sel-

dom came to New York. There was no one in Pittsburgh
whom Willa Cather cared to visit regularly. At Grand
Manan, without being unfriendly, she and Edith Lewis
kept to themselves; their stays on the island were intended to be a rest from the traffic and telephones of Manhattan, and its heat and harassments, not a participation
in the doings of a summer colony. It was at Grand Manan,
however, that Willa Cather found the nearest equivalent
to her stays in Red Cloud; at her cottage she was visited
on four different occasions by nieces and heartily enjoyed
having them. She could be a formidable aunt, but her interest in each of the Cathers in the next generation was serious and intense. Her letters concerning them are full of
perception and affection; and she would go to any pains
to arrange for their coming to stay with her. At the Jaffrey Inn, in New Hampshire, where she usually spent
some weeks each autumn, she was almost always at work
—from the time when she first discovered Jaffrey she had
been able to write and revise there more happily than
anywhere else. It meant a great deal to her when Ethel
Jones Litchfield decided, after the death of her husband,
to leave Pittsburgh and live in New York; with Mrs. Litchfield, whom she had first met in 1902 and whom she saw
almost every week, she could talk about music unre-
servedly and evoke many of the best happenings in the
Pittsburgh years. The friendship with Mr. and Mrs. Knopf
deepened with every year. It was through them that she
met two writers of her own generation to whose work and
personality she was drawn, Thomas Mann and Sigrid
Undset.

Madame Undset had always kept a photograph of Willa

Cather on her writing-table even before they had met; they had their literary careers in common and the same feeling for people and for nature. Sigrid Undset used to delight Willa Cather with her account of her continuing discoveries of American wild flowers and her forays into the field and wood to get them. And as a devout Catholic she felt, and often expressed, her admiration for the understanding way in which Willa Cather had written of Catholicism.

Still one cannot but feel that in the years after 1931 Willa Cather was erecting walls behind which she carried on a life that was essentially inward—retrospective, creative, and speculative. One main reason for her withdrawal was undoubtedly a decline in energy. Edith Lewis believes that the physical and emotional exertion in the years of her mother's illness was so great and sustained for so long a period that Willa Cather never overcame altogether its effects. She instinctively spared herself by avoiding new intimate relationships, knowing well that once she entered upon one of these, her imaginative and sympathetic nature could not be held in check. In the course of the 1930's Willa Cather did form one such relationship, with the Menuhin family; she could not have sustained many friendships so intense and so creative—no one of her years and temper could. Again and again in the letters written during the 1930's an impression and an awareness of deep fatigue appear.

Besides the failure in energy, her withdrawal was induced by what Harvey Newbranch, her friend from college times, describes as a slow spreading of the virus of pessimism. She was out of sympathy with the world about

her. The New Deal seemed to her to threaten the free activity of the strong individual by the kind of restrictive
influence that seemed to her the worst of all, restriction by
government. Government worked through civil servants,
and civil servants she had always believed were the culls
of their generation, dreary petty men who took a mean
pleasure in thwarting those who had energy, daring, and
originality. The age of the pioneers was quite over, and it
had been succeeded by an age of routine.

She was no less unhappy about the attitude to the arts
in modern American life. Even in the universities there
was an emphasis on what was done by contemporaries, a
growing indifference to the great performances of the past.
She was asked why during her years in Pittsburgh and
Allegheny high schools she had for a while taught Latin
as well as English; she appreciated with a shock that her
inquirer could not believe that it was because she liked
Latin—the language and the literature. Teachers of English in schools and colleges were constantly writing to her
about her works; and she observed that far more than half
of them did not respect their own language, could not use
it without gross errors, and had no sense whatever of its
possibilities as an instrument. Education seemed to her to
become more and more an exaltation of technology and an
aid to making money. This was not education at all, she
believed, and she wondered how anyone could be duped
into thinking it was. Shakespeare was less and less rightly
understood, inside schools and colleges and outside; and
what could be said for a people that did not care about
Shakespeare? The new paths of fiction in the 1930's did
not seem to her to lead anywhere worth going, though

she kept all her interest in what was written by those who seemed to her genuine artists, Ernest Hemingway, Thornton Wilder, Scott Fitzgerald, and, somewhat to one's surprise, Sinclair Lewis, whose pictures of Midwestern towns and cities seemed to her not only authentic but full of suggestion. There was no critic of power writing in these years, she felt: the last of the great American critics was Henry James, and the last of the good ones W. C. Brownell and H. L. Mencken.

What she wrote during the years after the publication of *Shadows on the Rock* reflected her withdrawal, the decline in her energy, and her tendency to retrospection.

II

A year after the publication of *Shadows on the Rock* Willa Cather collected three tales that stemmed from her early life and were filled with memories of Red Cloud and of her family. One of them, "Neighbour Rosicky," had been written in 1928 at the time of her father's death. The second, "Old Mrs. Harris," and the last, "Two Friends," were set down largely in the interval between completion and publication of her novel of Quebec, but the material in them had been in Willa Cather's mind since her tenth year. Her title for the volume is one of the simplest and most effective of all her titles: *Obscure Destinies*. From the portraits of Rosicky and Mrs. Harris to the two friends she remembered sitting on the sidewalk under the Western skies in the small town, the book is rich in affection for the characters and the life she depicted. Willa Cather felt that "Two Friends," with its story of their falling out over William Jennings Bryan, was a romantic kind of real-

ism—a painter's subject, which she had tried to do in a
painter's way. She told Alfred Knopf that she had in mind,
as she wrote the story, the paintings of Courbet, and indeed the memory we carry away from the sketch is the
static picture of the banker and the cattleman in their
chairs at evening, the small town flooded "by the rich in-
dolence of a full moon," and the young narrator (who is
clearly Willa Cather) beside them listening, always listening, to their worldly talk. But if the story is as static as
an old-time painting, it is filled with the emotion of the
sensitive young observer and an aching nostalgia for the
past.

Fine as this tale and "Neighbour Rosicky" are, they are
but sketches beside the richly developed story—it is really
a *nouvelle*—of "Old Mrs. Harris," which many consider
Willa Cather's finest short narrative. Reflected in it we
find her memories of the time when the Cathers moved
from the South to the West and when their way of living
was under the scrutiny of their new neighbors. With the
family has come the grandmother, a figure taken for
granted in the household, devoted to her daughter and
grandchildren, who seem almost unaware of her benign
presence.

In Tennessee every young married woman in good circumstances had an older woman in the house, a mother or mother-
in-law or an old aunt, who managed the household economies
and directed the help. . . .

To be sure, Mrs. Harris, and the other women of her age
who managed their daughter's house, kept in the background;
but it was their own background, and they ruled it jealously.
They left the front porch and the parlour to the young married

couple and their young friends; the old women spent most of
their lives in the kitchen and pantries and back dining-room.

But in Tennessee there was the old family house and here
"the little rented house was much too small for the family, and Mrs. Harris and her 'things' were almost required
to be invisible." Mrs. Harris represents those qualities of
quiet self-sacrificing and self-effacing heroism which Willa
Cather could never resist rendering homage to in her
work; as she moves through the story, accomplishing her
simple little daily tasks, she is at once a shadowy figure
behind the lively bustle of the new generation and also a
strong protagonist. Willa Cather's use of detail and small
dramatic incident was never more felicitous, whether in
giving us the portrait of Mrs. Harris through the kindly
eyes of the neighbor, Mrs. Rosen (drawn from Mrs.
Wiener), or describing the strivings of the daughter who
plans to go to the university. Such small matters as picnics
and serving tea, the routine of the kitchen, or the death of
the cat take on a distinct importance because they are important to Mrs. Harris, who goes about her appointed
tasks, emerging from her shadowy existence only to arrange quietly with her neighbor for Vickie to have a loan
to supplement the scholarship she has won that will take
her to college.

Sometimes, in the morning, if her feet ached more than usual,
Mrs. Harris felt a little low. . . . She would hang up her towel
with a sigh and go into the kitchen, feeling that it was hard to
make a start. But the moment she heard the children running
down the uncarpeted back stairs, she forgot to be low. Indeed,
she ceased to be an individual, an old woman with aching

feet; she became part of a group, became a relationship. She was drunk up into their freshness when they burst in upon her, telling her about their dreams, explaining their troubles with buttons and shoe-laces and underwear shrunk too small. The tired, solitary old woman grandmother had been at daybreak vanished; suddenly the morning seemed as important to her as it did to the children, and the mornings ahead stretched out sunshiny, important.

Obscure Destinies is Willa Cather's finest book of short stories and in its minute realism and sharpness of outline invites comparison with Flaubert's *Trois Contes*. The three tales are of a piece; they were the synthesis, after many years, of old experiences; and they are filled with a humanity and gentleness and feeling which demonstrated that if Willa Cather had in her two preceding novels turned to a distant past, she could still confront her own past and draw great art from it.

The stories in *Obscure Destinies* came from an impulse and a need to live again in imagination some passages in the early years in Nebraska. It was the same with *Lucy Gayheart*, the first novel to have a Nebraska setting since *A Lost Lady*. Willa Cather began to write it in the spring of 1933, in New York. She had not recovered from the strain and the losses of the preceding years; again and again she entered in the line-a-day she began to keep at this time "very tired" or "deadly tired." The early chapters, the first book, of the novel, were drafted in this exhausted mood, and no revision could free them from a heaviness, a lagging pace, for which there is no parallel in any of her earlier writings. During the summer, passed at Grand Manan, she could bring herself to work at the novel only intermittently. In the autumn, in the cool mountain air of Jaffrey, she began to feel her energy renewed; her spirits rose; and she felt, rightly, that at last she "could live with her story as she ought to do." The draft of the last book, which she always considered the best, was written as quickly and happily as anything she had ever done.

She had just begun to revise her draft when she suffered the greatest disability in her career as an author. Miss Lewis notes:

Her right wrist began to be painfully swollen; and when she went one day to the doctor with it, he diagnosed it as a serious inflammation of the sheath of the tendon, and said the hand must be completely immobilized. From this time on she was never free from the threat of this disability, which attacked sometimes her right hand, and less frequently her left. Often for months together she had to wear the steel and leather brace that Dr. Frank Ober, the great orthopedic surgeon, devised for her; it immobilized her thumb, but left her fingers free, so that she was able with some difficulty to sign her name, or to trace a few words at the end of a dictated letter. All this meant that for long periods she was unable to do any writing—she could not even typewrite. She never tried to dictate a piece of creative work. She felt it to be, for her, a psychological impossibility.

Although this affliction made the simplest acts of life, which ordinarily one performs unconsciously—taking a bath, dressing oneself, tying a knot, opening a letter—wearisomely difficult and irksome, Willa Cather rarely let it depress her spirits or affect her independence. I remember her telling once, when some one offered to help her, how when she was a very little child, and her parents would try to assist her in something, she would protest passionately: "Self-alone, self-alone!"

The recurrence of this disability, and its persistence for
weeks and even months, are one of the reasons why after
Lucy Gayheart she composed so little—only one novel and
less than half a dozen shorter fictions. In the spring of
1934 she was able to resume writing and to finish the revision of the manuscript; it was used as a serial by the
Woman's Home Companion, and appeared as a book in
1935.

Lucy Gayheart has likenesses with many of the earlier
writings about Nebraska. The most evident link, and also
the most intimate, is with *The Song of the Lark*. Like
Thea Kronborg, Lucy is a musician, who leaves a small
Nebraska town to study in Chicago, where she lives mea-
gerly, meets a great personage in the world of music, and
becomes severed from the society in which she grew up.
But unlike Thea's, Lucy's distinction is not a strength of
talent, her early death did not end a promising career; her
distinction is a fineness of nature, an intense response to
people, to life in people. What she always admired in
Harry Gordon, the man who could not forgive her until
she was dead, is the clue to what made her history worth
telling: "He rose and fell, he was alive, he moved. He was
not anchored, he was not lazy, he was not a sheep . . .
he wasn't tame at the core." The quick flow of life in Lucy
is caught in the beautiful introductory reminiscence of her
eager, happy walk, not faltering in the winter winds or
under the summer's heat. Thea Kronborg's story is that of
a talent and a career, Lucy's of a personality and a love.
It does not require a massive or elaborate treatment; it
can be rendered as Mrs. Forrester's was, in a few incidents and a few sketches of mood, lightly and without in-

sistence. In the early chapters there is sometimes too much insistence; the touch does not always have that swift and delicate sureness that was unfailing in *A Lost Lady*.

The relation between father and daughter that was at the center of *Shadows on the Rock* is again important in *Lucy Gayheart*. Again the mother is dead when the story opens, and again the father is out of place in the society of a town on the edge of civilization. Jacob Gayheart, a German-born watchmaker and flute-player, has the gentleness, the courtesy, the perceptive affection of Euclide Auclair and of Charles Cather. Like Auclair, by his gentleness and personal distinction he wins the friendship of men a generation younger who have in the highest degree the qualities prized in their societies—Harry Gordon is the hero of Haverford on the Platte as Pierre Charron and Father Hector St.-Cyr are the heroes of the Canadian rivers and woods. If Harry seems much less heroic, that is because the Nebraska of this novel—the action occurs in 1902 and 1903, with an epilogue in 1927—has lost the fire of the pioneer age and become almost submerged in dreary prose.

The idea of this novel had been in Willa Cather's mind a long time; she used to speak of it as *Blue Eyes on the Platte*, although when she came to write she determined that Lucy's eyes should be a startling brown—"they were not gentle brown eyes, but flashed with gold sparks like that Colorado stone we call the tiger-eye." The name of Gayheart, symbolic as names rarely were in the early novels about Nebraska,[1] was a reminiscence of a chance en-

---

[1] An exception is Wunsch, the name of Thea Kronborg's music teacher at Moonstone.

counter in the days when Willa Cather was a student at
the university. In early May 1896 she drove from Red
Cloud to Blue Hill for a dance and spent the night talking
with a young girl who had that name, a fine, delicate, sensitive creature who seemed to her pitiably unsuited to
teach school in that remote rough village.

The saturation of the novel in music and song was an
outcome of a new friendship, which meant at least as
much to Willa Cather as her association with Fremstad in
the years when she was writing *The Song of the Lark.* In
the summer of 1930 during her stay in Paris she met
through Jan and Isabelle Hambourg the Menuhin family
—Moshe and Marutha Menuhin, their two young daughters, Hephzibah and Yaltah, and their son, Yehudi. She
had always cared intensely for children, from the early
days in Red Cloud when like Thea Kronborg she asked
nothing better than drawing her young brother in his cart
along the narrow sidewalks of the town. The Menuhins
were the most gifted, the most sensitive children she had
known; and it is not too much to say that she fell in love
with the family as a whole, and with each member of it
individually. Mrs. Menuhin and the two girls came often
to see her the next winter in New York; and in the spring
of 1931, when she was with her mother in Pasadena, Willa
Cather often saw Yehudi, who was giving concerts in California. The Menuhin children had been brought up with
an Old World strictness and did not know very much of
the larger society outside their family; the friendship of
Willa Cather was as exciting and illuminating to them as
theirs was to her.

In 1927 Willa Cather and Edith Lewis had moved out of the Bank Street apartment, to which they had been deeply attached and where so many fruitful years had been spent; the building was being torn down, and they had no alternative. They sought refuge in the Grosvenor Hotel, at 35 Fifth Avenue, and what was intended to be a temporary *pied-à-terre* was protracted into a five-year residence. The Grosvenor was associated in Willa's mind with the painful period of the illness and death of her parents; it carried with it a sense of displacement and homelessness. In 1932 they resolved to escape from the irritations and confinements of hotel life and were able to find the space, privacy, and repose they longed for in an apartment in the quieter reaches of Park Avenue. The brightest element in Willa Cather's life in this apartment was her association with the Menuhins in the winters. During the years when she lived at the Grosvenor she had heard little opera or music of any kind; now, with the stimulus of the new friendship, it seemed she could never hear enough.

Miss Lewis notes:

I remember the Menuhin family's winter visits to New York, in the years that followed, as a sort of continuous festival, full of concerts and gay parties; orange trees and great baskets of flowers for Willa Cather arriving in the midst of snow-storms; birthday luncheons, with Russian caviare and champagne; excursions to the opera, where she took Yaltah and Hephzibah to hear *Parsifal* for the first time; long walks around the reservoir in Central Park, when the three children all wanted to walk beside her, and had to take turnabout. They discussed very abstract subjects together—art, religion, philosophy, life. If Willa Cather had been writing *War and Peace*, I am sure she would have abandoned it to take these walks.

She had a feeling that Hephzibah and Yaltah, travelling in so many countries, and learning something of the language of each, were never going to get a thorough sense of the English language; and this worried her. She asked Marutha Menuhin if she might organize a Shakespeare Club, with no one allowed to be present except herself and the little girls. Yehudi then asked if he might come too. They began with *Richard II*, and went on to *Macbeth* and *Henry IV*. Willa Cather hunted through the bookstores of New York to get each of the children a copy of these plays in the original Temple Edition, the only one she herself cared to read; it was then rapidly going out of print.

She was greatly touched when, many years afterward, Yehudi told her he had found and bought a complete second-hand set of the Temple Shakespeare, in a shop in New Orleans.

In *Lucy Gayheart* there is a reminiscence of these sessions and of the Temple Shakespeare. After he had sung a song from *Twelfth Night*, Clement Sebastian "ran his finger along a row of small red leather volumes, and pulled one out of its place." Lucy had thought the play "a rather foolish comedy where everybody was pretending, and nobody was in earnest." She had made this gross mistake because "until she began to play for Sebastian, she had never known that words had any value aside from their direct meaning." It was the words of Shakespeare that Willa Cather cared most to talk about. Gifted foreign people would, she thought, come to a mastery of English by learning and feeling what the language was in the use of its greatest master. For the background of the historical plays she read again J. R. Green's history, which is one of the few books in her library heavily scored and marked. The lifelong aversion to Lucius Sherman's severe and misleading analysis kept her touch glancing and informal. For the rest of her life she read Shakespeare more and more, and always with greater pleasure; but she did not care to acquaint herself with recent interpretations and criticisms.

To be with the Menuhins was to live in a world of music. Willa Cather did not go to the opera as often as in her early years in New York; she thought opera had declined; but the truth was that her taste had ripened over the years and she preferred now music by itself, without the trappings of drama, and, above all, orchestral and chamber music. One of her oldest friends, Mrs. Charles Weisz, with whom she often stayed when she was passing through Chicago, recalls her saying, especially when she was unhappy, under strain, or simply fatigued: "I must have music!" It was no longer Wagner but Beethoven or Schubert that she needed; and opera, which dominated *The Song of the Lark*, is in *Lucy Gayheart* secondary to the songs of Schubert.

What was essential to the art of Clement Sebastian, the great singer in this novel with whom Lucy falls in love, is, however, precisely what was essential to the art of Thea Kronborg in her maturity, as it was essential to Fremstad's. It was the classical austerity that Willa Cather found in the playing of Josef Lhevinne, whom she met in the early thirties and whose concerts she scarcely ever missed. In the calmness and serenity of Sebastian's rendering of Schubert there was "a kind of large enlightenment, like daybreak"; and hearing him, "one felt a long distance between the singer and the scenes he was recalling, a long perspective." Art such as Sebastian's depends most of all neither on training nor on the quality of a voice, but on the personality of the performer and what that personality has made of experience.

The art in *Lucy Gayheart* is of the same kind. The defect in *The Song of the Lark* had been in the closeness of the artist to the experiences thrown into the novel, in the absence of a long perspective, a large enlightenment. It offers quite another kind of pleasure, the pleasure that is given so often in the novels of H. G. Wells: the intellectual pleasure of following a mind of unusual sensitiveness and power as it comes to terms with experience. Nothing could be calmer than the manner of *Lucy Gayheart*, and in its finest part, where Harry Gordon surveys his life, his associations with the Gayhearts and above all with Lucy, by the long perspective and the large enlightenment a new depth is given to the incidents and musings which had come before us in the earlier sections. In those sections calmness had too often lapsed into heaviness, perspective faded to indifference.

III

Most of 1935 was given to Isabelle Hambourg, who came to America in March with her husband. She was gravely ill and Willa Cather, much alarmed, arranged for her to go into a New York hospital, and made a daily visit during the three weeks she was there. Willa Cather was told at once that Isabelle could not recover. The stay in the hospital brought unexpected improvement, however, and when Jan Hambourg undertook to conduct a summer course in Chicago, Isabelle insisted on going with him. Willa Cather accompanied the Hambourgs to lighten the journey and stayed to have an eye on Isabelle during weeks when Jan was much harried by working in a place that was unfamiliar to him, and in conditions less favorable than his hopeful and mercurial spirit had expected. The Hambourgs sailed in August; Willa Cather crossed a few days later and after a few weeks in Venice rejoined them for a final two months in Paris. The mortal illness of her friend, the wasting of her beauty, the decline in her intense response to life, left a mark on Willa Cather's writings during the next few years. Isabelle died three years afterward at Sorrento. Willa Cather never saw her again.

The very title of her next book suggested a sense of the falling away of the years, the fading of the world she had known. In a foreword to *Not Under Forty* that was belligerent, and by its brevity seemed even more belligerent than it was, she construed the title as a warning that those born in the present century would find the spirit of the book outside their range. Willa Cather was sure that she and her writings already belonged to the past. And out of this past she evoked the memory of two friends, long dead, Mrs. J. T. Fields and Sarah Orne Jewett; her recollections of the Charles Street days are at the core of *Not Under Forty*, which contains also the vivid account of her meeting with Madame Franklin Grout and papers on Thomas Mann and Katherine Mansfield. The essay on Miss Jewett was expanded from a preface written in 1925 to a selection Willa Cather had made of Miss Jewett's best stories, published in two volumes by Houghton Mifflin. She had been grieved and disturbed by the neglect of Miss Jewett's writings. She was sure they were indestructible, that a few persons with perfect taste would always turn to them as she did, taking down from her shelves now this book and now another, and always judging the pictures, the patterns, the phrases as fine as they had seemed in memory or finer. The essay is the most penetrating analysis ever written of the effects in Miss Jewett's prose, and of her sense of structure in fiction. It is also rich in provocative remarks about the prevailing climate of literary taste and opinion. With an asperity unusual in her mature critical writings Willa Cather defines the sort of reader and reviewer who seemed to her to be in the ascendant: a person born in Europe or of European parentage, reared in the jumble of a large Eastern city, drenched in the theories of Freud. Such a person would be completely impercipient of everything that mattered in the stories of Sarah Orne Jewett; his judgment on them would be that of invincible ignorance. More or less consciously Willa Cather was speaking for her own writings as much as for those of her friend. She had no confidence that her art could be understood where Miss Jewett's was neglected. They had worked in the same tradition; they belonged to the same period.

How strongly she had this feeling and some of the reasons for it appear in the next story she wrote, "The Old Beauty." This *nouvelle* was composed in 1936, probably in the autumn, and in 1937 was offered to the *Woman's Home Companion*. The editor, Gertrude Lane, who had been pleased by *Lucy Gayheart* and other shorter pieces, confessed that though she would publish "The Old Beauty," it did not stir her enthusiasm. Willa Cather asked for the return of the manuscript, made no other attempt to arrange for its publication in a magazine, and laid it aside for an eventual book of middle-length stories. That book, to which "The Old Beauty" gave the title, did not appear until after her death.

The disappointment of Miss Lane and Willa Cather's decision not to send the story elsewhere are both significant of the growing distance between her work and spirit and the temper of the age in which she was living out her last years. "I think one should go out with one's time," the Old Beauty says, and in that, as in so much else, spoke for her creator.

Nostalgia for an earlier period is a feeling that runs the length of Willa Cather's mature writing from *O Pioneers!* to the last story she finished, "The Best Years," with its title an echo of *"optima dies . . . prima fugit."* Up to 1936 she had been drawn chiefly, almost entirely, to what was creative and heroic in the past, to the breaking of "the wild land," to the preservation of what was fine in old ways by a bold adaptation to new circumstances, to the survival against huge odds of a great idea or feeling. In "The Old Beauty" she is more simply conservative: she is recalling people and a code neither creative nor heroic, not in any obvious way precious—the way of life of an upper class unaffected by art or religion, in the years of her own introduction to the world of great Eastern cities, in "the deep claret-coloured closing years of Victoria's reign." The narrator of the story, Henry Seabury, an Anglo-American, reproaches himself in 1922—the year when for

Willa Cather the world broke in two—for having taken
the end of the nineteenth century as an ordinary stretch
in time, for having lived the years of his youth without an
appreciation of what good fortune he had had in being
young then rather than a generation later. It is the same
with Gabrielle Longstreet, the old beauty. Her beauty
had drawn about her in the last two decades of the nineteenth century a multitude of the most remarkable men
of the period; she reproaches herself in 1922, and has
done so since the end of the war, for having supposed
that every period brought remarkable men, for having
taken the homage offered as what beauty may always expect. Now she travels with a gallery of photographs, reads
everything that appears about the statesmen and soldiers
who had flocked to her house in London or in New York
—one is clearly Earl Kitchener, another resembles Sir
Charles Dilke—and enjoys, rather grimly, "living her life
over again, more understandingly than she had lived it
for the first time."

The story is set at Aix-les-Bains, seen by Willa Cather
for the first time in 1923, and the place of her encounter
with Madame Franklin Grout in 1930. Seabury, who has
spent thirty years in China, has been unhappy on his return to Europe because of the almost universal changes,
and lingers at Aix because there both the place and many
of the visitors agree with his memories. Gabrielle stays
on for the same reason. Even at Aix things happen that
would not have happened in the 1890's; and it is one of
these things, a very slight thing, that leads to her death.
She has motored with Seabury to the Grande Chartreuse,
and on the way back their car collides with one that car-

ries two young American girls, "bobbed, hatless, clad in
dirty white knickers and sweaters." Gabrielle has a weak
heart, but the shock that ends her life is not the collision
but the subsequent encounter with the two girls, who are
at first noisy and then impudent. It was not the bruises that
did for her, Gabrielle believes, but the dirty white knickers of these "creatures." This final and fatal incident—Gabrielle dies that night—issued directly from an experience
of Willa Cather's, and the decisive role she gave it shows
much of her own feeling about the ways of her younger
contemporaries.

She thought well of "The Old Beauty." It is a finely conducted story, subdued in all its tones like the rest of her
fiction in the 1930's, and with a sureness about the right
dimensions and the pace that *Lucy Gayheart* lacked. It
does bear the impress of age and unhappiness, but gives
no ground for supposing there had been any failure in
power. There was no reason why the narrowing sympathies of Willa Cather should have threatened her art:
"The Old Beauty" might have been followed by a series
of sensitive, unhappy, perfectly executed works expressing not only her distance from the world about her but her
pleasure in imaginative recapture of an earlier time. The
artist who had written *My Ántonia* in her forties might be
expected to write such works as these in her sixties.

IV

What followed was one such work, the last of her novels,
Sapphira and the Slave Girl, in which she rendered the
quality of life in the Northern Neck of Virginia not in her
own childhood (only the epilogue does that), but in the

time when her grandmothers were young women. Willa Cather began this novel in the autumn of 1937. The strain and exhaustion that had left a mark on the earlier books of *Lucy Gayheart* had passed, though she was never to recover the energy that enabled her to write *Death Comes for the Archbishop* in two years of unalloyed happiness. It was three years since she had been at work on a novel, and she had missed the sense of unity and purpose a long fiction gave to life, and the happy companionship with creatures of memory and imagination. She had long intended to make a novel from her recollections of Virginia and from the countless stories about a yet earlier time she had heard of from older members of the family and their friends. She had promised her father she would do so. During the years when she was living in the Bank Street apartment she seldom had spoken of Virginia and it did not seem to belong to her imaginative life. The deaths of her father and mother and her own approach to old age led her to dwell with ever increasing pleasure and preoccupation on small incidents in the life of her childhood and on the stories she had heard so often. Miss Lewis recalls that when at last Willa Cather began *Sapphira and the Slave Girl* it was with her whole power and concentration.

It was [Miss Lewis notes] a novel written against circumstance. One catastrophe after another blocked its path; the sudden death of her brother Douglass—the most bitter, I think, of all her losses; the death of Isabelle Hambourg; the second World War. . . . Even Jaffrey, which she had always found such a happy refuge, was largely spoiled for her by the great hurricane of 1938, which wrecked the woods for miles around.

Against all these things, she worked at *Sapphira* with a reso-
luteness, a sort of fixed determination which I think was different from her ordinary working mood; as if she were bringing all her powers into play to save this, whatever else was
lost. She often worked far beyond her strength. In the summers
of 1938 and 1939 we stayed in New York through the heat until
the end of July, because she did not want to interrupt what she
was then doing. She finished the story at Grand Manan in September, 1940.

The invasion and the fall of France led her to say:
"There seems to be no future at all for people of my generation." In consoling Jan Hambourg for the loss of his
wife she declared that for persons like Isabelle there
could be no outcome of the war which could compensate
for what it had removed from the world—the buildings,
the people, the habits of life and thought. She seldom
spoke of the war, and never in casual conversation; she
felt it far more deeply than she had felt the First World
War; she felt it was the end of all. Like the deaths in her
own circle, and the devastation of her ideal scene for writing, but much more powerfully, the war bade her record
her memories while there was yet a little time.

In the early spring of 1938, accompanied by Edith
Lewis, she had gone to Virginia, and stayed for some
weeks at Winchester, to walk over the old ground and re-
new her sense of what it had meant to live there. Miss
Lewis notes:

It was as memorable an experience, as intense and thrilling
in its way, as those journeys to New Mexico, when she was
writing the *Archbishop*. Every bud and leaf and flower seemed
to speak to her with a peculiar poignancy, every slope of the

land, every fence and wall, rock and stream. I remember how she spoke of the limp, drooping acacia trees in bloom along all the roadsides—how they had the shiftless look that character- ized so many Southern things, but how their wood was the toughest of all, and was in great demand for fence-posts. She found again the wild azalea growing on the gravelly banks of the road up Timber Ridge, and gathered great bunches of it. The dogwood, in the almost leafless woods, had a dazzling beauty that spring. Her delight in these things gave, I think, a great freshness of detail to *Sapphira*.

The countryside was very much changed. But she refused to look at its appearance; she looked through and through it, as if it were transparent, to what she knew as its reality. Willow- shade, her old home, had been bought by a man who had al- ways borne a sort of grudge against the place; he chopped down the great willow trees that gave Willowshade its name, and destroyed the high box hedges that seemed so wonderful to Willa Cather when she was a child. The house itself had become so ruinous and forlorn that she did not go into it, only stood and looked down at it from a distance. All these trans- formations, instead of disheartening her, seemed to light a fierce inner flame that illumined all her pictures of the past.[2]

The rest was surprisingly like what it had been in her childhood. The suspension footbridge across Back Creek had gone; and the pedestrian, as is our modern way, had to expose himself on a solid structure that could carry the heavy truck, bus, and motor traffic from Winchester to Romney. At the mill farm, which is the center of the ac-

[2] The house has changed hands again. The present owner has re- paired it and freshened its appearance. Nothing can make up for the de- struction of the willows, but some trees are flourishing in front of it, and though the approach is certainly not a thing of beauty, it is much less dis- piriting than when Willa Cather refused to enter in 1938.

tion, the mill itself was disused and dilapidated. The mill house, where Willa Cather's maternal great-grandparents once lived, had suffered little change, though the slave cabins had disappeared. The markers in the private bury-ing-ground were still legible, though one had first to brush away the myrtle with which it was overgrown. The road from the farm to the village ran in another place, but when one reached the postmistress's house—where Mrs. Gore, Willa Cather's great-aunt, had lived—there was no great disappointment; and the other village house that ap-pears in the novel, her birthplace—the home of her grand-mother Mrs. Boak—shaded by maples, was also much as it had been. To be on the scene meant that Willa Cather could readily remount the half century that had passed since she lived there; and from many a family reminis-cence, told at the farm on the Divide or in the house in Red Cloud, she knew that the district as she had known it in childhood was almost exactly as it had been a quarter century earlier, in 1856, the year in which the action of *Sapphira and the Slave Girl* occurs.

More than any other of Willa Cather's novels this is a study of manners, a picture of how a little society lived in conditions that had vanished forever, painted by the one living person who had the knowledge and could transpose it into art. A number of the personages are included not for any role in the action, but simply because they were important parts of this society as it lived on in Willa Cath-er's memory. Mandy Ringer, the poor-white mountain woman, has no role at all in the action: she is in the book to remind us that women who could neither read nor write, and who depended for sustenance on the most

sketchy kind of farming, were among the most intelligent
and delightful in the countryside; by her vigor and good
humor in the midst of every kind of misfortune Mandy
Ringer becomes a witness for the Old South. It is the same
with Dr. Clevenger, the Baltimore physician who lives in
Winchester because his wife will live nowhere else; he has
nothing to do with the action, but every word he says, every tone in his voice, every movement of his body, is
treasured as it might be if he were the hero of the novel:
he is another witness for the Old South, and it is no surprise to learn that when the war came, his place was on
Robert E. Lee's personal staff.

Customs are remembered with the same intensity: the
waving of the fly-brush made of peacock feathers during
dinners in the hot season; the cutting into thin strips of all
worn-out garments and linen, the dyeing of these with log-
wood, copperas, or cochineal, and the weaving of them
into stout carpets; the driving out daily through June to
see the masses of wild laurel which covered the mountains with "drifts of rose or peach or flesh colour." Customs like these were a part of the way of life in Back
Creek Valley a hundred years ago; and always there is
the unspoken comment: was it not a gracious and a wise
way, would it not have been a pleasure to live in that
place at that time? Once the comment is spoken. The
richest massing of the laurel was on the main road west
of the village, where there was a double S of four great
loops around hills of rock. Even when the laurels were
not in bloom, this was a place of beauty. A peddler or a
poor farmer passing on foot paused to rest here or "walked
lingeringly"; when people in the district spoke of the dou-

ble S, "their voices took on something slow and dreamy, as if recalling the place itself; the shade, the unstained loveliness, the pleasant feeling one had there." Now the loops are denuded and ugly—a mechanical civilization did not set any store by them; and presently "the destroying armament of modern road-building" will blast them away. Once people came across the Atlantic to see the laurel bloom there; but that was in another time, which Willa Cather felt to be her own.

As its title suggests, the action in the novel turns upon slavery. When Sapphira Dodderidge, whose father was a large slave-owning landholder in Loudoun County, "took a long step down" and married Henry Colbert, a miller's son and an immigrant's grandson, she decided to put the Blue Ridge between herself and the aristocratic society in which she had lived until she was twenty-four. She terminated the lease of a mill farm in the Back Creek district of Frederick County which had been on the Dodderidge land roll since the days of Lord Fairfax, and began her married life there with a score of slaves. There she appears in the novel, thirty years later, still entirely a Loudoun County aristocrat, the representative of that element in the Old South to which slavery seemed—as it did not in the Back Creek Valley—an entirely natural institution. She treated her slaves as slaves, often with kindness, often with caprice, sometimes with cruelty, always as slaves. Her daughter, Rachel Blake, trying to account for the unhappiness she had felt during all the years when she was a girl at home, and for her deep disapproval of her mother, at last remembers "how she hated her mother's voice in sarcastic reprimand to the servants! And she hated it in contemptuous indulgence." It was the voice of the slave-owner. It was because she was wholly the slaveowner that Sapphira formed the nasty and petty design that produces the central situation in the book, as it is by their attitudes to slavery that the other characters respond to this design.

Sapphira, who is in her middle fifties, is in an advanced state of dropsy and has the easy suspicions of the immobilized. On the slightest of evidence she concludes that her husband has a personal interest in a young slave girl, the golden-colored mulatto, Nancy; that he either sleeps with her or will do so, since he will not allow Nancy to be sold. Sapphira then forms her design: she invites his nephew, Martin Colbert, a known woman-chaser, and bids Nancy care for his room. Martin, like Sapphira, has the attitudes of the slaveowners in Loudoun County; he attempts, as was expected, to make the best of his windfall. Nancy's confidante is Mrs. Blake, who had added to her instinctive dislike of slavery an intellectual disapproval as she absorbed the ideas of the postmistress, a local woman, who subscribes to an abolitionist paper. It is Mrs. Blake who foils her mother and her cousin and with the help of her neighbors puts Nancy on the underground railway and sees her across the Potomac. Between the extreme positions of Mrs. Blake and of Sapphira and Martin there are many gradations. Nancy's mother, Till, Sapphira's housekeeper, does not lift a finger; trained in Loudoun County, she accepts the institution of slavery as a natural fact; but after Nancy's escape her gratitude to Mrs. Blake lasts as long as life. Sampson, the foreman at the mill, is the most intelligent and independent of the slaves (he has, however, refused his freedom); he knows what is afoot, dares to show Martin Colbert that he knows, is dissatisfied that his master, usually so clear in his responses and quick in his decisions, temporizes and appears confused.

Henry Colbert's attitude toward slavery is the most complex of all. He had grown up in Loudoun County, but his father had never owned a slave. He had always obscurely felt slavery to be wrong; and a deeply religious man—reared a Lutheran and attending the Baptist chapel in Back Creek Valley—he constantly searched the Scriptures for an answer, marking all the passages that might have a bearing with a great "S," and reading them in sequence for what reciprocal illumination they might have. Joseph had been in slavery, and Daniel, and other prophets; and their escape had been hailed, but had the experience been all loss? There were exhortations to deal with slaves mercifully, and with tolerance, but there was no exhortation to get rid of slavery itself. The Scriptures gave no answer, even when one sat up the night through, reading and meditating. He knew no other source from which he could draw an answer he could depend upon. For Nancy he had a gentle paternal feeling, something more personal, if innocent, than for any other of his wife's slaves; he hated that she should come to ruin under his roof and by his nephew. But when his daughter Rachel asks him for the money needed in getting Nancy away, just as when Sampson had asked him to interpose, the strong man is parted from his strength. What he does is pathetically unlike his usual self—he falls into casuistry. Henry Colbert will not give the money, but he tells Ra-

chel it is in his coat, and the coat will be hanging that
night beside his open window; he lies awake, but silent,
until he has heard her take it and creep away. By laying
the responsibility on her, not only does he require her to
become a thief, he provokes a complete breach between
Rachel and Sapphira.

The evil of slavery is shown by its effects on individuals. There is an evidence of Willa Cather's persisting indifference to politics in the wide inaccuracy of her reference to the date when the Fugitive Slave Law was passed;
for the legal and political aspects of the institution she
has no interest. Her interest is in what slavery has done to
harden Sapphira and Martin, to inhibit Till's maternal
feelings, to take the edge off Sampson's will, to drive the
slave girl into exile, to paralyze the conscience and stultify
the intelligence of Henry Colbert. These are the disasters
that have the foreground; there are others, episodically
represented—a slave who loses his wits because the girl he
loves is taken to Baltimore, a family of poor whites pigging
it on the mountains because they will not take work that
would put them side by side with colored people. No one
is the better for slavery, and only those who oppose it
root and branch are safe from its poison.

The tract from the past rendered in *Sapphira* has upon
it the great spreading stain of slavery, and from the stain
the action arises. The reader is often persuaded to forget
the stain—the picture of slavery is framed in leisure, grace,
peace, and happiness. Because of the frame *Sapphira* does
not affect one in the manner of a problem novel. The problem is exhibited with no minimizing, but the other traits
of life in Back Creek Valley before the War between the

States are also exhibited not to deepen one's sense of the problem directly or by contrast, not to obliterate the problem—but without relation to the problem. The people in the valley were in no way remarkable—the last phrase in the novel is Till's and depends perhaps on a Loudoun County set of values: "here where nobody was anybody much"—but Willa Cather cared for them, as Till had always done, though like Till she thought it was better to live somewhere else. She cared for them as she cared for the people in "The Old Beauty," because in their way of life there were qualities that belonged to the age in which she had been young and that had disappeared in the age in which she was growing old. Now she no longer wished to contemplate the heroic moments in American life—the moment when the French made a civilization in the Canadian wilderness, the moment when the Southwest was at its apex, the moment when the wild land of Nebraska took the first impress of the pioneer. Now it was enough to evoke quite ordinary moments from the past; and these too had vanished, taking with them a burden of beauty for which there was nothing to compensate.

V

The retrospective mood of the last books coincided with a rereading of all her works as Willa Cather prepared them for the substantial, ornate "Library Edition" that Houghton Mifflin Company brought out during 1937 and 1938. There were twelve volumes, to which was added *Sapphira and the Slave Girl* in 1941. To reread her work was to relive her creative life and, rediscovering the work of her youth, she sought to bring it up to the level of her maturity. Willa Cather freely revised the first pages of *My Ántonia* and the last part of *The Song of the Lark*. To the latter she attached the brief preface she had written for the 1932 edition, explaining that she was well aware of the book's defects and in particular the way in which the story drops to a flat indeterminate ending. She might have said that life is often like this; but she defined the real reason for what she felt was an imbalance in the work when she said that "success is never so interesting as struggle— not even to the successful." Once Thea Kronborg's career ends in victory, everything else is anticlimax.

There were other changes in the edition. "A Death in the Desert" was dropped from *Youth and the Bright Medusa*, as well as the Christina Rossetti epigraph. *Not Under Forty* was meekly renamed *Literary Encounters*, and the defiant prefatory note that gave the book its original title was eliminated. The dedication of *One of Ours* to her mother and of *April Twilights* to her father were omitted, perhaps because her parents had died so recently that all dedication to them now seemed meaningless. She had already removed Jan Hambourg's name from the dedication of later editions of *A Lost Lady*, and the book remained undedicated here; she retained the dedication to him of *The Professor's House*, while *O Pioneers!* remained inscribed to the memory of Sarah Orne Jewett, and *The Song of the Lark* to Isabelle McClung. And finally she altered the chronology of her work. Although written after *Alexander's Bridge*, *O Pioneers!* received first place in the collection. She had once said in an article entitled "My First Novels (There Were Two)" that *O Pioneers!* was spontaneous and *Alexander's Bridge* contrived. In the end she could perhaps claim that of her two "first" novels, the novel about Alexandra Bergson was really the first.[3]

[3] Issued in 1937 were (I) *O Pioneers!* (II) *The Song of the Lark,* (III) *Alexander's Bridge* and *April Twilights,* (IV) *My Ántonia,* (V) *One of Ours,* (VI) *Youth and the Bright Medusa.* In 1938: (VII) *A Lost Lady,* (VIII) *The Professor's House,* (IX) *Death Comes for the Archbishop,* (X) *Shadows on the Rock,* (XI) *Lucy Gayheart* and *My Mortal Enemy,* (XII) *Obscure Destinies* and *Literary Encounters.* In 1941: *Sapphira and the Slave Girl.* A number of the sets were autographed and issued as the "Autograph Edition."

12

Epilogue: *A Cadence, a Quality of Voice . . .*

1941–1947

THE SEVEN YEARS that remained to Willa Cather after the publication of *Sapphira and the Slave Girl* were an epilogue to her career as a writer. Only two stories were completed, one no more than a sketch. A third, more ambitious but not intended as a full-length novel, was never brought beyond a fragment of a rough draft.

Throughout these years Willa Cather was in poor health. During her lifetime she had been relatively free from illness, save for a period in childhood when she had what may have been a mild attack of polio which affected her leg for some time, and periods when she suffered from extreme nervous fatigue; but not until 1940 did she have an illness that sapped her vitality. It was a condition to which she could not become accustomed. The vigorous woman who thought nothing of a twelve-mile walk on her Canadian island or an afternoon stroll around Central Park, now found herself reduced to comparative inaction. Work was impossible, and much of the discouragement of her last seven years had this simple physical origin.

She was ill in a world that was crumbling about her. To one who had lived through 1914–18 the experience of the new war was not unfamiliar; but now she was nearing seventy and the ever present sense of catastrophe was much harder to bear. As Hitler's bombs crashed ruin on places long loved in Europe, and America was increasingly regimented for a total war effort, Willa Cather felt that the German dictator was smashing not only the Old World but also the last vestiges of freedom in the New. The war, she told her younger friends, was hardest on older persons. The young, after all, had no beautiful past to regret. What brought the war close to her was correspondence with men in the armed forces. Most of her novels were republished in the rectangular army editions that could easily be carried in a soldier's pocket, and men in lonely outposts read her and wrote to her. She could not leave their letters unanswered, even though it taxed her strength to reply. And often she found herself writing as well to grieving parents when some of her correspondents fell in action. Nothing in the war stirred her so much as the liberation of her beloved France; and Joseph Kessel's account of the underground in *Army of Shadows* moved her to write enthusiastically to Blanche and Alfred Knopf, who published it, and to endorse the book (a rare thing for her) as telling "incident by incident, sacrifice by sacrifice, the courage and the constancy (and the resourcefulness) of all the unconquered and unbought people of France."

She was in ill health when she made her last trip across the continent to see her brother Roscoe in 1941. Her hand was in a brace and she was in a state of exhaustion. During the 1930's she and Roscoe had rarely met, but their letters, charged with the memories of the years, had brought them closer and closer together. Of all her brothers and sisters, he was the one who had been nearest to her, the one who understood her nature and her work the most fully. Willa Cather felt such a need to be with him now—he was suffering from a heart ailment—that despite her physical discomfort she traveled to San Francisco during the summer's heat, pausing only briefly at Chicago for much needed rest. Miss Lewis recalls that both Roscoe and his wife thought that Willa Cather looked "very frail." Nevertheless the reunion was a happy one and her hand improved sufficiently during her stay in California to enable her to remove the brace. She could not shake off the sense of fatigue, however, and rather than face the heat of Manhattan she journeyed on to British Columbia and spent a vacation at Victoria, where she did little but sit in the garden and read. She returned to New York in early autumn and promptly entered the French Hospital for a rest. This was her last long journey and the last time she saw Roscoe. He died in his sleep four years later. Willa Cather got the news while vacationing at Northeast Harbor, where she had just completed "The Best Years," a story intended for him and filled with memories of their common Nebraska childhood. She had been four when Roscoe was born and he figured in all her family memories, early and late. His passing was for her a time of deep heartbreak; in letter after letter to friends she could talk only of what he had meant to her. They had taken long trips together on horseback and in buck-wagons through the Northwest and Southwest before motor roads had been cut through the mountains. On one such journey Isabelle McClung had accompanied them. Willa Cather, alone of the three, now survived.

During the winter and spring of 1942 she showed

signs of increasing illness and in April she began to run a high fever. At Presbyterian Hospital a gall-bladder condition was diagnosed; and at the end of July she re-entered this hospital for an operation. Her convalescence was slow and she never regained her former health. In her letters she speaks in particular of her loss of weight and of the way in which her clothes no longer fitted her.

Because of the war it was impossible for her and Miss Lewis to return to their North Atlantic retreat at Grand Manan, and during these last years they finally found that the Asticou Inn, at Northeast Harbor in Maine, provided the most congenial summer surroundings. It was here that "The Best Years" and the brief sketch "Before Breakfast" were written, the latter a kind of *De senectute* in fictional form, an admission that "Plucky youth is more bracing than enduring age," but at the same time an assertion that however old one may be, life doesn't really change; if old age brings its trials and life has had its difficulties, the process of living is still a challenge and a delight. The elderly man who is set to musing about these matters by a geologist's chance remark about the hundred and thirty-six million years of life of the island where the tale is set— an island like Willa Cather's—contemplates a snowshoe hare nibbling clover, reaches for his eyedrops, and, leaning back his head to use them, glimpses the morning star. Lucy Gayheart with all life before her had looked at it in the evening sky feeling that recognition had flashed between her and its twinkling distance "that joy of saluting what is far above one was an eternal thing." So had it been for Willa Cather at Dieppe as the kite rose, and in Washington Square as the pigeons wheeled out of the dust; and now the elderly man, his head tilted back to receive the eyedrops of age, observes Venus. "Serene, impersonal splendor. Merciless perfection, ageless sovereignty. The poor hare and his clover, poor Grenfell and his eyedrops!" Like Willa Cather in the months after her operation he feels "limp." And he muses that man has "his little hour, with heat and cold and a time-sense suited to his endurance."

II

She might thus, at threescore and ten, muse on time's flight, but unlike other writers she had the distinct comfort of not outliving her reputation. Her books continued to sell and to be read; her public continued to grow; translations were made in many lands. There was a constant clamor from anthologists to republish her and every now and again some movie-producer would discover her novels and want to film them. One producer dreamed of a great panoramic *Death Comes for the Archbishop* (doubtless in technicolor) and another sought to obtain rights to *The Song of the Lark.* Willa Cather disliked being anthologized and disliked almost as much being used as a school text; she told Alfred Knopf that she felt literature was so badly taught now in the schools that children would grow up with unpleasant memories of being forced to read her writings, instead of discovering them for themselves. As for the dazzling offers from Hollywood, she had had her one experience with the Warner production of *A Lost Lady* and that sufficed; in her will she expressly prohibited theatrical or cinematic treatment of her fiction. Her artistic integrity was not for sale to the highest bidder to

be turned into "supercolossal" films, and her reason was
simple: she did not want her name attached to dialogue
written by some person whose name and ability she did
not know and to a product that would not be hers but
that of many hands. It offended her artist's sense, her belief in herself as a literary craftsman. She had worked in
a great medium after taking years to master it and saw
no need to be transposed into any other. This law she
made absolute also for radio. She permitted her work to
go into Braille for the blind, but not to be recorded for
them, fearing that through a reading of it in this way it
might some day be broadcast surrounded by commercials.
She relented only to repeated requests from composers
to set her early poem "Spanish Johnny" to music, and a
number of settings were made. Her concession to the
machine age, where art was concerned, was to the phono-
graph. It was a great comfort to be able to play record-
ings of great singers and the quartets of Beethoven. Music remained a passion to the last.

Honors continued to come. In 1944, her seventieth year,
she was awarded the gold medal of the National Institute
of Arts and Letters. She had been honored once before,
by the Academy, in 1930, with the Howells medal for fiction, and in 1933 had received the first annual Prix Fe-
mina Américaine for *Shadows on the Rock.* Now the total-
ity of her work was being crowned. What made the occasion of the presentation (on May 19, 1944) particularly
joyous for her was the presence on the dais of S. S. Mc-
Clure, who at the same time received the Institute's order
of merit for his services to literature. Those who were in
the audience still remember the spontaneity with which

Willa Cather spread out her arms and gave the veteran editor and her one-time boss a public hug as she met him on the stage. Also receiving awards on this occasion were Theodore Dreiser and Paul Robeson, the latter for "good diction on the stage."

The Institute honor was the last of a series that began as far back as 1917 with an honorary degree from her own University of Nebraska, followed in ensuing years with similar degrees from Michigan, Columbia, Yale, and New York universities and later California, Creighton in her home state, and Smith College. In June 1931 she received an honorary degree from Princeton at the same time as Colonel Charles A. Lindbergh, Frank B. Kellogg, and Newton D. Baker, but, said the *New York Times*, the conferring of the Doctorate of Letters on Willa Cather "seemed to attract the greatest attention." This was a tribute alike to her art and to the fact that she was the first woman to receive an honorary degree from the university.

III

There remained at the end certain of the steadfast friends of other years, the loyal companionship and devotion of Edith Lewis, and the visits, when they were in New York, of such long-standing musical intimates as Myra Hess or the Menuhins, now grown to maturity. High among these friends were Blanche and Alfred Knopf and Ethel Jones Litchfield. Knopf still, as during all the years, carefully remembered festive occasions, such as birthdays and of course Christmases, and sent Willa Cather the rare sherries and vintage wines she relished; he had from far back ministered not only to her artistic sensibilities and literary

interests but to her highly developed palate. There had
been times when, from her summer's isolation at Grand
Manan, she would suddenly appeal to him, sometimes by
urgent wire, for candy or for such comestibles as wild
rice, tins of Italian tomato paste, and supplies of garlic to
be artfully compounded into a *risotto* washed down by an
appropriate wine. Knopf had always respected to the full
Willa Cather's tastes and had never made demands on her
for the publicizing of her work, knowing her aversion to
public encounters. There had also been a common interest in the manufacturing problems involved in her books.
From the time of her *Home Monthly* days the smell of
print and the problems of the composing-room were familiar to Willa Cather. More often than not it was she who
dictated the kind of type to be used, demanding, for instance, that *Lucy Gayheart* be set in exactly the same type
face as *A Lost Lady*; or choosing the Monotype Old Style
No. 31 in which *Death Comes for the Archbishop* was set
because, in her rationale of printing, she felt this particular book had to have the air of being printed on a country
press for old people to read. Legibility was therefore all-
important. Her decisions were always deliberate and carefully made. When objections were raised that the dialogue
in *Shadows on the Rock* was stiff and stilted she explained
that this had been her intention; she had translated every
conversation in her mind back into French, to give to the
readers the effect of characters talking the Quebec French
of 1697.

During a quarter of a century what began as a cordial
business relationship between publisher and author had
long ago become a mellow friendship of shared interests

and social occasions (Willa Cather for instance attended regularly the annual reception the Knopfs held for Serge Koussevitsky after his opening Boston Symphony concert in New York). To Knopf fell also the never ending process of warding off from Willa Cather demands for speech-making and attendance at innumerable functions, which are the inevitable lot of the successful writer. Above all, Knopf had promptly published her work, defended it in the marketplace, and helped maintain and augment her reputation with all the resources of a modern publishing house. To the last she was grateful for his loyalty and care and for his deeply founded belief that "close personal and friendly bonds . . . should hold publisher and author together."

Sigrid Undset continued to come over from Brooklyn, where she lived, for an occasional dinner with Willa Cather, and of the younger generation a warm friendship had developed with Stephen Tennant, an English artist and writer who had written to her about *A Lost Lady* when he was still a student at the Slade School in London. The son of Lord and Lady Glenconner and a nephew of the late Lord Asquith, he had known many of the older writers in England—Yeats, Hardy, Barrie—as well as some of the newer, including Virginia Woolf. When in America, he would have long talks with Willa Cather, and often he brought her personal messages from her transatlantic colleagues. It was he who wrote the preface for the posthumous volume *Willa Cather on Writing*.

Mrs. Litchfield, whom she saw regularly during her last winter as she had done for a number of years, remembers the grace and spirit of Willa Cather's talk, the unaltered ritual with which she entertained her intimate friends, her continued interest in music and books and food; there were sometimes casual meals in restaurants and leisurely, if now abbreviated, walks in Central Park. At the end of March 1947 there was a morning in which Yehudi and Hephzibah Menuhin came to see her with their children a few hours before sailing for England. They were going to give a series of popularly priced concerts. Willa Cather had known them for sixteen years and, as did her nieces, they filled the apartment on Park Avenue with the voices of youth. She thought that the beauty in the natures of the Menuhin children transcended mere "giftedness," and she confided to one correspondent that she would rather have almost any other chapter of her life left out than the Menuhin chapter, which had brought her so much happiness. At the end of that morning the Menuhins quietly slipped on their things, the appointed cabs were waiting, and they drove away. This was the last time they saw Willa Cather.

Of these last months Miss Lewis writes: "During the winter and spring of 1946–1947 up to the time of her death she never lived the life of an invalid; she went out nearly every day, walked, read a great deal, dictated letters, saw a few friends, attended to all the small chores of life. Her interest in things, her talk, were full of life and spirit. It was only her bodily strength that failed."

Twelve days before the end she talked of her plans for the summer. She had begun to think of a trip to the West, but there was a hope of doing some writing again; the cottage at Northeast Harbor seemed to her most likely to meet her best needs. On April 24 she remained late in bed

and had her lunch brought in to her. She chatted of a
number of things with Miss Lewis and then fell into a
sleep from which she awoke in midafternoon complaining of a severe head pain. Death came for Willa Cather
with a single swift step at about four o'clock on that day.
Four days later she was laid to rest, as she had asked, in
the quiet burial ground of Jaffrey, in New Hampshire, in
the shadow of Mount Monadnock, in the stubborn soil of
New England.

IV

"To note an artist's limitations is but to define his talent,"
Willa Cather once wrote in discussing Sarah Orne Jewett.
And she went on to make a highly significant distinction
between *reportage* and creative writing, by which I suppose she meant imaginative writing. "A reporter," she observed, "can write equally well about everything that is
presented to his view, but a creative writer can do his
best only with what lies within the range and character of
his talent." What she may have had in mind were the criticisms that had been addressed to her repeatedly in American journals in which reviewers accused her of neglecting
the world around her by writing only of the past. There
has been for a long time a tendency among book-review-
ers to lecture novelists for "turning their back" on this
subject and on that—as if the novelist must create his novels on prescribed subjects like reporters sent out to cover
a disaster or a political meeting. The great novelists have
always been those who wrote about the world to which
they were drawn and which they deeply experienced and
not those who "collect" what passes for "local color" and

then "work up" a subject. Willa Cather had neither the capacious imagination of the Balzacian, the Dickensian, or the Jamesian novelist nor a gift for elaborating fictional panoramas; she deliberately arrived at a novel unfurnished, almost bare by comparison with the fiction of her immediate predecessors. She had no capacity or desire to construct tight and intricate plots. She was not a writer of "love stories"; indeed "love," in the conventional literary sense, scarcely figures in her novels. These are not, perhaps, strictly the limitations of the artist; they *are* distinctly the things she was not. She limited herself to a narrative of people seeking to master their environment, to farm-folk or missionaries or colonists, or, at the opposite pole, to artists (and mainly singers), seeking in their fugitive world to maintain their integrity amid the tensions of modern life. The passion in her books is for the process of living and conquering, for preserving things as they are; and the intensity in her books rises from her own feelings about her people. Motive and image, carefully organized in compact, dramatic statement, are central to her narrative.

Willa Cather was unyielding—sometimes belligerently so—in her refusal to accept change. Yet by some curious alchemy of the spirit her inflexibility was transmuted into the very core of her art. Her ultimate symbol was the stratified, immovable rock, "the utmost expression of human need"; and this is understandable when we think of her, in the end, as a kind of monolith of rugged individualism, an exalter of the pioneer and the builder. The enduring rock knows only the slowest change; it yields only to earthquake or the blast of man-made explosive. Willa

Cather's inner malaise in a world that underwent violent change during her lifetime caused her to look ever backward at what was enduring. "It has changed less than most places," Flaubert's niece remarked to Willa Cather at Aix-les-Bains, where they had their chance encounter. She remembered the remark. She spoke of herself as having written certain of her essays in *Not Under Forty* "for the backward, and by one of their number," suggesting that the forward-looking, who were under forty, were perhaps in the truest sense the most backward. In the sketch "Before Breakfast" the note of joy at the end is that Grenfell finds "Nothing had changed. Everything was the same. . . ." To look forward meant acceptance of the ephemeral things of daily life and acceptance too of the inevitable wear of the decades. It meant growing old. Therefore Willa Cather looked only to where there had been youth and high hope and bright beginning; her novels are in effect a reverie, a "remembrance of things past." Her famous remark about the world breaking in two was made as she neared her fiftieth year and the rock of her life had been blasted with the dynamite of the First World War. A new generation of little goblin men had succeeded the pioneers. The past could give Willa Cather a sense of consorting with the heroic men, a sense of clarity and order undiscoverable in the rushing present. In the past, as Sir Max Beerbohm once observed, all is "a work of art free from irrelevancies and loose ends. There are, for our vision, comparatively few people in it, and all of them are interesting people. The dullards have all disappeared—all but those whose dullness was so pronounced as to be in itself for us an amusing virtue. And in the past there is so

blessedly nothing for us to worry about. Everything is settled. There's nothing to be done about it—nothing but to
contemplate it and blandly form theories about this or
that aspect of it."

In "the precious, the incommunicable" past there was
nothing for Willa Cather to worry about. The eternal flux
could be frozen and immovable, unchangeable. The Rock
stands as it always has stood; the cliff dwellings survive;
the ancient men have wrought and their handiwork remains even after they and the vanities of their daily lives
have perished. Between the tight society of French Canada (symbolized by the Rock of Quebec, and the steep
old streets of the Catholic city) and the placid pre-Civil
War society in Back Creek, Timber Ridge, or Hayfield
there was an affinity that Willa Cather could appreciate;
the ordered, the hierarchic, the parochial society, where
the game of life is played according to hard and fast rules,
with no tolerance of change or nonconformity, as Willa
Cather well knew. She had been one of the nonconform-
ing in her youth; yet in the later years she found in that
society certain eternal values that seemed to transcend its
intolerance.

This love for the ordered and regulated mode of life in
a small society sprang undoubtedly in part from the violence of Willa Cather's early uprooting from Virginia to
the Divide, so that ever after she felt acutely what it
means to be torn from cherished things and transported
to scenes unfamiliar and wild. Willa Cather's childhood
pilgrimage, and her adult pilgrimage eastward, could
make her sensitive, and it did, to those pilgrims who had
come from the Old World to a new land; and she could

experience in all its intensity their longing for things left behind in their forsaken worlds. There was also the reverse of this: in the New World order was being created out of chaos, a new life replaced the old. Trees transplanted were nourished and grew in alien soil. One has only to remember the role that gardens play in Willa Cather's work to understand this. To have been brought up on the sprawling prairie had given her a deep fondness for the small cultivated plot, the well-kept garden that is also a well-kept work of art. She always remembered how the Germans in the West planted trees and hauled water and labored to make them flourish. Garden succeeds garden: the Troll Garden, the garden at Uplands, the Wunsch garden, Ántonia's grape-arbor, the evil garden at Ácoma, the professor's French garden set in the Middle West. . . .

The Professor had succeeded in making a French garden in Hamilton. There was not a blade of grass; it was a tidy half-acre of glistening gravel and glistening shrubs and bright flowers. There were trees, of course; a spreading horse-chestnut, a row of slender Lombardy poplars at the back, along the white wall, and in the middle two symmetrical, round-topped linden trees. Masses of green-briar grew in the corners, the prickly stems interwoven and clipped until they were like great bushes. There was a bed for salad herbs. Salmon-pink geraniums dripped over the wall. The French marigolds and dahlias were just now at their best—such dahlias as no one else in Hamilton could grow. St. Peter had tended this bit of ground for over twenty years, and had got the upper hand of it.

The transplanting of graces and traditions, like the transplanting of trees, was in fact a bringing of the unchanged, the old, into the new; not only was something of the past kept alive in the process, but it grew and flourished and took on new life. So the transplanted Bohemians and Swedes and French and Germans sought to recapture what had gone before in the midst of the wild land.

Willa Cather wanted life to be an arranged garden, she liked an *achieved* order; and this inevitably meant the conquest of disorder. The emphasis must be on the word *conquest,* for Willa Cather's books were built around the central theme of her own life—"the passionate struggle of a tenacious will." Her heroes and heroines were Alexanders and Alexandras whose names were synonymous with conquest, and it is no accident that of all of Plutarch's lives, little Cécile reads in the evenings at Quebec the life of Alexander the Great; and when, in Pittsburgh, Willa Cather wrote an essay on her actress friend Lizzie Hudson Collier, she gave the article the Meredithian title of "One of Our Conquerors." Her stories are stories of conquest; sometimes there is defeat, but mostly there is the timeless victory of the spirit. To conquer meant to rise above the petty men, the little conniving spirits, the baleful goblins of this world, always whittling greatness down to their own spiteful mediocrity. She, Willa Cather, had conquered by tearing herself away from the inarticulate vastness of Nebraska and rendered it articulate in a competitive and brutal world. "What I cared about," she wrote in her late preface to *The Song of the Lark,* "and still care about," she added, "was the girl's escape; the play of blind chance, the way in which commonplace occurrences fell together to liberate her from commonness." But what Willa Cather forgot to mention was that Thea had been uncommon and endowed with great inner resources, which would ultimately lead her to what James once spoke of as the artist's "free possession of himself." The fortuitous circumstances had been there in Willa Cather's life as well—Mr. Ducker, Dr. Tyndale, the eagerness and curiosity that attracted certain professors to her, the chance meeting that led to her escape to Pittsburgh, that other chance meeting which led to her friendship with Isabelle McClung, the interest of Sam McClure in her first tales. Above all, there had been—and this was not fortuitous—the way in which she had learned by the costly process of trial and error that what mattered most was "the loyalty of young hearts to some exalted ideal, and the passion with which they strive."

That passion is written into all her books. Within the heroic personages she created, leading simple lives, there was the tension and emotion with which she was able to suffuse so many of her pages; the feelings well up almost imperceptibly into the acute experience that Brownell recorded on his first reading of *My Ántonia* or Mr. Justice Oliver Wendell Holmes when he wrote to Willa Cather that she had the "gift of the transfiguring touch." If we retain the image of the Rock and Willa Cather's devotion to the unalterable, we must recognize that her great gift was her capacity to observe and record the shadows on her own spiritual rock and endow it with light and color and a play of feeling. Her unfinished fragment describing the effect of light on adobe walls in the south expresses this. The artist, she wrote, cannot paint the sun or the sunlight, "he can only paint the tricks that shadows play with it, or what it does to forms," and, she adds, it is not even that so much as "some emotion they give him, some man-made arrangement of them that happens to give him personal delight." At bottom, she said, all the artist could give was "the thrill of his own poor little nerve." She ventured the belief that in the end some great artists outgrow their own art; "the men were bigger than the game." Tolstoy did, and Leonardo. "When I hear the last opuses, I think Beethoven did." In *The Tempest* Shakespeare gave the "awful veiled threat" that he too felt "he had outgrown his toys, was about to put them away and free that spirit of Comedy and Lyrical Poetry and all the rest he held captive—quit play-making and verse-making for ever and turn his attention—to what, he did not hint, but it was probably merely to enjoy with all his senses that Warwickshire country which he loved to weakness—with a warm physical appetite. But he died before he had tried to grow old, never became a bitter old man wrangling with abstractions or creeds. . . ."

Willa Cather never wrangled with abstractions or creeds, never struggled with politics or the pressing history of the front pages. She was concerned with the concrete process of observing life. In her later years, however, a note of bitterness crept increasingly into her work. It came first as a vigorous note of criticism: her sense that new generations were adulterating the pioneer spirit, possessing neither the standards nor the values of those who had gone before. The pioneers were creators. What had followed was a decline in creativity. The pampered new generation waxed fat on the capital created by the old without adding anything new save cluttering machinery, baubles that could not really replace the old valued things and were soon enough relegated to basement or attic as a child discards obsolescent playthings. Willa Cather had no use for a gadget civilization. "You Americans are always looking for something outside yourselves to warm you up and it is no way to do," the Bohemian boy tells Claude in *One of Ours*. In the old countries "we learn to make the most of little things." What Claude discovers in the life of the Erlich family in Lincoln is that "they merely knew how to live . . . and spent their money on themselves, instead of on machines to do the work and machines to entertain people." And Eusabio, speaking of the railroad from Gallup to Santa Fe in *Death Comes for the Archbishop*, observes: "Men travel faster now, but I do not know if they go to better things."

Men indeed traveled faster, as Willa Cather saw in her old age. They had soared from the earth into the astronomical spaces, and Willa Cather was no longer sure even of the freedom of the skies; there were moments when her tone became petulant and merely irritable not only against those who had watered down American life but against change itself, the inevitable flow and forward movement of the years. It was then that the strong voice, which could be addressed against decay and corrosion, faltered and at times became shrill. She could no longer face with equanimity a group of callow and unfeeling girls in knickers, as in *The Old Beauty*, without identifying them with the destruction of the world of grace and politeness she had known, rather than with perhaps some part of the Willa Cather of Red Cloud and Lincoln who had affected unconventional attire and sought to *épater les bourgeois*.

Posterity will overlook, I think, the moments of petu-lance and irritation and recognize that Willa Cather's picture of American achievement and its subsequent met-amorphosis into a technical and material gadget civiliza-tion was a view from an artist's great height of transition from the nineteenth to the twentieth century, the obliter-ation of early promise and man-made deeds by the imper-sonal machine. And posterity will also recognize that in her extraordinary craftsmanship, as in her vision, she achieved an enduring artistic synthesis of this transforma-tion of a country and a way of life.

What we have gained by her craftsmanship is, above all, a beautiful lightening of the novel form. From George Eliot's time down to ours, the load upon the novel has been steadily increasing until in works like *The Financier* or *The World of William Clissold*—to choose examples from two of Willa Cather's contemporaries—the form broke beneath the stress. For the popular fiction of a semi-serious sort, and for fiction that aspires to distinction without fully attaining it, the characteristic formula has been during the past quarter of a century the memoir of a crowded life, abounding in rather crude sexual experience and with somewhat hasty reflections on education, indus-try, the social system, coming to a climax in a melodra-matic ethical regeneration or else in an equally melodra-matic recognition of life's futility, the entire story often crowded with violence and brutality. Examples of such fiction, written for the day, or at best for the decade, will be in everyone's mind. In most of them character and story are mere props and are handled with an almost un-believable clumsiness; structure and tone are scarcely considered; and in style the model appears to be the manner of the more lively foreign correspondent or the court reporter. Against such a degradation of the art of fiction to mere journalism Miss Cather's craftsmanship stands out with an alien definiteness and firmness of beauty.

Her vision is of essences. In her earlier novels the essential subject, a state of mind or of feeling, was enveloped in the massiveness of the conventional modern realist novel. It was there, but it was muffled. Then she saw that if she abandoned the devices of massive realism, if she depended on picture and symbol and style, she could disengage her essential subject and make it tell upon the reader with a greater directness and power, help it to remain uncluttered in his mind. The things that pass, the things that merely adhere to states of mind and feeling, she began to use with a severe and rigid economy. Her fiction became a kind of symbolism, with the depths and suggestions that belong to symbolist art, and with the devotion to a music of style and structure for which the great literary symbolists strove, Pater and Moore and the later Henry James. What she cares for in humanity and in nature many sensitive and cultivated people have cared for in every time. She was aware of this. Amid the discouragements of her last years, her belief could never be shaken that whatever the war had done to the past—the destruction of the Tolstoy memorial by the Nazis, the breaking up of the estate of Madame Franklin-Grout—it could not destroy the works themselves. Time and circumstance and indifference might disperse the material relics of a writer, but they could not annihilate what the writer left of himself or herself in books. Sarah Orne Jewett came alive every time Willa Cather took one of her volumes from the shelf. *The Pilgrim's Progress* had survived the centuries. The enduring works needed no justification for their continued existence. "One might say," Willa Cather had written in her essay on Miss Jewett, "that every fine story must leave in the mind of the sensitive reader an intangible residuum of pleasure; a cadence, a quality of voice that is exclusively the writer's own, individual, unique. A quality which one can remember without the volume at hand, can experience over and over again in the mind but can never absolutely define, as one can experience in memory a melody, or the summer perfume of a garden."

"*A cadence, a quality of voice . . .*" and what this voice, so singular and intense, tells us in the case of Willa Cather is that America was created not only by sheer vitality projected from the Old World, but by a heroism alike sensitive and perceptive; that it took men and women of large imagination and unbending faith to achieve a pioneer greatness which a later generation accepted without comprehending. Her theme, as Henry Seidel Canby has said, was unique in our formative time, "the overflow of vigorous men and women from the Old World into the new country, after one thousand years of stability." To write of it Willa Cather described the arc in reverse, and having learned the world she discovered that she knew the village. Of American artists she was the first who wooed the muse in her particular wild land, and because it was an authentic muse, the art is authentic and pure, almost classical in form, built of the rocklike materials that endure.

Acknowledgment

E. K. BROWN traveled widely and talked to many persons in the process of piecing together the record of Willa Cather's creative life. One clue led to another, and long before the end he was carrying on an extensive and exacting correspondence. In going over his voluminous notes and papers I have found the names of a number of persons to whom he was clearly indebted for generous assistance at various stages of his research, and I give them here neither in alphabetical order nor indeed in any special sequence, but as I come upon them. He was particularly indebted to Mariel C. Gere; Elsie Margaret Cather; Mary Virginia Mellen; William Linn Westermann; Helen McAfee; Mrs. Robert W. Millar; George Seibel; James R. Shively; Norman Foerster; Earl A. Dimmick, superintendent of Pittsburgh Public Schools; the late Dr. George W. Gerwig of the Allegheny Central Board of Education; the late Benjamin D. Hitz; Mrs. W. W. Ray; Mrs. W. A. Sherwood; Mr. and Mrs. Sydney Florance; Ferris Greenslet; Mrs. L. C. Dillon; Louise and Olivia Pound; Mrs. Forman; Miss Sarah Bloom; Ned C. Abbott; George Kibbe Turner; and Napier Wilt, of the University of Chicago. A generous grant from the Carl and Lily Pforzheimer Fund facilitated the necessary travel and searches in libraries for much buried material.

In completing the work I had the assistance of a number of persons who had also aided Brown, and the gratitude here expressed is therefore on my behalf as well as his—to Mrs. Ethel Jones Litchfield; F. B. Adams, Jr., of the Pierpont Morgan Library; Elizabeth Shepley Sergeant; Miss Rose Demorest, of the Carnegie Library of Pittsburgh; and Preston Farrar. In especial I single out Dorothy Canfield Fisher, who with great patience and unvarying promptness answered in full detail all my queries concerning Willa Cather's early years in Pittsburgh and abroad; without her copious notes and generous searching of her papers and memories, that portion of this biography would lack much of the precise detail it now possesses. I wish also to express thanks to Mrs. Jessica Cather Auld, Mrs. E. H. Anderson, A. S. P. Woodhouse, Ernest Sirluck, Morton Dauwen Zabel, and Mrs. Edward K. Brown for assistance given me in the difficult task of taking up and completing an unfinished work. Harry Finestone, a graduate student at the University of Chicago, who worked under Professor Brown, generously supplied material from a thesis he is preparing on Miss Cather's Pittsburgh years. I am indebted also to my wife, Roberta Roberts Edel, for her guidance in matters pertaining to her native Nebraska.

E. K. Brown would have specially singled out for his thanks Alfred A. Knopf, Miss Cather's publisher of many years, for the interest he displayed in the project from the outset. This interest was proffered just as generously to the solution of the problems I encountered in completing the book. He placed his archives at my disposal and in every way facilitated my task.

Miss Edith Lewis's contribution to a project she first conceived and to which she gave its essential design is amply attested by the passages of reminiscence which she set down for E. K. Brown and which he incorporated in his text. What cannot emerge for the reader of the book, however, is the fine quality of attention and loyalty she brought to bear on the research problems and to the questions we brought to her. No small detail was too insignificant to be pursued and evaluated. In the fullest and friendliest sense of the word, Miss Lewis must be considered as a collaborator, alike generous and devoted, in this book.

L. E.

Bibliographical Note

THE WORKS OF WILLA CATHER

April Twilights, 1903.
The Troll Garden, 1905.
Alexander's Bridge, 1912.
O, Pioneers! 1913.
The Song of the Lark, 1915.
My Ántonia, 1918.
Youth and the Bright Medusa, 1920.
One of Ours, 1922.
A Lost Lady, 1923.
The Professor's House, 1925.
My Mortal Enemy, 1926.
Death Comes for the Archbishop, 1927.
Shadows on the Rock, 1931.
Obscure Destinies, 1932.
Lucy Gayheart, 1935.
Not Under Forty, 1936.
Sapphira and the Slave Girl, 1940.

THE NOVELS AND STORIES OF WILLA CATHER were published as a "Library Edition" in 13 volumes (Boston: Houghton Mifflin Company; 1937–41). Unless otherwise indicated, all quotations are from Willa Cather's work included in this collected edition and conform to the edition's text. *April Twilights and Other Poems* (New York, 1933) is a new edition of the 1903 volume with several poems omitted and others added. Reprints include *Alexander's Bridge* (Boston, 1922) with a preface by the author; *O, Pioneers!* (Boston, 1929) in the Riverside Library; *The Song of the Lark* (New York, 1932) in the Traveller's Library with a preface by the author; *One of Ours* (New York, 1926) with an introduction by Stanley T. Williams and *Death Comes for the Archbishop* (New York, 1931, in the Modern Library, and also New York, 1945). A number of Miss Cather's novels have been translated into Dutch, German, French, Czech, Japanese, Swedish, Danish, Norwegian, Spanish, Hungarian, and Italian. English editions exist of a majority of the works.

Posthumously there appeared *The Old Beauty* (New York, 1948), containing three stories left completed at the time of Miss Cather's death, and *Willa Cather on Writing* (New York, 1949), with a foreword by Stephen Tennant. During Willa Cather's lifetime there were a number of de luxe and limited editions of some of her novels and a limited signed edition of her poems. A list of first editions is to be found in Jacob Blanck: *Merle Johnson's American First Editions* (fourth edition, New York, 1942). A listing of secondary items is contained in Fred B. Millett: *Contemporary American Authors* (New York, 1940, pp. 289–92). Frederick B. Adams, Jr.: "Willa Cather, Middle Years: The Right Road Taken," *Colophon* (New Graphic Series, I, 1939, No. 4, 103–8) contains comment and data on editions. See also the bibliography in *Literary History of the United States* (New York, 1948, III, 436–8.)

Students of Willa Cather will find that a search of the
journals for which she wrote during her years at Lincoln
and later in Pittsburgh will yield much material concerning the young Willa Cather serving her apprenticeship in
letters. In particular the files of the *State Journal* and the
Courier in Lincoln and the *Leader* in Pittsburgh, 1897–
1901, are filled with examples of Miss Cather's energetic
journalism and early critical attitudes. James R. Shively in
Writings from Willa Cather's Campus Years (Lincoln,
1950) brought together much early material as well as
recollections from her classmates. The Pittsburgh *Home
Monthly*, 1896–7, contains a considerable body of miscel-
laneous writing, but due attention must be paid to the fact
that Miss Cather was here producing, in accordance with
strict editorial requirements, material often distasteful to
her and designed to fit the publisher's special concept of
what a "family" magazine should be.

The short-lived *Library*, published during 1900 in Pittsburgh, contains some twenty items by Willa Cather, some
pseudonymous, and the column "The Passing Show" in the
Lincoln *Courier*, appears from October 23, 1897 and
weekly thereafter, with some interruptions, until April 30,
1898; it is resumed January 7, 1899 and again weekly,
with occasional interruptions, until May 12, 1900. The
files of the newspaper also contain stories, poems, mis-
cellaneous contributions, and reprints of some of her contributions to magazines.

A number of Willa Cather's stories, published in the
magazines and recorded in the periodical index, were
never republished by her. Notable among these is "The
Enchanted Bluff" (*Harper's Monthly*, April 1909); "The

Bohemian Girl" (*McClure's*, June 1912); and "Uncle Valentine" (*Woman's Home Companion*, February-March 1925). Her key essay, "The Novel *Démeublé*," first published in the *New Republic* (April 12, 1922), has been reprinted a number of times and is to be found both in *Not Under Forty* and in *Willa Cather on Writing*. For the *Nation* (September 5, 1923) she wrote "Nebraska: The End of the First Cycle." This was reprinted in *These United States*, edited by Ernest Henry Gruening (New York, 1923).

In 1933, in reply to increasing demands for biographical data concerning Miss Cather, Alfred A. Knopf published a twenty-eight page pamphlet which contained a biographical sketch, an English estimate by Alexander Porterfield originally published in the London *Mercury*, March 1926; Robert Morss Lovett's review of *Death Comes for the Archbishop*, originally published in the *New Republic*; Willa Cather's letter to the *Commonweal* on how she came to write this novel; an unsigned review of *Shadows on the Rock*, originally published in the *Irish Press*, January 22, 1932; Miss Cather's letter to Governor Wilbur Cross concerning this novel, originally published in the *Saturday Review of Literature*, October 17, 1932; a *Manchester Guardian* review of *Obscure Destinies*, December 16, 1932 and an estimate of Miss Cather's fiction by Frank Kendon, which first appeared in *John O'London's Weekly*. The pamphlet also contained an abridged bibliography.

It is significant that most of the reviews used in this pamphlet were from British pens. This was not because of any special preference of Mr. Knopf's or Miss Cather's for them. Although the American public had unhesitatingly accepted her novels, American criticism, preoccupied with the jazz age of the twenties and the depression in the thirties, had lagged seriously in appreciating and comprehending the art of Miss Cather. A finer perspective prevailed on the other side of the water. The earliest American estimate of significance was a discriminating article by Lloyd Morris, "Willa Cather" in the *North American Review* (CCXIX, 1924), and the first significant literary portrait was sketched by Elizabeth Shepley Sergeant in *Fire under the Andes* (New York, 1927, pp. 261–82).

Other estimates include Thomas K. Whipple: *Spokesmen* (New York, 1928, pp. 139–60); René Rapin: *Willa Cather* (New York, 1930, in the "Modern American Writers" series); Rebecca West: *The Strange Necessity* (New York, 1931, pp. 215–28); Louis Kronenberger, in *Bookman* (LXXIV, 134–40, October 1931); Harry Hartwick: *The Foreground of American Fiction* (New York, 1934, pp. 389–404); Lionel Trilling, in Malcolm Cowley, ed.: *After the Genteel Tradition* (New York, 1937, pp. 52–63); Carl Van Doren: *The American Novel* (New York, 1940, pp. 281–93); Alfred Kazin: *On Native Grounds* (New York, 1942, pp. 247–57); Maxwell Geismar: *The Last of the Provincials* (Boston, 1947, pp. 153–220); Edward A. and Lillian D. Bloom: "Willa Cather's Novels of the Frontier," *American Literature* (XXI, 71–93, March 1949). David Daiches: *Willa Cather: A Critical Introduction* (Ithaca, N.Y., 1951) is the most recent critical estimate to appear.

Reminiscences of Miss Cather's life in Pittsburgh are to be found in *These Too Were Here*, by Elizabeth Moorhead (Pittsburgh, 1950, pp. 45–62), and "Miss Willa Cather from Nebraska," by George Seibel, the *New Colo-*

phon, Vol. II, Part 7 (1949), pp. 195–208. John P. Hinz in "Willa Cather in Pittsburgh," in the *New Colophon*, Vol. III (1950), pp. 198–207, has appended a bibliography covering the novelist's extensive pseudonymous writings during this period. Light on "Willa Cather's Call on Housman" was shed by Carl J. Weber in *Colby College Quarterly*, Series II, No. 4, pp. 61–4 (November 1947).

Mildred R. Bennett's *World of Willa Cather* (New York, 1951) is devoted largely to the writer's Red Cloud years.

E. K. Brown's first estimate of Willa Cather appeared in the *University of Toronto Quarterly*, July 1936 (V, 544–66); his essay in the *Yale Review*, "Homage to Willa Cather," September 1946 (XXXVI, 77–92). He also contributed a note on the Benjamin Hitz Collection of Cather Material in the *Newberry Library Bulletin* (Chicago, December 1950, pp. 158–60). His third in the series of Alexander Lectures delivered at the University of Toronto, in *Rhythm in the Novel* (Toronto, 1950), contains a discussion of *The Professor's House*, pp. 71–8.

Index

A NOTE ON THE

T Y P E

IN WHICH THIS BOOK IS SET

THE TEXT of this book is set in Caledonia, a Linotype face that belongs to the family of printing types called "modern face" by printers—a term used to mark the change in style of type-letters that occurred about 1800. Caledonia borders on the general design of Scotch Modern, but is more freely drawn than that letter.

The book was composed, printed, and bound by The Plimpton Press, Norwood, Massachusetts. The typography and binding design are by W. A. Dwiggins.

WAD